Bilingual
VISUAL
dictionary

Bilingual

VISUAL

dictionary

DK | Penguin
Random
House

DK LONDON
Senior Editors Angeles Gavira, Angela Wilkes
Senior Art Editor Ina Stradins
Jacket Editor Claire Gell
Jacket Design Development Manager Sophia MTT
Preproduction Producer Andy Hilliard
Producer Alex Bell
Picture Researcher Anna Grapes
Project Manager Christine Stroyan
Art Director Karen Self
Publisher Liz Wheeler
Publishing Director Jonathan Metcalf

DK INDIA
Editor Arpita Dasgupta
Assistant Editor Priyanjali Narain
Art Editor Yashashvi Choudhary
DTP Designers Anita Yadav, Jaypal Chauhan Singh
Jacket Designer Tanya Mehrotra
Jackets Editorial Coordinator Priyanka Sharma
Preproduction Manager Balwant Singh
Production Manager Pankaj Sharma

Designed for DK by WaltonCreative.com
Art Editor Colin Walton, assisted by Tracy Musson
Designers Peter Radcliffe, Earl Neish, Ann Cannings
Picture Research Marissa Keating

Language content for DK by g-and-w PUBLISHING
Managed by Jane Wightwick, assisted by Ana Bremón
Translation and editing by Christine Arthur
Additional input by Dr Arturo Pretel, Martin Prill,
Frédéric Monteil, Meinrad Prill, Mari Bremón,
Oscar Bremón, Anunchi Bremón, Leila Gaafar

First published in Great Britain in 2005
This revised edition published in 2018 by
Dorling Kindersley Limited,
80 Strand, London WC2R 0RL

Copyright © 2005, 2015, 2018 Dorling Kindersley Limited
A Penguin Random House Company

Content first published as
5 Language Visual Dictionary in 2003

2 4 6 8 10 9 7 5 3 1
001 – 308057 – Feb/18

A CIP catalogue record for this
book is available from the British Library.

ISBN: 978-0-2413-1754-9

Printed and bound in China

A WORLD OF IDEAS:
SEE ALL THERE IS TO KNOW

www.dk.com

содержание
soderzhaniye
contents

42
здоровье
zdorov'ye
health

146
питание вне дома
pitaniye vne doma
eating out

252
досуг
dosug
leisure

о словаре

Доказано, что использование изображений способствует пониманию и запоминанию информации. Данный принцип был положен в основу создания этого красочно иллюстрированного англо-русского словаря, представляющего широкий спектр полезной актуальной лексики.

В словаре подробно отражено большинство аспектов повседневной жизни, от ресторана до спортзала, от дома до работы, от космоса до животного мира. Вы также найдете дополнительные слова и выражения для использования в беседе и расширения своего словарного запаса.

Некоторые замечания
Русская лексика в словаре представлена в кириллическом написании и сопровождается системой упрощенной транслитерации. При чтении транслитерации ставьте ударение на подчеркнутые гласные буквы в словах. Записи представлены в одном и том же порядке – на русском, транслитерация, английский эквивалент:

лук	дети
luk	deti
onion	children

У глаголов после английского слова в скобках указано (v), например:
тренироваться treni<u>ro</u>vat'sya | train (v)

Для каждого из языков в конце книги приводится алфавитный указатель. Вы можете найти там слово на английском или русском языках и узнать номер(а) страницы(ы), на которой или на которых имеется данное слово. Род обозначен следую-щими сокращениями:

m = мужской
f = женский
n = средний

как пользоваться словарем

Для каких целей вы бы ни изучали язык – для бизнес-контактов, удовольствия или при подготовке к отпуску за рубежом, данный словарь станет ценным инструментом обучения, которым вы можете пользоваться различными способами.

Активные методы обучения
Находясь дома, на работе или в университете, просмотрите страницы словаря, относящиеся к соответствующей обстановке. Затем закройте книгу, оглянитесь вокруг и проверьте, сколько предметов или деталей обстановки вы можете назвать.
• Изготовьте флеш-карточки с английским текстом с одной стороны и русским переводом с другой. Носите их с собой ипроверяйте свои знания, тасуя карточки перед каждой проверкой.
• Напишите рассказ или диалог, используя как можно больше слов и выражений с определенной страницы. Это поможет вам сохранить словарный запас и запомнить правильное написание. Хотите усовершенствовать свои знания и перейти к созданию более длинных текстов? Начинайте с предложений из 2-3 слов.
• Если у вас хорошая зрительная память, попробуйте нарисовать изображения предметов из книги на листе бумаги, а затем подпишите картинки по памяти.
• Набравшись уверенности, перейдите к работе с указателем. Выберите из него слова и проверьте, знаете ли вы их значение, перед тем как обратиться к соответствующей странице и проверить себя.

Бесплатное аудиоприложение

это Аудио-приложение содержит все слова и фразы из книге, которые используются в русском и английском языках, что увеличить ваш словарные запаз и поможет улучшить произношение.

Как пользоваться аудиоприложением

• Найдите «Bilingual Visual Dictionary» и загрузите бесплатное приложение на свой смартфон или планшет из выбранного магазина приложений.
• Откройте приложение и сканируйте штрих-код (или введите ISBN), чтобы разблокировать визуальный словарь в библиотеке.
• Загрузите аудиофайлы для вашей книги.
• Введите номер страницы, затем прокрутите вверх и вниз по списку, чтобы найти слово или фразу. Слова можно заказать по алфавитному порядку, на русском или английском.
• Нажмите на слово чтобы услышать произношение.
• Проведите пальцем по экрану влево или вправо, чтобы посмотреть предыдущую или следующую страницу.
• Добавьте слова к вашей странички "Избранное".

about the dictionary

Using pictures is proven to aid understanding and the retention of information. Working on this principle, this highly-illustrated English–Russian bilingual dictionary presents a large range of useful current vocabulary.

The dictionary covers most aspects of the everyday world in detail, from the restaurant to the gym, the home to the workplace, outer space to the animal kingdom. You will also find additional words and phrases for conversational use and for extending your vocabulary.

A few things to note

The Russian in the dictionary is in the Cyrillic alphabet.

The pronunciation for the Russian words follows a systematic coding of transliterations that English speakers should find easy to follow. When reading the transliteration, stress the vowel that is underlined. The entries are always in the same order – Russian, transliteration, then English:

лук	**дети**
luk	d<u>e</u>ti
onion	**children**

Verbs are indicated by a **(v)** after the English, for example:
тренироваться treniro<u>va</u>t'sya | **train (v)**

Each language also has its own index at the back of the book. Here you can look up a word in either English or Russian and be referred to the page number(s) where it appears. The gender is shown using the following abbreviations:

m = masculine
f = feminine
n = neuter

how to use this book

Whether you are learning a new language for business, pleasure, or in preparation for a holiday abroad, or are hoping to extend your vocabulary in an already familiar language, this dictionary is a valuable learning tool which you can use in a number of different ways.

Practical learning activities

• As you move about your home, workplace, or college, try looking at the pages which cover that setting. You could then close the book, look around you and see how many of the objects and features you can name.
• Make flashcards for yourself with English on one side and Russian on the other side. Carry the cards with you and test yourself frequently, making sure you shuffle them between each test.
• Challenge yourself to write a story, letter, or dialogue using as many of the terms on a particular page as possible. This will help you retain the vocabulary and remember the spelling. If you want to build up to writing a longer text, start with sentences incorporating two to three words.
• If you have a very visual memory, try drawing or tracing items from the book onto a piece of paper, then close the book and see if you can fill in the words below the picture.
• Once you are more confident, pick out words in the foreign language index and see if you know what they mean before turning to the relevant page to check if you were right.

free audio app

The audio app contains all the words and phrases in the book, spoken by native speakers in both Russian and English, making it easier to learn important vocabulary and improve your pronunciation.

how to use the audio app

• Search for "Bilingual Visual Dictionary" and download the free app on your smartphone or tablet from your chosen app store.
• Open the app and scan the barcode (or enter the ISBN) to unlock your Visual Dictionary in the Library.
• Download the audio files for your book.
• Enter a page number, then scroll up and down through the list to find a word or phrase. Words can be ordered alphabetically in Russian or English.
• Tap a word to hear it.
• Swipe left or right to view the previous or next page.
• Add words to your Favourites.

люди lyudi
people

тело t̲e̲lo • **body**

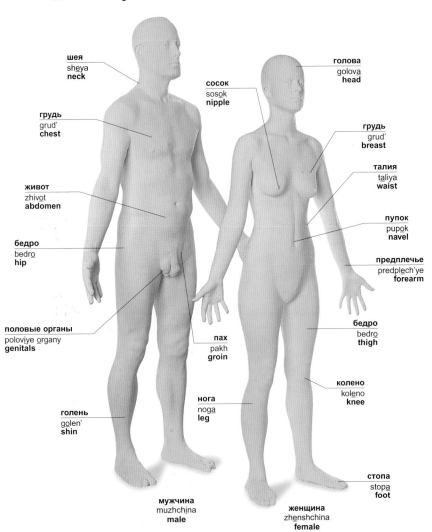

шея
sheya
neck

сосок
sosok
nipple

голова
golova
head

грудь
grud'
chest

грудь
grud'
breast

талия
taliya
waist

живот
zhivot̲
abdomen

пупок
pupok
navel

бедро
bedro̲
hip

предплечье
predplech'ye
forearm

половые органы
poloviye o̲rgany
genitals

пах
pakh
groin

бедро
bedro̲
thigh

колено
kole̲no
knee

голень
go̲len'
shin

нога
no̲ga
leg

стопа
stopa̲
foot

мужчина
muzhchi̲na
male

женщина
zh̲enshchina
female

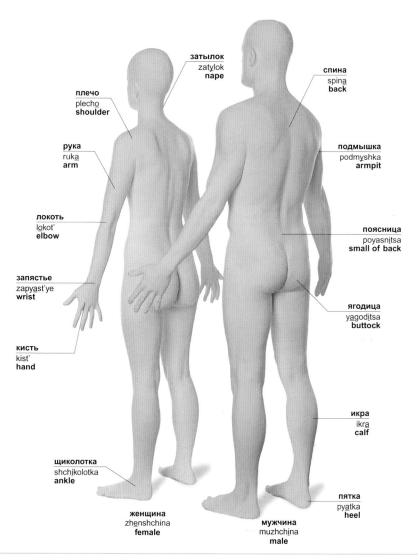

затылок
zatylok
nape

спина
spina
back

плечо
plecho
shoulder

подмышка
podmyshka
armpit

рука
ruka
arm

локоть
lokot'
elbow

поясница
poyasnitsa
small of back

запястье
zapyast'ye
wrist

ягодица
yagoditsa
buttock

кисть
kist'
hand

икра
ikra
calf

щиколотка
shchikolotka
ankle

пятка
pyatka
heel

женщина
zhenshchina
female

мужчина
muzhchina
male

лицо litso · face

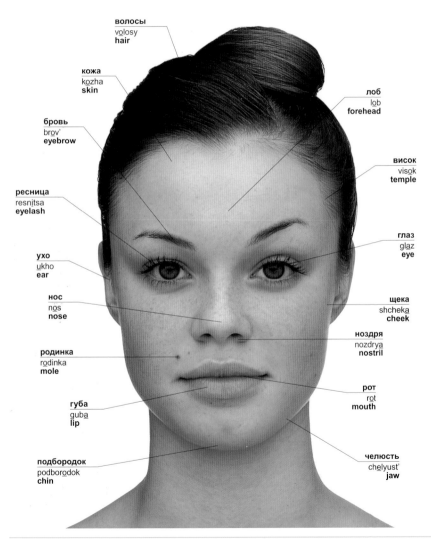

волосы
volosy
hair

кожа
kozha
skin

лоб
lob
forehead

бровь
brov'
eyebrow

висок
visok
temple

ресница
resnitsa
eyelash

глаз
glaz
eye

ухо
ukho
ear

щека
shcheka
cheek

нос
nos
nose

ноздря
nozdrya
nostril

родинка
rodinka
mole

рот
rot
mouth

губа
guba
lip

подбородок
podborodok
chin

челюсть
chelyust'
jaw

морщина
morshchina
wrinkle

веснушка
vesnushka
freckle

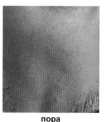

пора
pora
pore

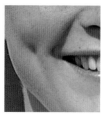

ямочка
yamochka
dimple

кисть kist' • hand

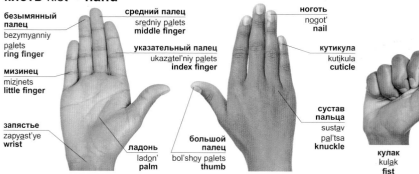

безымянный палец
bezymyanniy palets
ring finger

средний палец
sredniy palets
middle finger

указательный палец
ukazatel'niy palets
index finger

мизинец
mizinets
little finger

запястье
zapyast'ye
wrist

ладонь
ladon'
palm

большой палец
bol'shoy palets
thumb

ноготь
nogot'
nail

кутикула
kutikula
cuticle

сустав пальца
sustav pal'tsa
knuckle

кулак
kulak
fist

стопа stopa • foot

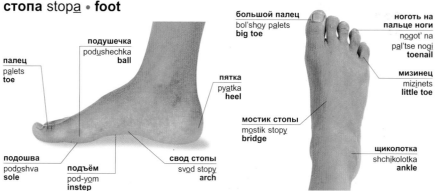

палец
palets
toe

подушечка
podushechka
ball

подошва
podoshva
sole

подъём
pod-yom
instep

свод стопы
svod stopy
arch

пятка
pyatka
heel

большой палец
bol'shoy palets
big toe

ноготь на пальце ноги
nogot' na pal'tse nogi
toenail

мизинец
mizinets
little toe

мостик стопы
mostik stopy
bridge

щиколотка
shchikolotka
ankle

мышцы myshtsy • **muscles**

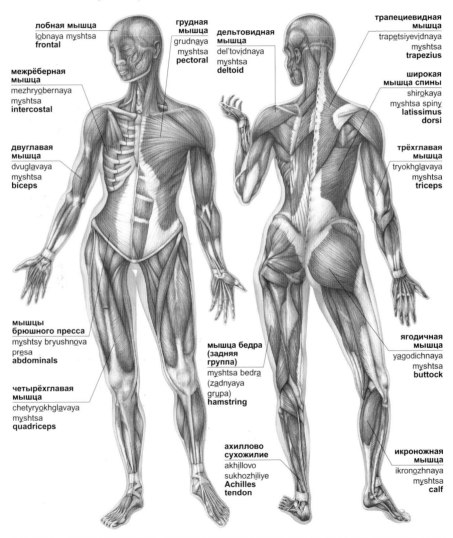

лобная мышца
lobnaya myshtsa
frontal

грудная мышца
grudnaya myshtsa
pectoral

дельтовидная мышца
del'tovidnaya myshtsa
deltoid

трапециевидная мышца
trapetsiyevidnaya myshtsa
trapezius

межрёберная мышца
mezhryobernaya myshtsa
intercostal

широкая мышца спины
shirokaya myshtsa spiny
latissimus dorsi

двуглавая мышца
dvuglavaya myshtsa
biceps

трёхглавая мышца
tryokhglavaya myshtsa
triceps

мышцы брюшного пресса
myshtsy bryushnova presa
abdominals

мышца бедра (задняя группа)
myshtsa bedra (zadnyaya grupa)
hamstring

ягодичная мышца
yagodichnaya myshtsa
buttock

четырёхглавая мышца
chetyryokhglavaya myshtsa
quadriceps

ахиллово сухожилие
akhillovo sukhozhiliye
Achilles tendon

икроножная мышца
ikronozhnaya myshtsa
calf

скелет skel<u>e</u>t • **skeleton**

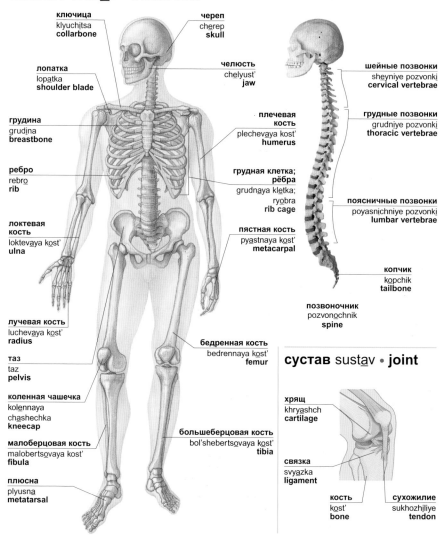

ключица
klyuch<u>i</u>tsa
collarbone

череп
ch<u>e</u>rep
skull

челюсть
chelyust'
jaw

лопатка
lop<u>a</u>tka
shoulder blade

грудина
grud<u>i</u>na
breastbone

ребро
rebr<u>o</u>
rib

**локтевая
кость**
loktev<u>a</u>ya k<u>o</u>st'
ulna

лучевая кость
luchev<u>a</u>ya k<u>o</u>st'
radius

таз
t<u>a</u>z
pelvis

коленная чашечка
kol<u>e</u>nnaya
ch<u>a</u>shechka
kneecap

малоберцовая кость
maloberts<u>o</u>vaya k<u>o</u>st'
fibula

плюсна
plyusn<u>a</u>
metatarsal

**плечевая
кость**
plechev<u>a</u>ya k<u>o</u>st'
humerus

**грудная клетка;
рёбра**
grudn<u>a</u>ya kl<u>e</u>tka;
ry<u>o</u>bra
rib cage

пястная кость
py<u>a</u>stnaya k<u>o</u>st'
metacarpal

бедренная кость
bedr<u>e</u>nnaya k<u>o</u>st'
femur

большеберцовая кость
bol'sheberts<u>o</u>vaya k<u>o</u>st'
tibia

шейные позвонки
sh<u>e</u>yniye pozvonk<u>i</u>
cervical vertebrae

грудные позвонки
grudn<u>i</u>ye pozvonk<u>i</u>
thoracic vertebrae

поясничные позвонки
poyasn<u>i</u>chniye pozvonk<u>i</u>
lumbar vertebrae

копчик
k<u>o</u>pchik
tailbone

позвоночник
pozvon<u>o</u>chnik
spine

сустав sust<u>a</u>v • **joint**

хрящ
khry<u>a</u>shch
cartilage

связка
svy<u>a</u>zka
ligament

кость
k<u>o</u>st'
bone

сухожилие
sukhozh<u>i</u>liye
tendon

внутренние органы vnutrenniye organy • internal organs

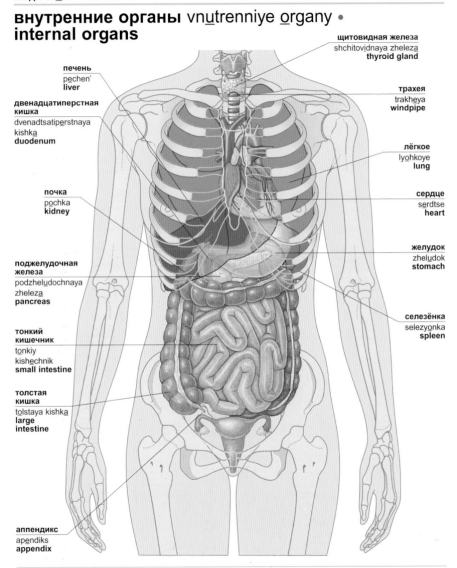

щитовидная железа
shchitovidnaya zheleza
thyroid gland

печень
pechen'
liver

двенадцатиперстная кишка
dvenadtsatiperstnaya kishka
duodenum

трахея
trakheya
windpipe

лёгкое
lyohkoye
lung

почка
pochka
kidney

сердце
serdtse
heart

поджелудочная железа
podzheludochnaya zheleza
pancreas

желудок
zheludok
stomach

селезёнка
selezyonka
spleen

тонкий кишечник
tonkiy kishechnik
small intestine

толстая кишка
tolstaya kishka
large intestine

аппендикс
apendiks
appendix

голова golova • head

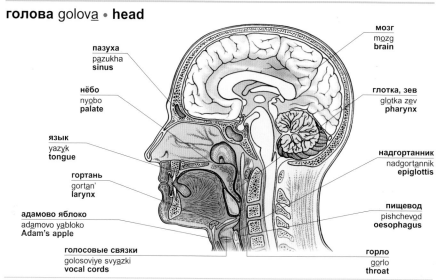

пазуха
pazukha
sinus

нёбо
nyobo
palate

язык
yazyk
tongue

гортань
gortan'
larynx

адамово яблоко
adamovo yabloko
Adam's apple

голосовые связки
golosoviye svyazki
vocal cords

мозг
mozg
brain

глотка, зев
glotka zev
pharynx

надгортанник
nadgortannik
epiglottis

пищевод
pishchevod
oesophagus

горло
gorlo
throat

системы организма sistemy organizma • body systems

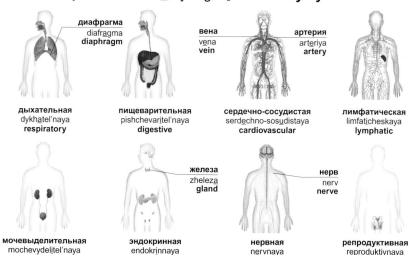

диафрагма
diafragma
diaphragm

дыхательная
dykhatel'naya
respiratory

пищеварительная
pishchevaritel'naya
digestive

вена
vena
vein

артерия
arteriya
artery

сердечно-сосудистая
serdechno-sosudistaya
cardiovascular

лимфатическая
limfaticheskaya
lymphatic

мочевыделительная
mochevydelitel'naya
urinary

железа
zheleza
gland

эндокринная
endokrinnaya
endocrine

нерв
nerv
nerve

нервная
nervnaya
nervous

репродуктивная
reproduktivnaya
reproductive

половые органы poloviye organy • reproductive organs

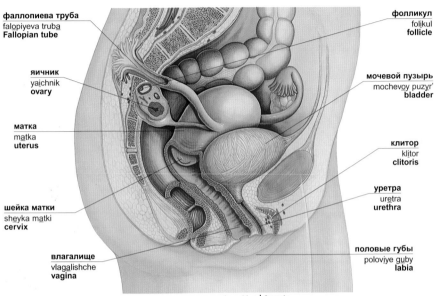

фаллопиева труба
falopiyeva truba
Fallopian tube

яичник
yaichnik
ovary

матка
matka
uterus

шейка матки
sheyka matki
cervix

влагалище
vlagalishche
vagina

фолликул
folikul
follicle

мочевой пузырь
mochevoy puzyr'
bladder

клитор
klitor
clitoris

уретра
uretra
urethra

половые губы
poloviye guby
labia

женские zhenskiye | **female**

размножение razmnozheniye • reproduction

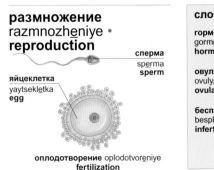

сперма
sperma
sperm

яйцеклетка
yaytsekletka
egg

оплодотворение oplodotvoreniye
fertilization

словарь slovar' • vocabulary

гормон gormon **hormone**	**импотент** impotent **impotent**	**способный к деторождению** sposobniy k detorozhdeniyu **fertile**
овуляция ovulyatsiya **ovulation**	**зачать** zachat' **conceive**	**менструация** menstruatsiya **menstruation**
бесплодный besplodniy **infertile**	**половой акт** polovoy akt **intercourse**	**ЗППП** ze-pe-pe-pe **sexually transmitted disease**

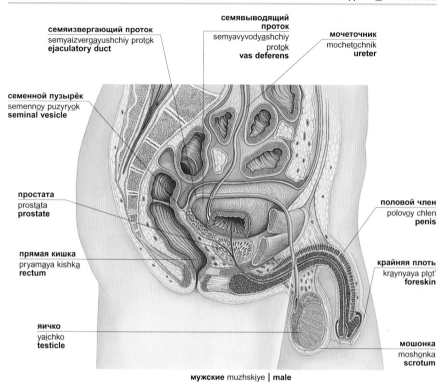

семяизвергающий проток
semyaizvergayushchiy protok
ejaculatory duct

семявыводящий
проток
semyavyvodyashchiy
protok
vas deferens

мочеточник
mochetochnik
ureter

семенной пузырёк
semennoy puzyryok
seminal vesicle

простата
prostata
prostate

половой член
polovoy chlen
penis

прямая кишка
pryamaya kishka
rectum

крайняя плоть
kraynyaya plot'
foreskin

яичко
yaichko
testicle

мошонка
moshonka
scrotum

мужские muzhskiye | male

контрацепция kontratseptsiya •
contraception

колпачок
kolpachok
cap

диафрагма
diafragma
diaphragm

презерватив
prezervativ
condom

ВМС
ve-em-es
IUD

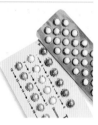

противозачаточные
таблетки
protivozachatochniye
tabletki
pill

семья sem'ya • **family**

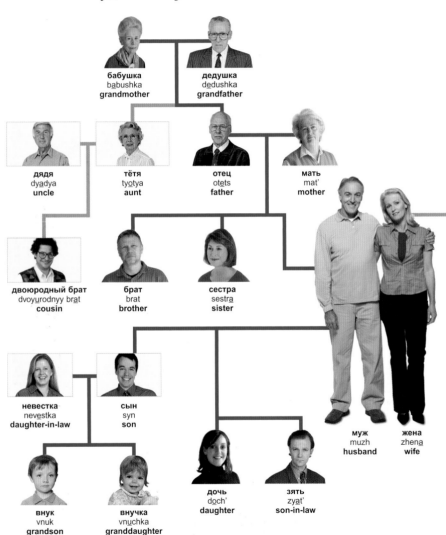

бабушка
babushka
grandmother

дедушка
dedushka
grandfather

дядя
dyadya
uncle

тётя
tyotya
aunt

отец
otets
father

мать
mat'
mother

двоюродный брат
dvoyurodnyy brat
cousin

брат
brat
brother

сестра
sestra
sister

невестка
nevestka
daughter-in-law

сын
syn
son

муж
muzh
husband

жена
zhena
wife

внук
vnuk
grandson

внучка
vnuchka
granddaughter

дочь
doch'
daughter

зять
zyat'
son-in-law

словарь slovar' • vocabulary

родственники rodstvenniki **relatives**	**родители** roditeli **parents**	**внуки** vnuki **grandchildren**	**мачеха** machekha **stepmother**	**пасынок** pasynok **stepson**	**партнёр** partnyor **partner**
поколение pokoleniye **generation**	**дети** deti **children**	**бабушка и дедушка** babushka i dedushka **grandparents**	**отчим** otchim **stepfather**	**падчерица** padcheritsa **stepdaughter**	**близнецы** bliznetsy **twins**

тёща
tyoshcha
mother-in-law

тесть
test'
father-in-law

шурин
shurin
brother-in-law

свояченица
svoyachenitsa
sister-in-law

племянница
plemyannitsa
niece

племянник
plemyannik
nephew

госпожа
gospozha
Mrs

обращения
obrashcheniya •
titles

господин
gospodin
Mr

девочка
devushka
Miss/Ms

этапы etapy • **stages**

младенец
mladenets
baby

ребёнок
rebyonok
child

мальчик
mal'chik
boy

девочка
devochka
girl

подросток
podrostok
teenager

взрослый
vzrosliy
adult

мужчина
muzhchina
man

женщина
zhenshchina
woman

отношения otnosheniya • relationships

ассистент	менеджер	деловой партнер	работодатель	подчиненный	коллега
assistent	menedzher	delovoy partnyor	rabotodatel'	podchinyonniy	kollega
assistant	**manager**	**business partner**	**employer**	**employee**	**colleague**

офис ofis | office

сосед/соседка
sosed/sosedka
neighbour

друг/подруга
drug/podruga
friend

знакомый/знакомая
znakomiy/znakomaya
acquaintance

друг по переписке
drug po perepiske
penfriend

парень
paryen'
boyfriend

девушка
devushka
girlfriend

жених
zhenikh
fiancé

невеста
nevesta
fiancée

пара para | couple

помолвленная пара pomolvlennaya para | engaged couple

эмоции emotsiyi • emotions

улыбка
ulybka
smile

радостный
radosniy
happy

грустный
grusniy
sad

возбужденный
vozbuzhdyonniy
excited

скучающий
skuchayushchiy
bored

удивленный
udivlyonniy
surprised

испуганный
ispuganniy
scared

хмурый
взгляд
khmuriy
vzglyad
frown

сердитый
serditiy
angry

сбитый с толку
sbitiy s tolku
confused

взволнованный
vzvolnovanniy
worried

нервный
nervniy
nervous

гордый
gordiy
proud

уверенный
uverenniy
confident

смущенный
smushchyonniy
embarrassed

застенчивый
zastenchiviy
shy

словарь slovar' • vocabulary

расстроенный rastroyenniy **upset**	**смеяться** smeyatsa **laugh (v)**	**вздыхать** vzdykhat' **sigh (v)**	**кричать** krichat' **shout (v)**
пораженный porazhonniy **shocked**	**плакать** plakat' **cry (v)**	**падать в обморок** padat' v obmorok **faint (v)**	**зевать** zevat' **yawn (v)**

события в жизни sobytiya v zhizni • life events

родиться
roditsa
be born (v)

пойти в школу
poyti v shkolu
start school (v)

подружиться
podruzhitsa
make friends (v)

окончить университет
okonchit' universitet
graduate (v)

получить работу
poluchit' rabotu
get a job (v)

влюбиться
vlyubitsa
fall in love (v)

жениться/выйти замуж
zhenitsa/viyti zamuzh
get married (v)

родить ребёнка
rodit' rebyonka
have a baby (v)

свадьба svad'ba | **wedding**

развод
razvod
divorce

похороны
pokhorony
funeral

словарь slovar' • vocabulary

крещение
kreshcheniye
christening

юбилей
yubiley
anniversary

эмигрировать
emigrirovat'
emigrate (v)

выйти на пенсию
viyti na pensiyu
retire (v)

умереть
umeret'
die (v)

составить завещание
sostavit' zaveshchaniye
make a will (v)

свидетельство о рождении
svidetel'stvo o rozhdenii
birth certificate

свадебный приём
svadebniy priyom
wedding reception

медовый месяц
medoviy mesyats
honeymoon

бар-мицва
barmitsva
bar mitzvah

праздники pr<u>a</u>zniki • celebrations

**вечеринка в честь
дня рождения**
vecher<u>i</u>nka v chest'
dnya rozhd<u>e</u>niya
birthday party

открытка
otkr<u>y</u>tka
card

подарок
pod<u>a</u>rok
present

день рождения
den' rozhd<u>e</u>niya
birthday

Рождество
rozhdestv<u>o</u>
Christmas

Песах (Пасха)
p<u>e</u>sakh (p<u>a</u>skha)
Passover

Новый год
n<u>o</u>viy g<u>o</u>d
New Year

карнавал
karnav<u>a</u>l
carnival

процессия
prots<u>e</u>ssiya
procession

Рамадан
ramad<u>a</u>n
Ramadan

лента
l<u>e</u>nta
ribbon

День Благодарения
den' blagodar<u>e</u>niya
Thanksgiving

Пасха
p<u>a</u>skha
Easter

Хеллоуин
khell<u>o</u>uin
Halloween

Дивали (Праздник огней)
div<u>a</u>li (pr<u>a</u>znik ogn<u>e</u>y)
Diwali

внешность vn<u>e</u>shnost'
appearance

детская одежда detskaya odezhda • children's clothing

младенец mladenets • baby

зимний комбинезон
zimniy kombinezon
snowsuit

боди
bodi
vest

слип
slip
babygro

кнопка
knopka
popper

комбинезон для сна
kombinezon dlya sna
sleepsuit

ромпер
romper
romper suit

нагрудник
nagrudnik
bib

рукавички
rukavichki
mittens

пинетки
pinetki
booties

подгузник
podguznik
terry nappy

одноразовый подгузник
odnorazoviy podguznik
disposable nappy

пластиковые трусы
plastikoviye trusy
plastic pants

малыш malysh • toddler

футболка
futbolka
T-shirt

комбинезон
kombinezon
dungarees

панама
panama
sunhat

фартук
fartuk
apron

шорты
shorty
shorts

юбка
yubka
skirt

ребёнок rebyonok • child

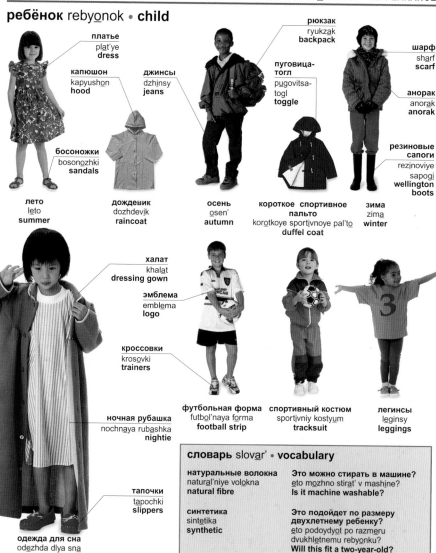

платье
plat'ye
dress

капюшон
kapyushon
hood

джинсы
dzhinsy
jeans

рюкзак
ryukzak
backpack

пуговица-тогл
pugovitsa-togl
toggle

шарф
sharf
scarf

анорак
anorak
anorak

босоножки
bosonozhki
sandals

резиновые сапоги
rezinoviye sapogi
wellington boots

лето
leto
summer

дождевик
dozhdevik
raincoat

осень
osen'
autumn

короткое спортивное пальто
korotkoye sportivnoye pal'to
duffel coat

зима
zima
winter

халат
khalat
dressing gown

эмблема
emblema
logo

кроссовки
krosovki
trainers

ночная рубашка
nochnaya rubashka
nightie

тапочки
tapochki
slippers

футбольная форма
futbol'naya forma
football strip

спортивный костюм
sportivniy kostyum
tracksuit

легинсы
leginsy
leggings

одежда для сна
odezhda dlya sna
nightwear

словарь slovar' • vocabulary

натуральные волокна
natural'niye volokna
natural fibre

синтетика
sintetika
synthetic

Это можно стирать в машине?
eto mozhno stirat' v mashine?
Is it machine washable?

Это подойдет по размеру двухлетнему ребенку?
eto podoydyot po razmeru dvukhletnemu rebyonku?
Will this fit a two-year-old?

мужская одежда muzhsk<u>a</u>ya od<u>e</u>zhda • **men's clothing**

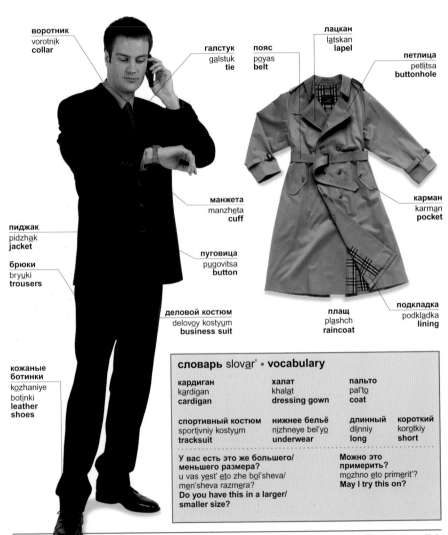

воротник
vorotn<u>i</u>k
collar

галстук
g<u>a</u>lstuk
tie

пояс
p<u>o</u>yas
belt

лацкан
l<u>a</u>tskan
lapel

петлица
petl<u>i</u>tsa
buttonhole

манжета
manzh<u>e</u>ta
cuff

карман
karm<u>a</u>n
pocket

пиджак
pidzh<u>a</u>k
jacket

брюки
bry<u>u</u>ki
trousers

пуговица
p<u>u</u>govitsa
button

деловой костюм
delov<u>o</u>y kosty<u>u</u>m
business suit

плащ
pl<u>a</u>shch
raincoat

подкладка
podkl<u>a</u>dka
lining

кожаные ботинки
k<u>o</u>zhaniye bot<u>i</u>nki
leather shoes

словарь slov<u>a</u>r' • **vocabulary**

кардиган k<u>a</u>rdigan **cardigan**	**халат** khal<u>a</u>t **dressing gown**	**пальто** pal't<u>o</u> **coat**
спортивный костюм sport<u>i</u>vniy kosty<u>u</u>m **tracksuit**	**нижнее бельё** n<u>i</u>zhneye bel'y<u>o</u> **underwear**	**длинный** **короткий** dl<u>i</u>nniy kor<u>o</u>tkiy **long** **short**

У вас есть это же большего/
меньшего размера?
u vas y<u>e</u>st' <u>e</u>to zhe b<u>o</u>l'sheva/
m<u>e</u>n'sheva razm<u>e</u>ra?
**Do you have this in a larger/
smaller size?**

Можно это
примерить?
m<u>o</u>zhno <u>e</u>to primer<u>i</u>t'?
May I try this on?

блейзер
bleyzer
blazer

спортивный пиджак
sportivniy pidzhak
sports jacket

жилет
zhilet
waistcoat

треугольный вырез
treugol'niy vyrez
V-neck

круглый вырез
krugliy
vyrez
**round
neck**

футболка
futbolka
T-shirt

анорак
anorak
anorak

толстовка
tolstovka
sweatshirt

рубашка
rubashka
shirt

джинсы
dzhinsy
jeans

свитер
sviter
sweater

пижама
pizhama
pyjamas

майка без рукавов
mayka bez rukavov
vest

повседневная одежда
povsednevnaya odezhda
casual wear

длинные трусы, шорты
dlinniye trusy, shorty
shorts

трусы-плавки, брифы
trusy-plavki, brify
briefs

трусы-боксёры
trusy-boksyory
boxer shorts

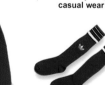

носки
noski
socks

женская одежда zhenskaya odezhda •
women's clothing

жакет
zhaket
jacket

шов
shov
seam

без шлеек
bez shleyek
strapless

без рукавов
bez rukavov
sleeveless

рукав
rukav
sleeve

в пол
v pol
ankle length

вечернее платье
vecherneye plat'ye
evening dress

платье
plat'ye
dress

юбка
yubka
skirt

блузка
bluzka
blouse

брюки
bryuki
trousers

подол
podol
hem

по колено
po koleno
knee length

колготки
kolgotki
tights

туфли
tufli
shoes

**деловой
(костюм)**
delovoy (kostyum)
formal

повседневный
povsednevniy
casual

бельё bel'yo • lingerie

халат
khalat
dressing gown

комбинация
kombinatsiya
slip

шлейка
shleyka
strap

топик
topik
camisole

подвязки
podvyazki
suspenders

майка-корсет
mayka-korset
basque

чулок
chulok
stocking

колготки
kolgotki
tights

бюстгальтер
byustgal'ter
bra

трусы
trusy
knickers

ночная рубашка
nochnaya rubashka
nightdress

свадьба svad'ba • wedding

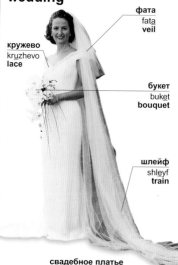

фата
fata
veil

кружево
kruzhevo
lace

букет
buket
bouquet

шлейф
shleyf
train

свадебное платье
svadebnoye plat'ye
wedding dress

словарь slovar' • vocabulary

корсет
korset
corset

подвязка
podvyazka
garter

подплечник
podplechnik
shoulder pad

пояс
poyas
waistband

сшитый на заказ
sshitiy na zakaz
tailored

воротник хомутиком (на открытом платье)
vorotnik khomutikom (na otkrytom plat'ye)
halter neck

на косточках
na kostochkakh
underwired

спортивный лифчик
sportivniy lifchik
sports bra

аксессуары aksessu<u>a</u>ry • **accessories**

пряжка
pry<u>a</u>zhka
buckle

ручка
r<u>u</u>chka
handle

кепка
k<u>e</u>pka
cap

шляпа
shly<u>a</u>pa
hat

шарф
sharf
scarf

ремень
rem<u>e</u>n'
belt

наконечник
nakon<u>e</u>chnik
tip

носовой платок
nos<u>o</u>voy plat<u>o</u>k
handkerchief

галстук-бабочка
g<u>a</u>lstuk-b<u>a</u>bochka
bow tie

булавка для галстука
bul<u>a</u>vka dlya g<u>a</u>lstuka
tie-pin

перчатки
perch<u>a</u>tki
gloves

зонт
z<u>o</u>nt
umbrella

ювелирные изделия yuvel<u>i</u>rniye izd<u>e</u>liya • **jewellery**

нитка жемчуга
n<u>i</u>tka
zh<u>e</u>mchuga
string of pearls

кулон
kul<u>o</u>n
pendant

брошь
br<u>o</u>sh
brooch

запонка
z<u>a</u>ponka
cuff links

звено
zv<u>e</u>no
link

фермуар
fermu<u>a</u>r
clasp

серьга
ser'g<u>a</u>
earrings

кольцо
kol'ts<u>o</u>
ring

камень
k<u>a</u>men'
stone

ожерелье
ozher<u>e</u>l'ye
necklace

часы
chas<u>y</u>
watch

браслет
brasl<u>e</u>t
bracelet

цепочка
tsep<u>o</u>chka
chain

ювелирная шкатулка yuvel<u>i</u>rnaya shkat<u>u</u>lka
jewellery box

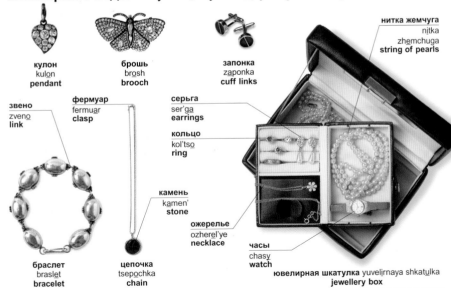

сумки su_mki • bags

бумажник
bum_azhnik
wallet

кошелёк
koshelyok
purse

сумка через плечо
su_mka che_rez plecho_
shoulder bag

застёжка
zastyo_zhka
fastening

ручки
ru_chki
handles

лямка
lya_mka
shoulder strap

дорожная сумка
doro_zhnaya su_mka
holdall

портфель
portfel'
briefcase

сумочка
su_mochka
handbag

рюкзак
ryukz_ak
backpack

обувь o_buv' • shoes

отверстие для шнурка
otve_rstiye dlya shnurka_
eyelet

шнурок
shnur_ok
lace

подошва
podo_shva
sole

язык
yaz_yk
tongue

туристические ботинки
turist_icheskiye bot_inki
walking boot

кроссовки
kros_ovki
trainer

каблук
kabl_uk
heel

ботинки на шнуровке
bot_inki na shnur_ovke
lace-up

сапоги
sapog_i
boot

вьетнамки
v'yetn_amki
flip-flop

**броги,
полуботинки**
br_ogi, polubot_inki
brogue

туфли на каблуке
t_ufli na kabluk_e
high-heeled shoe

туфли на танкетке
t_ufli na tank_etke
wedge

босоножки
boson_ozhki
sandal

**туфли без
шнуровки**
t_ufli bez shnur_ovki
slip-on

балетки
bal_etki
pump

волосы volosy • hair

расчёска
raschoska
comb

расчёсывать
raschosyvat'
comb (v)

щётка
shchotka
brush

расчесать щёткой
raschesat' shchotkoy
brush (v)

парикмахер
parikmakher
hairdresser

раковина
rakovina
sink

клиент/клиентка
kliyent / kliyentka
client

мыть myt' | **wash (v)**

накидка
nakidka
robe

ополаскивать
opolaskivat'
rinse (v)

стричь
strich'
cut (v)

уложить феном
ulozhit' fenom
blow dry (v)

делать укладку
delat' ukladku
set (v)

аксессуары aksesuary • accessories

фен
fen
hairdryer

шампунь
shampun'
shampoo

кондиционер
konditsioner
conditioner

гель
gel'
gel

лак для волос
lak dlya volos
hairspray

плойка
ployka
curling tongs

ножницы
nozhnitsy
scissors

ободок
obodok
hairband

выпрямитель для волос
vypryamitel' dlya volos
hair straighteners

невидимка
nevidimka
hairpin

причёски prich_o_ski • styles

конский хвост
k_o_nskiy khv_o_st
ponytail

коса
kos_a_
plait

ракушка
r_a_kushka
French pleat

пучок
puch_o_k
bun

хвостики
khv_o_stiki
pigtails

боб
bob
bob

короткая стрижка
kor_o_tkaya str_i_zhka
crop

кудрявые
kudr_ya_viye
curly

химическая завивка
khim_i_cheskaya zav_i_vka
perm

прямые
pry_a_miye
straight

корни
k_o_rni
roots

мелирование
melir_o_vaniye
highlights

лысый
l_y_siy
bald

парик
par_i_k
wig

цвета tsvet_a_ • colours

блонд
blond
blonde

тёмно-каштановый
ty_o_mno-kasht_a_noviy
brunette

тёмно-рыжий
ty_o_mno-r_y_zhiy
auburn

рыжий
r_y_zhiy
ginger

чёрный
ch_o_rniy
black

седой
sed_o_y
grey

белый
b_e_liy
white

крашеный
kr_a_sheniy
dyed

красота krasota • **beauty**

краска для волос
kraska dlya volos
hair dye

тени для век
teni dlya vek
eye shadow

тушь для ресниц
tush dlya resnits
mascara

подводка для глаз
podvodka dlya glaz
eyeliner

румяна
rumyana
blusher

тональный крем
tonal'niy krem
foundation

помада
pomada
lipstick

макияж makiyazh • **make-up**

карандаш для бровей
karandash dlya brovey
eyebrow pencil

щёточка для бровей
shchotochka dlya brovey
eyebrow brush

пинцет
pintset
tweezers

блеск для губ
blesk dlya gub
lip gloss

кисточка для губ
kistochka dlya gub
lip brush

контурный карандаш для губ
konturniy karandash dlya gub
lip liner

кисть
kist'
brush

консилер
konsiler
concealer

зеркало
zerkalo
mirror

пудра
pudra
face powder

пуховка
pukhovka
powder puff

пудреница pudrenitsa | **compact**

косметические процедуры
kosmeticheskiye protsedury •
beauty treatments

маска для лица
maska dlya litsa
face pack

солярий
solyariy
sunbed

уход за кожей лица
ukhod za kozhey litsa
facial

отшелушивать
otshelushivat'
exfoliate (v)

эпиляция воском
epilyatsiya voskom
wax

педикюр
pedikyur
pedicure

маникюр manikyur • **manicure**

жидкость для снятия лака
zhidkost' dlya snyatiya laka
nail varnish remover

пилка для ногтей
pilka dlya nogtey
nail file

лак для ногтей
lak dlya nogtey
nail varnish

маникюрные
ножницы
manikyurniye
nozhnitsy
nail scissors

книпсеры
knipsery
nail clippers

гигиена и уход gigiyena i ukhod • **toiletries**

очищающее
средство
ochishchayushcheye
sredstvo
cleanser

тоник
tonik
toner

увлажняющий
крем
uvlazhnyayushchiy
krem
moisturizer

автозагар
avtozagar
self-tanning cream

духи
dukhi
perfume

туалетная вода
tualetnaya voda
eau de toilette

словарь slovar' • **vocabulary**

цвет и тип
кожи лица
tsvet i tip
kozhi litsa
complexion

светлая
svetlaya
fair

тёмная
tyomnaya
dark

сухая
sukhaya
dry

жирная
zhirnaya
oily

чувствительная
chuvstvitel'naya
sensitive

гипоаллергенный
gipoallergenniy
hypoallergenic

оттенок
ottenok
shade

загар
zagar
tan

татуировка
tatuirovka
tattoo

от морщин
ot morshchin
antiwrinkle

ватные
шарики
vatniye shariki
cotton balls

здоровье zdor<u>o</u>v'ye
health

болезнь bolezn' • illness

температура temperatura | **fever**

ингалятор
ingalyator
inhaler

головная боль
golovnaya bol'
headache

носовое кровотечение
nosovoye krovotecheniye
nosebleed

кашель
kashel'
cough

чихание
chikhaniye
sneeze

простуда
prostuda
cold

грипп
grip
flu

астма
astma
asthma

колики
koliki
cramps

тошнота
toshnota
nausea

ветряная оспа
vetryanaya ospa
chickenpox

сыпь
syp'
rash

словарь slovar' • vocabulary

инсульт insul't **stroke**	**диабет** diabet **diabetes**	**экзема** ekzema **eczema**	**озноб** oznob **chill**	**страдать рвотой** stradat' rvotoi **vomit (v)**	**понос** ponos **diarrhoea**
давление davleniye **blood pressure**	**аллергия** allergiya **allergy**	**инфекция** infektsiya **infection**	**боль в животе** bol' v zhivote **stomach ache**	**эпилепсия** epilepsiya **epilepsy**	**корь** kor' **measles**
инфаркт infarkt **heart attack**	**сенная лихорадка** sennaya likhoradka **hay fever**	**вирус** virus **virus**	**падать в обморок** padat' v obmorok **faint (v)**	**мигрень** migren' **migraine**	**свинка** svinka **mumps**

врач vrach • doctor

консультация konsul'tatsiya • consultation

врач
vrach
doctor

негатоскоп
negatoskop
x-ray viewer

рецепт
retsept
prescription

медсестра
medsestra
nurse

**пациент/
пациентка**
patsiyent/
patsiyentka
patient

весы
vesy
scales

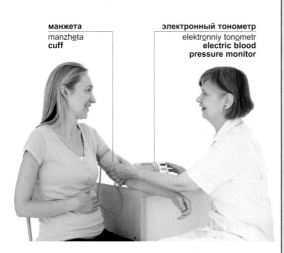

манжета
manzheta
cuff

электронный тонометр
elektronniy tonometr
**electric blood
pressure monitor**

словарь slovar' • vocabulary

**запись на
приём**
zapis' na priyom
appointment

кабинет
kabinet
surgery

приёмная
priyomnaya
waiting room

прививка
privivka
inoculation

градусник
gradusnik
thermometer

**медицинский
осмотр**
meditsinskiy
osmotr
**medical
examination**

Мне нужен врач.
mne nuzhen vrach
I need to see a doctor.

Здесь болит.
zdes' bolit
It hurts here.

травмы travmy • injury

косыночная
повязка
kosynochnaya
povyazka
sling

шейный
ортез
sheyniy
ortez
neck brace

растяжение связок rastyazheniye svyazok | **sprain**

перелом
perelom
fracture

травма шеи
travma shei
whiplash

порез
porez
cut

ссадина
ssadina
graze

синяк
sinyak
bruise

заноза
zanoza
splinter

солнечный ожог
solnechniy ozhog
sunburn

ожог
ozhog
burn

укус
ukus
bite

укус насекомого
ukus nasekomogo
sting

словарь slovar' • vocabulary

несчастный
случай
neschasniy sluchay
accident

неотложная
помощь
neotlozhnaya
pomoshch
emergency

рана
rana
wound

кровоизлияние
krovoizliyaniye
haemorrhage

волдырь
voldyr'
blister

сотрясение мозга
sotryaseniye mozga
concussion

отравление
otravleniye
poisoning

поражение электротоком
porazheniye elektrotokom
electric shock

травма головы
travma golovy
head injury

С ним/ней всё будет хорошо?
s nim/ney vsyo budet khorosho?
Will he/she be all right?

Где больно?
gde bol'no?
Where does it hurt?

Пожалуйста, вызовите
скорую помощь.
pozhalusta, vyzovite skoruyu
pomoshch'
Please call an ambulance.

первая помощь p<u>e</u>rvaya p<u>o</u>moshch' • first aid

мазь
maz'
ointment

пластырь
pl<u>a</u>styr'
plaster

булавка
bul<u>a</u>vka
safety pin

перевязочный материал
perevy<u>a</u>zochniy material
bandage

обезболивающие
obezb<u>o</u>livayushchiye
painkillers

антибактериальная салфетка
antibakteri<u>a</u>l'naya salf<u>e</u>tka
antiseptic wipe

пинцет
pints<u>e</u>t
tweezers

ножницы
n<u>o</u>zhnitsy
scissors

антисептик
antis<u>e</u>ptik
antiseptic

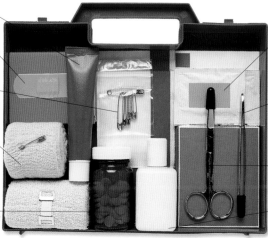

аптечка apt<u>e</u>chka | **first-aid box**

марля/бинт
m<u>a</u>rlya/b<u>i</u>nt
gauze

повязка
pov<u>ya</u>zka
dressing

шина sh<u>i</u>na | **splint**

лейкопластырь
leykopl<u>a</u>styr'
adhesive tape

реанимация
reanim<u>a</u>tsiya
resuscitation

словарь slov<u>a</u>r' • vocabulary

шок sh<u>o</u>k **shock**	**пульс** p<u>u</u>l's **pulse**	**задыхаться/ подавиться** zadykh<u>a</u>tsa/ podav<u>i</u>tsa **choke (v)**	**Вы можете помочь?** vy m<u>o</u>zhete pom<u>o</u>ch'? **Can you help?**
без сознания bez sozn<u>a</u>niya **unconscious**	**дыхание** dykh<u>a</u>niye **breathing**	**стерильный** ster<u>i</u>l'niy **sterile**	**Вы умеете оказывать первую помощь?** vy um<u>e</u>yete ok<u>a</u>zyvat' p<u>e</u>rvuyu pom<u>o</u>shch'? **Do you know first aid?**

больница bol'nitsa • hospital

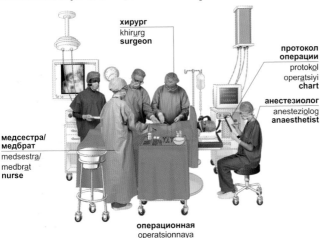

хирург
khirurg
surgeon

**протокол
операции**
protokol
operatsiyi
chart

анестезиолог
anesteziolog
anaesthetist

**медсестра/
медбрат**
medsestra/
medbrat
nurse

операционная
operatsionnaya
operating theatre

анализ крови
analiz krovi
blood test

укол
ukol
injection

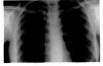

рентген
rentgen
x-ray

каталка
katalka
trolley

кнопка вызова персонала
knopka vyzova personala
call button

пункт скорой помощи
punkt skoroy pomoshchi
emergency room

палата
palata
ward

кресло-каталка
kreslo-katalka
wheelchair

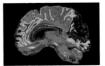

томография (КТ)
tomografiya (kate)
scan

словарь slovar' • vocabulary

операция operatsiya **operation**	**выписан** vypisan **discharged**	**время посещений** vremya poseshcheniy **visiting hours**	**детское отделение** detskoye otdeleniye **children's ward**	**отделение реанимации и интенсивной терапии** otdeleniye reanimatsii i intensivnoy terapii **intensive care unit**
госпитализирован gospitalizirovan **admitted**	**клиника** klinika **clinic**	**родильное отделение** rodil'noye otdeleniye **maternity ward**	**отдельная палата** otdel'naya palata **private room**	**амбулаторный пациент** ambulatorniy patsiyent **outpatient**

отделения otdeleniya • departments

лор
lor
ENT

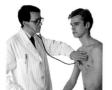

кардиология
kardiologiya
cardiology

ортопедия
ortopediya
orthopaedics

гинекология
ginekologiya
gynaecology

физиотерапия
fizioterapiya
physiotherapy

дерматология
dermatologiya
dermatology

педиатрия
pediatriya
paediatrics

рентгенология
rentgenologiya
radiology

хирургия
khirurgiya
surgery

роддом
roddom
maternity

психиатрия
psikhiatriya
psychiatry

офтальмология
oftal'mologiya
ophthalmology

словарь slovar' • vocabulary

неврология nevrologiya **neurology**	**урология** urologiya **urology**	**эндокринология** endokrinologiya **endocrinology**	**патология** patologiya **pathology**	**результат** rezul'tat **result**
онкология onkologiya **oncology**	**пластическая хирургия** plasticheskaya khirurgiya **plastic surgery**	**направление** napravleniye **referral**	**анализ** analiz **test**	**консультант** konsul'tant **consultant**

зубной врач zubnoy vrach • dentist

зуб zub • tooth

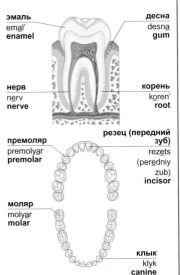

эмаль
emal'
enamel

десна
desna
gum

нерв
nerv
nerve

корень
koren'
root

премоляр
premolyar
premolar

резец (передний зуб)
rezets (peredniy zub)
incisor

моляр
molyar
molar

клык
klyk
canine

осмотр osmotr • checkup

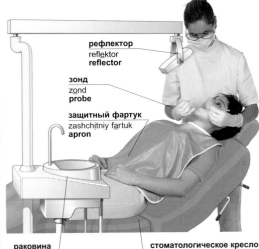

рефлектор
reflektor
reflector

зонд
zond
probe

защитный фартук
zashchitniy fartuk
apron

раковина
rakovina
basin

стоматологическое кресло
stomatologicheskoye kreslo
dentist's chair

словарь slovar' • vocabulary

зубная боль
zubnaya bol'
toothache

зубной налёт
zubnoy nalyot
plaque

кариес
kariyes
decay

пломба
plomba
filling

бормашина
bormashina
drill

зубная нить
zubnaya nit'
dental floss

удаление (зуба)
udaleniye (zuba)
extraction

коронка
koronka
crown

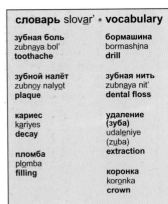

чистить зубной нитью
chistit' zubnoy nit'yu
floss (v)

чистить
chistit'
brush (v)

брекеты
brekety
braces

рентгеновский снимок зуба
rentgenovskiy snimok zuba
dental x-ray

рентгеновская плёнка
rentgenovskaya plyonka
x-ray film

зубные протезы
zubniye protezy
dentures

окулист okulist • **optician**

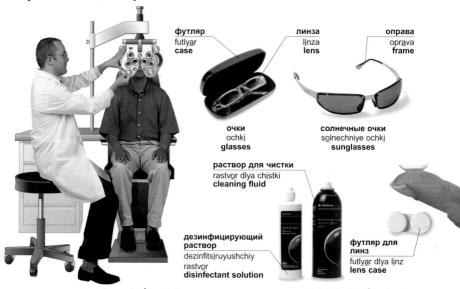

футляр
futlyar
case

линза
linza
lens

оправа
oprava
frame

очки
ochki
glasses

солнечные очки
solnechniye ochki
sunglasses

раствор для чистки
rastvor dlya chistki
cleaning fluid

дезинфицирующий раствор
dezinfitsiruyushchiy rastvor
disinfectant solution

футляр для линз
futlyar dlya linz
lens case

проверка зрения proverka zreniya | **eye test**

контактные линзы kontaktniye linzy | **contact lenses**

глаз glaz • **eye**

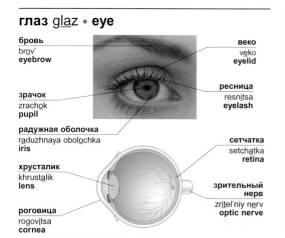

бровь
brov'
eyebrow

веко
veko
eyelid

зрачок
zrachok
pupil

ресница
resnitsa
eyelash

радужная оболочка
raduzhnaya obolochka
iris

сетчатка
setchatka
retina

хрусталик
khrustalik
lens

зрительный нерв
zritel'niy nerv
optic nerve

роговица
rogovitsa
cornea

словарь slovar' • **vocabulary**

зрение
zreniye
vision

астигматизм
astigmatizm
astigmatism

диоптрия
dioptriya
diopter

дальнозоркость
dal'nozorkost'
long sight

слеза (слёзы)
sleza (slyozy)
tear

близорукость
blizorukost'
short sight

катаракта
katarakta
cataract

бифокальный
bifokal'niy
bifocal

беременность beremennost' • **pregnancy**

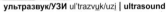

УЗИ
uzi
scan

тест на беременность
test na beremennost'
pregnancy test

ультразвук/УЗИ ul'trazvuk/uzi | **ultrasound**

пуповина
pupovina
umbilical cord

плацента
platsenta
placenta

шейка матки
sheyka matki
cervix

матка
matka
uterus

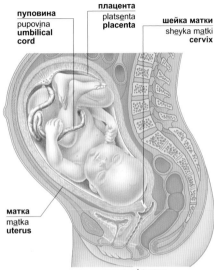

плод plod | **foetus**

словарь slovar' • **vocabulary**

овуляция ovulyatsiya **ovulation**	пренатальный prenatal'niy **antenatal**	схватка skhvatka **contraction**	раскрытие raskrytiye **dilation**	роды rody **delivery**	ягодичное (предлежание) yagodichnoye (predlezhaniye) **breech birth**
зачатие zachatiye **conception**	эмбрион embrion **embryo**	отошли воды otoshli vody **break waters (v)**	эпидуральная анестезия epidural'naya anesteziya **epidural**	рождение rozhdeniye **birth**	преждевременные (роды) prezhdevremenniye (rody) **premature**
беременная beremennaya **pregnant**	матка matka **womb**	околоплодные воды okoloplodniye vody **amniotic fluid**	эпизиотомия epiziotomiya **episiotomy**	выкидыш vykidysh **miscarriage**	гинеколог ginekolog **gynaecologist**
готовящаяся стать матерью gotovyashchayasya stat' mater'yu **expectant**	триместр trimestr **trimester**	амниоцентез amniotsentez **amniocentesis**	кесарево сечение kesarevo secheniye **caesarean section**	швы shvy **stitches**	акушер akusher **obstetrician**

роды rody • childbirth

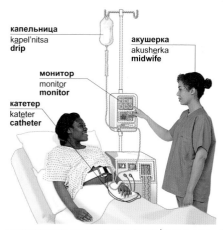

капельница
kapel'nitsa
drip

акушерка
akusherka
midwife

монитор
monitor
monitor

катетер
kateter
catheter

закрытый кувез zakrytiy kuvez | **incubator**

стимулировать роды stimulirovat' rody | **induce labour (v)**

вес при рождении ves pri rozhdeniyi
birth weight

акушерские щипцы
akusherskiye shchiptsy
forceps

вакуум-экстрактор
vakuum-ekstraktor
ventouse cup

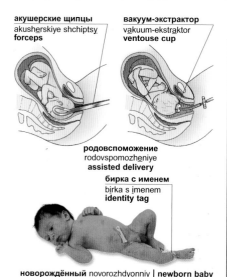

родовспоможение
rodovspomozheniye
assisted delivery

бирка с именем
birka s imenem
identity tag

новорождённый novorozhdyonniy | **newborn baby**

кормление kormleniye • nursing

молокоотсос
molokootsos
breast pump

бюстгальтер для кормящих
byustgal'ter dlya kormyashchikh
nursing bra

кормить грудью
kormit' grud'yu
breastfeed (v)

прокладки для груди
prokladki dlya grudi
pads

нетрадиционная медицина netraditsionnaya meditsina • alternative therapy

позы йоги
poza iogi
yoga pose

коврик
kovrik
mat

массаж
massazh
massage

шиацу
shiatsu
shiatsu

йога yoga | **yoga**

хиропрактика
khiropraktika
chiropractic

остеопатия
osteopatiya
osteopathy

рефлексология
refleksologiya
reflexology

медитация
meditatsiya
meditation

психолог-консультант
psikholog-konsul'tant
counsellor

рейки
reyki
reiki

иглоукалывание
igloukalyvaniye
acupuncture

групповая психотерапия
gruppovaya psikhoterapiya
group therapy

аюрведа
ayurveda
ayurveda

гипнотерапия
gipnoterapiya
hypnotherapy

эфирные масла
efirniye masla
essential oils

фитотерапия
fitoterapiya
herbalism

ароматерапия
aromaterapiya
aromatherapy

гомеопатия
gomeopatiya
homeopathy

акупрессура
akupressura
acupressure

психотерапевт
psikhoterapevt
therapist

психотерапия
psikhoterapiya
psychotherapy

словарь slovar' • vocabulary

(пищевая) добавка (pishchevaya) dobavka **supplement**	**натуропатия** naturopatiya **naturopathy**	**релаксация, отдых** relaksatsiya, otdykh **relaxation**	**лекарственное растение** lekarstvennoye rasteniye **herb**
водолечение vodolecheniye **hydrotherapy**	**фэншуй** fenshuy **feng shui**	**стресс** stress **stress**	**кристаллотерапия** kristalloterapiya **crystal healing**

дом d<u>o</u>m
home

дом dom • house

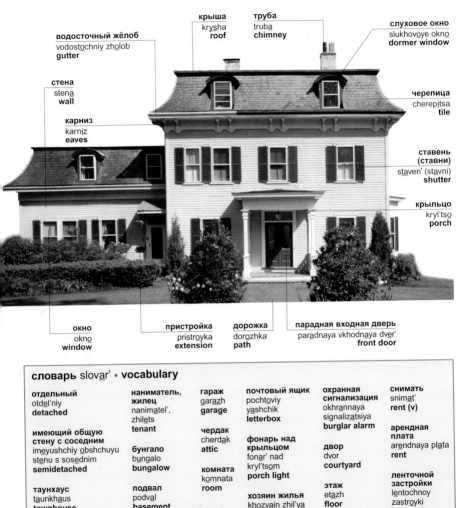

крыша
krysha
roof

труба
truba
chimney

слуховое окно
slukhovoye okno
dormer window

водосточный жёлоб
vodostochniy zholob
gutter

стена
stena
wall

карниз
karniz
eaves

черепица
cherepitsa
tile

**ставень
(ставни)**
staven' (stavni)
shutter

крыльцо
kryl'tso
porch

окно
okno
window

пристройка
pristroyka
extension

дорожка
dorozhka
path

парадная входная дверь
paradnaya vkhodnaya dver'
front door

словарь slovar' • vocabulary

отдельный otdel'niy **detached**	**наниматель, жилец** nanimatel', zhilets **tenant**	**гараж** garazh **garage**	**почтовый ящик** pochtoviy yashchik **letterbox**	**охранная сигнализация** okhrannaya signalizatsiya **burglar alarm**	**снимать** snimat' **rent (v)**
имеющий общую стену с соседним imeyushchiy obshchuyu stenu s sosednim **semidetached**	**бунгало** bungalo **bungalow**	**чердак** cherdak **attic**	**фонарь над крыльцом** fonar' nad kryl'tsom **porch light**	**двор** dvor **courtyard**	**арендная плата** arendnaya plata **rent**
таунхаус taunkhaus **townhouse**	**подвал** podval **basement**	**комната** komnata **room**	**хозяин жилья** khozyain zhil'ya **landlord**	**этаж** etazh **floor**	**ленточной застройки** lentochnoy zastroyki **terraced**

вход vkh<u>o</u>d • entrance

поручень
poruchen'
hand rail

лестничная площадка
l<u>e</u>snichnaya ploshch<u>a</u>dka
landing

перила
per<u>i</u>la
banister

лестница
l<u>e</u>snitsa
staircase

прихожая
prikh<u>o</u>zhaya
hallway

дверной звонок
dvern<u>o</u>y zvon<u>o</u>k
doorbell

коврик для ног
k<u>o</u>vrik dlya n<u>o</u>g
doormat

дверной молоток
dvern<u>o</u>y molot<u>o</u>k
door knocker

ключ
kly<u>u</u>ch
key

дверная цепочка
dvern<u>a</u>ya tsep<u>o</u>chka
door chain

замок
zam<u>o</u>k
lock

задвижка
zadv<u>i</u>zhka
bolt

квартира
kvart<u>i</u>ra • **flat**

балкон
balk<u>o</u>n
balcony

многоквартирный дом
mnogokv<u>a</u>rtirniy dom
block of flats

домофон
domof<u>o</u>n
intercom

лифт
lift
lift

внутренние системы vnutrenniye sistemy • internal systems

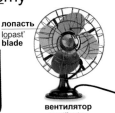

лопасть
lopast'
blade

вентилятор
ventilyator
fan

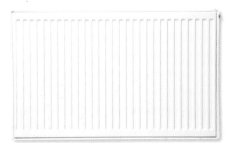

конвектор
konvektor
convector heater

батарея
batareya
radiator

обогреватель
obogrevatel'
heater

электричество elektrichestvo • electricity

нулевой
nulevoy
neutral

заземление
zazemleniye
earthing

штекер
shteker
pin

под напряжением
pod napryazheniyem
live

энергосберегающая
лампочка
energosberegayushchaya
lampochka
energy-saving bulb

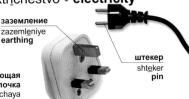

штепсельная вилка
shtepsel'naya vilka | **plug**

проводка provodka | **wires**

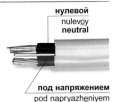

словарь slovar' • vocabulary

напряжение napryazheniye **voltage**	предохранитель predokhranitel' **fuse**	розетка rozetka **socket**	прямой ток pryamoy tok **direct current**	отключение электроэнергии otklyucheniye elektroenergii **power cut**
ампер amper **amp**	блок плавких предохранителей blok plavkikh predokhraniteley **fuse box**	выключатель vyklyuchatel' **switch**	трансформатор transformator **transformer**	питание от сети pitaniye ot seti **mains supply**
электроэнергия elektroenergiya **power**	генератор generator **generator**	переменный ток peremenniy tok **alternating current**	электросчётчик elektroschotchik **electricity meter**	

водопровод vodoprovod • plumbing

вход холодной воды
vkhod kholodnoy vody
inlet

предохранительный клапан
predokhranitel'niy klapan
pressure valve

переливная труба
perelivnaya truba
overflow pipe

водосборник
vodosbornik
water chamber

термостат
termostat
thermostat

газовая горелка
gazovaya gorelka
gas burner

бойлер
boyler
boiler

выход горячей воды
vykhod goryachey vody
outlet

теплоизоляция
teploizolyatsiya
insulation

бак
bak
tank

сливной кран
slivnoy kran
drain cock

нагревательный элемент
nagrevatel'niy element
heating element

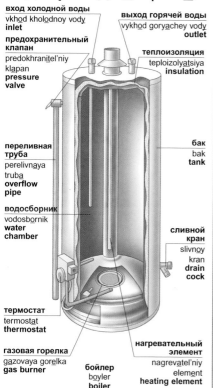

раковина rakovina • sink

кран
kran
tap

рычаг
rychag
lever

прокладка
prokladka
gasket

подводящая труба
podvodyashchaya truba
supply pipe

стопорный вентиль
stoporniy ventil'
shutoff valve

сливная труба
slivnaya truba
drain

измельчитель отходов
izmel'chitel' otkhodov
waste disposal unit

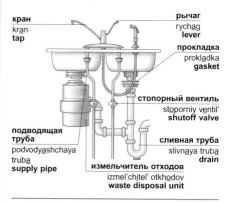

туалет tualet • toilet

поплавок
poplavok
float ball

сиденье
siden'ye
seat

чаша унитаза
chasha unitaza
bowl

сливной бачок
slivnoy bachok
cistern

канализационный спуск
kanalizatsionniy spusk
waste pipe

утилизация мусора utilizatsiya musora • waste disposal

бутылка
butylka
bottle

педаль
pedal'
pedal

крышка
kryshka
lid

контейнер для мусора
konteyner dlya musora
recycling bin

мусорка
musorka
rubbish bin

сортировочный ящик
sortirovochniy yashchik
sorting unit

органические отходы
organicheskiye otkhody
organic waste

гостиная gos**ti**naya • **living room**

бра
bra
wall light

камин
kam**i**n
fireplace

потолок
pot**o**l**o**k
ceiling

ваза
v**a**za
vase

диванная
подушка
div**a**nnaya
pod**u**shka
cushion

лампа
l**a**mpa
lamp

журнальный
столик
zhurn**a**l'niy
st**o**lik
coffee table

диван
div**a**n
sofa

пол
p**o**l
floor

рама
rama
frame

картина
kartina
painting

штора
shtora
curtain

тюлевая занавеска
tyulevaya zanaveska
net curtain

жалюзи
zhalyuzi
Venetian blind

рольштора
rol'shtora
roller blind

лепной карниз
lepnoy karniz
moulding

кресло
kreslo
armchair

книжная полка
knizhnaya polka
bookshelf

диван-кровать
divan-krovat'
sofa bed

ковёр
kovyor
rug

кабинет kabinet | **study**

столовая stol<u>o</u>vaya • dining room

перец
perets
pepper

соль
s<u>o</u>l'
salt

стол
st<u>o</u>l
table

посуда
pos<u>u</u>da
crockery

столовые приборы
stol<u>o</u>viye pribory
cutlery

стул
st<u>u</u>l
chair

спинка
sp<u>i</u>nka
back

сиденье
sid<u>e</u>n'ye
seat

ножка
n<u>o</u>zhka
leg

словарь slov<u>a</u>r' • vocabulary

накрывать на стол nakryv<u>a</u>t' na st<u>o</u>l **lay the table (v)**	**голодный** gol<u>o</u>dniy **hungry**	**обед/ланч** ob<u>e</u>d/lanch **lunch**	**сыт(ый)** syt(iy) **full**	**хозяин** khoz<u>ya</u>in **host**	**Можно мне добавки?** m<u>o</u>zhno mne dob<u>a</u>vki? **Can I have some more, please?**
подавать podav<u>a</u>t' **serve (v)**	**скатерть** sk<u>a</u>tert' **tablecloth**	**ужин / обед** <u>u</u>zhin / ob<u>e</u>d **dinner**	**порция** p<u>o</u>rtsiya **portion**	**хозяйка** khoz<u>ya</u>yka **hostess**	**Спасибо, мне достаточно.** spas<u>i</u>bo, mne dost<u>a</u>tochno **I've had enough, thank you.**
есть y<u>e</u>st' **eat (v)**	**завтрак** z<u>a</u>vtrak **breakfast**	**салфетка-подложка под прибор** salf<u>e</u>tka-podl<u>o</u>zhka pod prib<u>o</u>r **place mat**	**прием пищи** pri<u>yo</u>m p<u>i</u>shchi **meal**	**гость** g<u>o</u>st' **guest**	**Это было очень вкусно.** eto bylo <u>o</u>chen' vk<u>u</u>sno **That was delicious.**

посуда и столовые приборы posuda i stoloviye pribory • crockery and cutlery

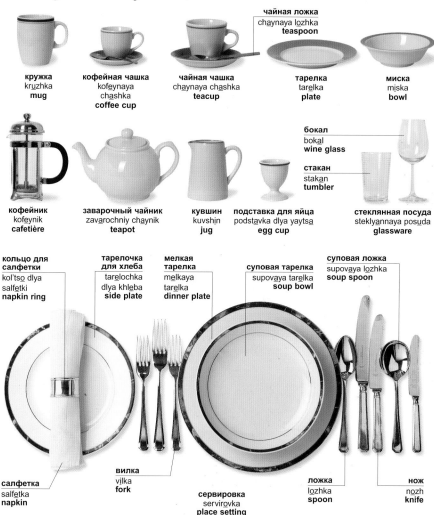

чайная ложка
chaynaya lozhka
teaspoon

кружка
kruzhka
mug

кофейная чашка
kofeynaya chashka
coffee cup

чайная чашка
chaynaya chashka
teacup

тарелка
tarelka
plate

миска
miska
bowl

бокал
bokal
wine glass

стакан
stakan
tumbler

кофейник
kofeynik
cafetière

заварочный чайник
zavarochniy chaynik
teapot

кувшин
kuvshin
jug

подставка для яйца
podstavka dlya yaytsa
egg cup

стеклянная посуда
steklyannaya posuda
glassware

кольцо для салфетки
kol'tso dlya salfetki
napkin ring

тарелочка для хлеба
tarelochka dlya khleba
side plate

мелкая тарелка
melkaya tarelka
dinner plate

суповая тарелка
supovaya tarelka
soup bowl

суповая ложка
supovaya lozhka
soup spoon

салфетка
salfetka
napkin

вилка
vilka
fork

сервировка
servirovka
place setting

ложка
lozhka
spoon

нож
nozh
knife

кухня k<u>u</u>khnya • **kitchen**

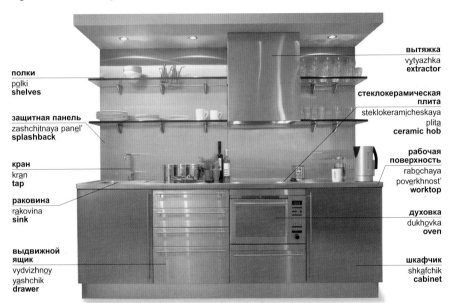

полки
polki
shelves

защитная панель
zashchitnaya pan<u>e</u>l'
splashback

кран
kran
tap

раковина
r<u>a</u>kovina
sink

выдвижной ящик
vydvizhn<u>o</u>y
y<u>a</u>shchik
drawer

вытяжка
vyty<u>a</u>zhka
extractor

стеклокерамическая плита
steklokeram<u>i</u>cheskaya
pl<u>i</u>ta
ceramic hob

рабочая поверхность
rab<u>o</u>chaya
pov<u>e</u>rkhnost'
worktop

духовка
dukh<u>o</u>vka
oven

шкафчик
shk<u>a</u>fchik
cabinet

бытовые приборы bytov<u>i</u>ye prib<u>o</u>ry • **appliances**

чаша для смешивания
ch<u>a</u>sha dlya sm<u>e</u>shivaniya
mixing bowl

крышка
kr<u>y</u>shka
lid

лезвие ножа
l<u>e</u>zviye nozh<u>a</u>
blade

микроволновая печь
mikrovoln<u>o</u>vaya p<u>e</u>ch'
microwave oven

чайник
ch<u>a</u>ynik
kettle

тостер
t<u>o</u>ster
toaster

кухонный комбайн
k<u>u</u>khonniy komb<u>a</u>yn
food processor

блендер
bl<u>e</u>nder
blender

посудомоечная машина
posudom<u>o</u>yechnaya mash<u>i</u>na
dishwasher

льдогенератор
l'dogenerator
ice maker

холодильник
kholodil'nik
refrigerator

полка
polka
shelf

морозильник
morozil'nik
freezer

отделение
для овощей и
фруктов
otdeleniye dlya
ovoshchey i
fruktov
crisper

холодильник-морозильник kholodil'nik-morozil'nik | **fridge-freezer**

словарь slovar' ·
vocabulary

подставка для
сушки
podstavka dlya
sushki
draining board

конфорка
газовой плиты
konforka
gazovoy plity
burner

варочная
панель
varochnaya
panel'
hob

мусорка
musorka
rubbish bin

замораживать
zamorazhivat'
freeze (v)

размораживать
razmorazhivat'
defrost (v)

готовить на
пару
gotovit' na paru
steam (v)

пассеровать
passerovat'
sauté (v)

приготовление пищи prigotovleniye pishchi · **cooking**

чистить
chistit'
peel (v)

резать (ломтиками)
rezat' (lomtikami)
slice (v)

тереть на тёрке
teret' na tyorke
grate (v)

лить, сыпать
lit', sypat'
pour (v)

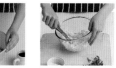
смешивать
smeshivat'
mix (v)

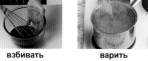
взбивать
vzbivat'
whisk (v)

варить
varit'
boil (v)

жарить
zharit'
fry (v)

раскатывать
raskatyvat'
roll (v)

помешивать
pomeshivat'
stir (v)

**медленно
кипятить**
medlenno kipyatit'
simmer (v)

**варить на
слабом огне**
varit' na slabom ogne
poach (v)

печь
pech'
bake (v)

жарить, запекать
zharit', zapekat'
roast (v)

жарить на гриле
zharit' na grile
grill (v)

кухонная утварь k**u**khonnaya **u**tvar' • **kitchenware**

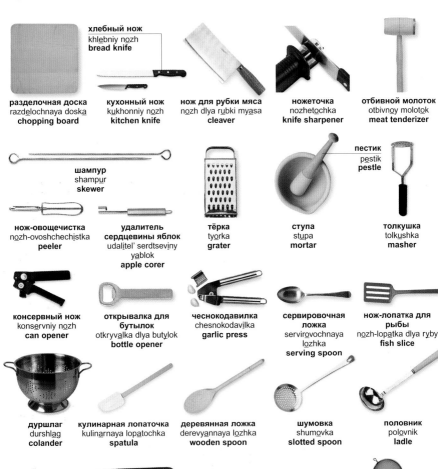

хлебный нож
khl**e**bniy n**o**zh
bread knife

разделочная доска
razd**e**lochnaya dosk**a**
chopping board

кухонный нож
k**u**khonniy n**o**zh
kitchen knife

нож для рубки мяса
n**o**zh dlya r**u**bki my**a**sa
cleaver

ножеточка
nozhet**o**chka
knife sharpener

отбивной молоток
otbivn**o**y molot**o**k
meat tenderizer

шампур
shamp**u**r
skewer

нож-овощечистка
n**o**zh-ovoshchech**i**stka
peeler

**удалитель
сердцевины яблок**
udal**i**tel' serdtsev**i**ny
y**a**blok
apple corer

тёрка
ty**o**rka
grater

пестик
p**e**stik
pestle

ступа
st**u**pa
mortar

толкушка
tolk**u**shka
masher

консервный нож
kons**e**rvniy n**o**zh
can opener

**открывалка для
бутылок**
otkryv**a**lka dlya but**y**lok
bottle opener

чеснокодавилка
chesnokod**a**vilka
garlic press

**сервировочная
ложка**
servir**o**vochnaya
l**o**zhka
serving spoon

**нож-лопатка для
рыбы**
n**o**zh-lop**a**tka dlya r**y**by
fish slice

дуршлаг
durshl**a**g
colander

кулинарная лопаточка
kulin**a**rnaya lopat**o**chka
spatula

деревянная ложка
derevy**a**nnaya l**o**zhka
wooden spoon

шумовка
shum**o**vka
slotted spoon

половник
pol**o**vnik
ladle

разделочная вилка
razd**e**lochnaya v**i**lka
carving fork

ложка для мороженого
l**o**zhka dlya mor**o**zhenogo
scoop

венчик для взбивания
v**e**nchik dlya vzbiv**a**niya
whisk

дуршлаг-сеточка
durshl**a**g-s**e**tochka
sieve

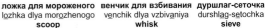

крышка
kryshka
lid

антипригарный
antiprigarniy
non-stick

сковорода
skovoroda
frying pan

кастрюля
kastryulya
saucepan

сковорода для гриля
skovoroda dlya grilya
grill pan

вок
vok
wok

керамическая
кастрюля
keramicheskaya kastryulya
earthenware dish

стекло
Steklo
glass

жаропрочный
zharoprochniy
ovenproof

миска
miska
mixing bowl

форма для суфле
forma dlya sufle
soufflé dish

форма для запеканки
forma dlya zapekanki
gratin dish

рамекин
ramekin
ramekin

кастрюля-
кассероль
kastryulya-kasserol'
casserole dish

выпечка vypechka • baking cakes

весы
vesy
scales

мерный кувшин
merniy kuvshin
measuring jug

форма для торта
forma dlya torta
cake tin

форма для пирога
с начинкой
forma dlya piroga s
nachinkoy
pie tin

форма для флана
forma dlya flana
flan tin

кисточка для смазки
kistochka dlya smazki
pastry brush

скалка skalka | **rolling pin**

кондитерский мешок
konditerskiy meshok | **piping bag**

форма для
маффинов
forma dlya mafinov
muffin tray

противень
protiven'
baking tray

решётка (для
охлаждения)
reshotka (dlya
okhlazhdeniya)
cooling rack

рукавица-
прихватка
rukavitsa-prikhvatka
oven glove

передник
perednik
apron

спальня spal'nya • **bedroom**

платяной шкаф
platyanoy shk**af**
wardrobe

настольная лампа
nast**ol**'naya l**a**mpa
bedside lamp

изголовье
izgolov'ye
headboard

тумбочка
t**u**mbochka
bedside table

комод
kom**o**d
chest of drawers

выдвижной ящик	**кровать**	**матрас**	**покрывало, плед**	**подушка**
vydvizhn**oy** y**a**shchik	krov**at**'	matr**as**	pokryv**a**lo, pl**ed**	pod**u**shka
drawer	**bed**	**mattress**	**bedspread**	**pillow**

грелка
gr**e**lka
hot-water bottle

часы-радио
chasy-r**a**dio
clock radio

будильник
bud**il**'nik
alarm clock

коробка салфеток
kor**o**bka salf**e**tok
box of tissues

вешалка
v**e**shalka
coat hanger

постельное бельё postel'noye bel'yo • bed linen

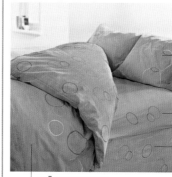

наволочка
navolochka
pillowcase

простыня
prostynya
sheet

подзор
podzor
valance

зеркало
zerkalo
mirror

туалетный столик
tualetniy stolik
dressing table

стёганое одеяло
styoganoye odeyalo
duvet

лоскутное одеяло, квилт
loskutnoye odeyalo, kvilt
quilt

шерстяное одеяло
sherstyanoye odeyalo
blanket

пол
pol
floor

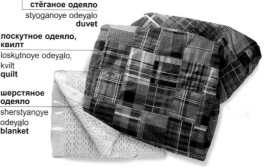

словарь slovar' • vocabulary

односпальная кровать
odnospal'naya krovat'
single bed

двуспальная кровать
dvuspal'naya krovat'
double bed

электроодеяло
elektroodeyalo
electric blanket

изножье кровати
iznozh'ye krovati
footboard

пружина
pruzhina
bedspring

ковёр
kovyor
carpet

бессонница
bessonnitsa
insomnia

идти спать
idti spat'
go to bed (v)

заснуть
zasnut'
go to sleep (v)

проснуться
prosnut'sya
wake up (v)

вставать
vstavat'
get up (v)

застилать постель
zastilat' postel'
make the bed (v)

ставить будильник
stavit' budil'nik
set the alarm (v)

храпеть
khrapet'
snore (v)

встроенный шкаф
vstroyenniy shkaf
built-in wardrobe

ванная комната vannaya komnata • bathroom

вешалка для полотенца
veshalka dlya polotentsa
towel rail

раковина
rakovina
washbasin

пробка
probka
plug

дверца душа
dvertsa dusha
shower door

кран с холодной водой
kran s kholodnoy vodoy
cold tap

кран с горячей водой
kran s goryachey vodoy
hot tap

головка душа
golovka dusha
shower head

душ
dush
shower

сливное отверстие
slivnoye otverstiye
drain

сиденье
siden'ye
toilet seat

унитаз
unitaz
toilet

ёршик для унитаза
yorshik dlya unitaza
toilet brush

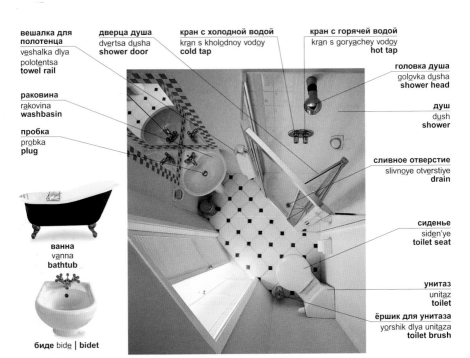

ванна
vanna
bathtub

биде bide | **bidet**

словарь slovar' • vocabulary

аптечка
aptechka
medicine cabinet

туалетная бумага
tualetnaya bumaga
toilet roll

принимать душ
prinimat' dush
take a shower (v)

коврик для ванной
kovrik dlya vannoy
bath mat

занавеска для душа
zanaveska dlya dusha
shower curtain

принимать ванну
prinimat' vannu
take a bath (v)

гигиена полости рта gigiyena polosti rta • dental hygiene

зубная щётка
zubnaya shchotka
toothbrush

зубная нить
zubnaya nit'
dental floss

зубная паста
zubnaya pasta
toothpaste

ополаскиватель для рта
opolaskivatel' dlya rta
mouthwash

русский ruskiy • english

пемза
pemza
pumice stone

губка
gubka
sponge

щётка для спины
shchotka dlya spiny
back brush

дезодорант
dezodorant
deodorant

мыло
mylo
soap dish

гель для душа
gel' dlya dusha
shower gel

мыло
mylo
soap

крем для лица
krem dlya litsa
face cream

пена для ванн
pena dlya vann
bubble bath

**полотенце
для рук**
polotentse dlya ruk
hand towel

**банное
полотенце**
bannoye
polotentse
bath towel

полотенца
polotentsa
towels

молочко для тела
molochko dlya tela
body lotion

тальк
tal'k
talcum powder

банный халат
banniy khalat
bathrobe

бритьё brit'yo • shaving

электробритва
elektrobritva
electric razor

пена для бритья
pena dlya brit'ya
shaving foam

**одноразовый станок для
бритья**
odnorazoviy stanok dlya brit'ya
disposable razor

лезвие
lezviye
razor blade

лосьон после бритья
los'yon posle brit'ya
aftershave

детская detskaya • nursery

уход за младенцем ukhod za mladentsem • baby care

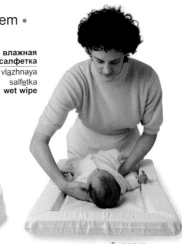

губка
gubka
sponge

крем от опрелостей
krem ot oprelostey
nappy rash cream

влажная салфетка
vlazhnaya salfetka
wet wipe

ванночка
vannochka
baby bath

горшок
gorshok
potty

пеленальный коврик
pelenal'niy kovrik
changing mat

сон son • sleeping

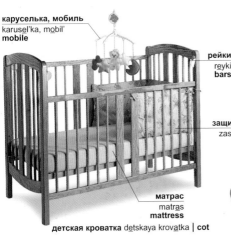

каруселька, мобиль
karusel'ka, mobil'
mobile

рейки
reyki
bars

защитные бортики
zashchitniye bortiki
bumper

матрас
matras
mattress

детская кроватка detskaya krovatka | **cot**

простыня
prostynya
sheet

одеяльце
odeyal'tse
blanket

овчинка
ovchinka
fleece

постельные принадлежности
postel'niye prinadlezhnosti
bedding

погремушка
pogremushka
rattle

колыбелька с ручками
kolybel'ka s ruchkami
Moses basket

игры igry • playing

кукла
kukla
doll

кукольный домик
kukol'niy domik
doll's house

домик для игр
domik dlya igr
playhouse

безопасность bezopasnost' • safety

блокиратор от детей
blokirator ot detey
child lock

радионяня
radionyanya
baby monitor

мишка
mishka
teddy bear

игрушка
igrushka
toy

корзина для игрушек
korzina dlya igrushek
toy basket

мяч
myach
ball

манеж
manezh
playpen

воротца
vorottsa
stair gate

мягкая игрушка
myakhkaya igrushka
soft toy

еда yeda • eating

стульчик для кормления
stul'chik dlya kormleniya
high chair

соска
soska
teat

поильник
poil'nik
drinking cup

бутылочка
butylochka
bottle

прогулка progulka • going out

прогулочная коляска
progulochnaya kolyaska
pushchair

коляска с люлькой
kolyaska s lyul'koy
pram

капюшон
kapyushon
hood

переносная люлька
perenosnaya lyul'ka
carrycot

подгузник
podguznik
nappy

сумка для смены подгузника
sumka dlya smeny podguznika
changing bag

рюкзак-кенгуру
ryukzak-kenguru
baby sling

подсобное помещение podsobnoye pomescheniye • utility room

стирка stirka • laundry

чистая одежда
chistaya
odezhda
clean clothes

грязное бельё
gryaznoye
bel'yo
**dirty
washing**

**корзина для
грязного белья**
korzina dlya
gryaznogo bel'ya
laundry basket

**стиральная
машина**
stiral'naya mashina
washing machine

**стирально-сушильная
машина**
stiral'no-sushil'naya
mashina
washer-dryer

**сушильная
машина**
sushil'naya mashina
tumble dryer

**бельевая
корзина**
bel'yevaya korzina
linen basket

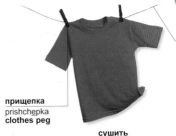

верёвка для белья
veryovka dlya bel'ya
clothes line

утюг
utyug
iron

прищепка
prishchepka
clothes peg

сушить
sushit'
dry (v)

гладильная доска gladil'naya doska | **ironing board**

словарь slovar' • vocabulary

загружать zagruzhat' **load (v)**	**отжимать (в центрифуге)** otzhimat' (v tsentrifuge) **spin (v)**	**гладить** gladit' **iron (v)**	**Как пользоваться этой стиральной машиной?** kak pol'zovat'sya etoy stiral'noy mashinoy? **How do I operate the washing machine?**
полоскать poloskat' **rinse (v)**	**центрифуга** tsentrifuga **spin dryer**	**кондиционер для белья** konditsioner dlya bel'ya **fabric conditioner**	**Какой режим предназначен для цветного/белого белья?** kakoy rezhim prednaznachen dlya tsvetnova/belova bel'ya? **What is the setting for coloureds/whites?**

оборудование для уборки oborudovaniye dlya ub_orki • cleaning equipment

всасывающий шланг
vs_asyvayushchiy shlang
suction hose

щётка
shch_otka
brush

совок
sov_ok
dust pan

отбеливатель
otb_elivatel'
bleach

ведро
vedr_o
bucket

порошок
porosh_ok
powder

жидкость
zhidkost'
liquid

тряпка для (вытирания) пыли
try_apka dlya (vytir_aniya) pyli
duster

пылесос
pyles_os
vacuum cleaner

швабра
shv_abra
mop

моющее средство
m_oyushcheye sr_edstvo
detergent

полироль
polir_ol'
polish

действия d_eystviya • activities

протирать, очищать
protir_at', ochishch_at'
clean (v)

мыть
m_yt'
wash (v)

вытирать
vytir_at'
wipe (v)

тереть
ter_et'
scrub (v)

скрести
skrest_i
scrape (v)

щётка
schy_otka
broom

подметать
podmet_at'
sweep (v)

вытирать пыль
vytir_at' pyl'
dust (v)

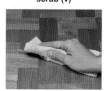

полировать, натирать
polirov_at', natir_at'
polish (v)

мастерская mastersk<u>a</u>ya • workshop

патрон
patr<u>o</u>n
chuck

сверло
sverl<u>o</u>
drill bit

аккумулятор
akumuly<u>a</u>tor
battery pack

электрический лобзик
elektr<u>i</u>cheskiy l<u>o</u>bzik
jigsaw

аккумуляторная дрель
akumuly<u>a</u>tornaya dr<u>e</u>l'
cordless drill

электродрель
elektrodr<u>e</u>l'
electric drill

клеевой пистолет
kleyev<u>o</u>y pistol<u>e</u>t
glue gun

струбцина
strubts<u>i</u>na
clamp

лезвие
l<u>e</u>zviye
blade

тиски
tisk<u>i</u>
vice

шлифовальная машинка
shlifov<u>a</u>l'naya mash<u>i</u>nka
sander

циркулярная пила
tsirkuly<u>a</u>rnaya pil<u>a</u>
circular saw

верстак
verst<u>a</u>k
workbench

клей для дерева
kl<u>e</u>y dlya d<u>e</u>reva
wood glue

стеллаж для
инструментов
stell<u>a</u>zh dlya
instrum<u>e</u>ntov
tool rack

фрезерный станок
fr<u>e</u>zerniy stan<u>o</u>k
router

коловорот
kolovor<u>o</u>t
bit brace

стружка
str<u>u</u>zhka
wood shavings

удлинитель
udlin<u>i</u>tel'
extension lead

виды обработки v̲idy obrab̲otki • techniques

резать
rez̲at'
cut (v)

пилить
pil̲it'
saw (v)

сверлить
sverl̲it
drill (v)

прибивать
pribiv̲at'
hammer (v)

строгать strog̲at'
plane (v)

точить toch̲it' | **turn (v)**

припой
prip̲oy
solder

вырезать vyrez̲at'
carve (v)

паять pay̲at' | **solder (v)**

материалы material̲y • materials

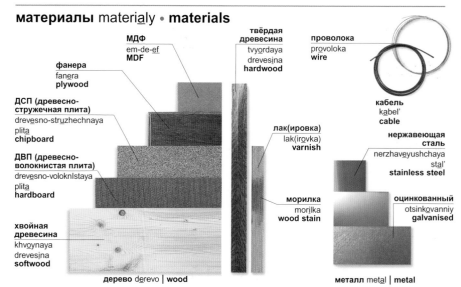

МДФ
em-de-̲ef
MDF

фанера
fan̲era
plywood

**ДСП (древесно-
стружечная плита)**
drev̲esno-struzhechnaya
plit̲a
chipboard

**ДВП (древесно-
волокнистая плита)**
drevesno-volokn̲lstaya
plit̲a
hardboard

**хвойная
древесина**
khv̲oynaya
drev̲esina
softwood

**твёрдая
древесина**
tvy̲ordaya
drev̲esina
hardwood

лак(ировка)
lak(ir̲ovka)
varnish

морилка
mor̲ilka
wood stain

дерево d̲erevo | wood

проволока
prov̲oloka
wire

кабель
kab̲el'
cable

**нержавеющая
сталь**
nerzhav̲eyushchaya
stal'
stainless steel

оцинкованный
otsink̲ovanniy
galvanised

металл met̲al | metal

набор инструментов nabor instrumentov • **toolbox**

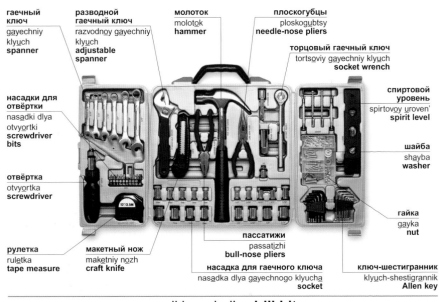

гаечный ключ
gayechniy klyuch
spanner

разводной гаечный ключ
razvodnoy gayechniy klyuch
adjustable spanner

молоток
molotok
hammer

плоскогубцы
ploskogubtsy
needle-nose pliers

торцовый гаечный ключ
tortsoviy gayechniy klyuch
socket wrench

насадки для отвёртки
nasadki dlya otvyortki
screwdriver bits

спиртовой уровень
spirtovoy uroven'
spirit level

отвёртка
otvyortka
screwdriver

шайба
shayba
washer

гайка
gayka
nut

рулетка
ruletka
tape measure

макетный нож
maketniy nozh
craft knife

пассатижи
passatizhi
bull-nose pliers

насадка для гаечного ключа
nasadka dlya gayechnogo klyucha
socket

ключ-шестигранник
klyuch-shestigrannik
Allen key

насадки на дрель nasadki na drel' • **drill bits**

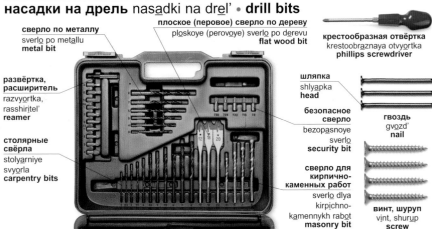

сверло по металлу
sverlo po metallu
metal bit

плоское (перовое) сверло по дереву
ploskoye (perovoye) sverlo po derevu
flat wood bit

крестообразная отвёртка
krestoobraznaya otvyortka
phillips screwdriver

развёртка, расширитель
razvyortka, rasshiritel'
reamer

шляпка
shlyapka
head

столярные свёрла
stolyarniye svyorla
carpentry bits

безопасное сверло
bezopasnoye sverlo
security bit

гвоздь
gvozd'
nail

сверло для кирпично-каменных работ
sverlo dlya kirpichno-kamennykh rabot
masonry bit

винт, шуруп
vint, shurup
screw

стриппер (устройство для зачистки проводов)
stripper (ustroystvo dlya zachistki provodov)
wire strippers

кусачки-бокорезы
kusachki-bokorezy
wire cutters

паяльник
payal'nik
soldering iron

изолента
izolenta
insulating tape

нож-скальпель
nozh-skal'pel'
scalpel

лобзик
lobzik
fretsaw

припой
pripoy
solder

наградка; пасовочная пила
nagradka; pasovochnaya pila | **tenon saw**

защитные очки
zashchitniye ochki
safety goggles

рубанок
rubanok
plane

ручная пила
ruchnaya pila
handsaw

усорез
usorez
mitre block

слесарная ножовка
slesarnaya nozhovka
hacksaw

ручная дрель
ruchnaya drel'
hand drill

стальная вата
stal'naya vata
wire wool

разводной ключ
razvodnoy klyuch
wrench

наждачная бумага
nazhdachnaya bumaga
sandpaper

стамеска
stameska
chisel

вантуз
vantuz
plunger

напильник
napil'nik
file

точильный камень
tochil'niy kamen'
sharpening stone

труборез truborez | **pipe cutter**

отделочные работы otd<u>e</u>lochniye rab<u>o</u>ty • **decorating**

ножницы
n<u>o</u>zhnitsy
scissors

макетный нож
mak<u>e</u>tniy n<u>o</u>zh
craft knife

отвес
otv<u>e</u>s
plumb line

скребок
skreb<u>o</u>k
scraper

мастер (по внутренней отделке), маляр-обойщик
m<u>a</u>ster (po vn<u>u</u>trenney otd<u>e</u>lke), malyar-ob<u>o</u>yshchik
decorator

обои
ob<u>o</u>i
wallpaper

стремянка
stremy<u>a</u>nka
stepladder

щётка для обоев
shch<u>o</u>tka dlya ob<u>o</u>yev
wallpaper brush

стол для поклейки обоев
st<u>o</u>l dlya pokl<u>e</u>yki ob<u>o</u>yev
pasting table

кисть для клея
k<u>i</u>st' dlya kl<u>e</u>ya
pasting brush

клей для обоев
kl<u>e</u>y dlya ob<u>o</u>yev
wallpaper paste

ведро
ved<u>r</u>o
bucket

оклеивать обоями okl<u>e</u>ivat' ob<u>o</u>yami | **wallpaper (v)**

сдирать sdir<u>a</u>t' | **strip (v)**

шпаклевать shpaklev<u>a</u>t' | **fill (v)**

шлифовать shlifov<u>a</u>t'
sand (v)

штукатурить shtukatur<u>i</u>t'
plaster (v)

оклеивать (обоями)
okl<u>e</u>ivat' (ob<u>o</u>yami) | **hang (v)**

облицовывать плиткой
oblits<u>o</u>vyvat' pl<u>i</u>tkoy | **tile (v)**

валик
valik
roller

поддон для краски
poddon dlya kraski
paint tray

краска
kraska
paint

кисть
kist'
brush

губка
gubka
sponge

малярная лента
malyarnaya lenta
masking tape

наждачная бумага
nazhdachnaya bumaga
sandpaper

банка с краской
banka s kraskoy
paint tin

рабочий комбинезон
rabochiy kombinezon
overalls

защитное покрытие от пыли
zashchitnoye pokrytiye ot pyli
dustsheet

скипидар
skipidar
turpentine

шпатлёвка
shpatlyovka
filler

растворитель, уайт-спирит
rastvoritel', uayt-spirit
white spirit

красить krasit' | **paint (v)**

словарь slovar' · vocabulary

штукатурка shtukaturka **plaster**	**глянцевый** glyantseviy **gloss**	**тиснёные обои** tisnyoniye oboi **embossed paper**	**нижний слой покрытия** nizhniy sloy pokrytiya **undercoat**	**герметик** germetik **sealant**
лак lak **varnish**	**матовый** matoviy **matte**	**оклеечная бумага** okleyechnaya bumaga **lining paper**	**верхний слой покрытия** verkhniy sloy pokrytiya **top coat**	**растворитель** rastvoritel' **solvent**
эмульсия emul'siya **emulsion**	**трафарет** trafaret **stencil**	**грунтовка** gruntovka **primer**	**защитная пропитка** zashchitnaya propitka **preservative**	**жидкий строительный раствор/затирка** zhidkiy stroitel'niy rastvor/zatirka **grout**

сад <u>sad</u> • garden

садовые стили sad<u>o</u>viye st<u>i</u>li • garden styles

патио p<u>a</u>tio | **patio garden**

сад на крыше
sad na kryshe
roof garden

сад камней
s<u>a</u>d kamney
rock garden

внутренний двор
vn<u>u</u>trenniy dv<u>o</u>r | **courtyard**

детали сада
det<u>a</u>li s<u>a</u>da •
garden features

подвесное кашпо
podvesn<u>o</u>ye kashp<u>o</u>
hanging basket

трельяжная опора
trel'y<u>a</u>zhnaya op<u>o</u>ra | **trellis**

английский сад angl<u>i</u>yskiy sad | **formal garden**

дачный английский сад
d<u>a</u>chniy angl<u>i</u>yskiy sad
cottage garden

садик пряных трав
s<u>a</u>dik pry<u>a</u>nykh tr<u>a</u>v
herb garden

водный сад
v<u>o</u>dniy sad
water garden

пергола
p<u>e</u>rgola
pergola

мощёное покрытие
moshchonoye pokrytiye
paving

клумба
klumba
flowerbed

дорожка
dorozhka
path

компостная куча
kompostnaya kucha
compost heap

калитка
kalitka
gate

сарай
saray
shed

парник
parnik
greenhouse

забор
zabor
fence

лужайка
luzhayka
lawn

пруд
prud
pond

изгородь
izgorod'
hedge

арка
arka
arch

сад
sad
vegetable garden

цветочный бордюр
tsvetochniy bordyur
herbaceous border

настил
nastil
decking

фонтан fontan | **fountain**

почва
pochva • **soil**

верхний слой почвы
verkhniy sloy pochvy
topsoil

песок
pesok
sand

мел
mel
chalk

илистый грунт
ilistiy grunt
silt

глина
glina
clay

растения в саду rasteniya v sadu • garden plants

виды растений vidy rasteniy • types of plants

однолетник
odnoletnik
annual

двулетник
dvuletnik
biennial

многолетник
mnogoletnik
perennial

луковичное
lukovichnoye
bulb

папоротник
paporotnik
fern

камыш
kamysh
rush

бамбук
bambuk
bamboo

сорняки
sornyaki
weeds

пряная трава
pryanaya trava
herb

водное растение
vodnoye rasteniye
water plant

дерево
derevo
tree

пальма
pal'ma
palm

хвойное растение
khvoynoye rasteniye
conifer

вечнозелёное растение
vechnozelyonoye
rasteniye
evergreen

лиственное дерево
listvennoye derevo
deciduous

**фигурная стрижка,
топиарий**
figurnaya stri_zh_ka, topi_a_riy
topiary

альпийское растение
al'p_i_yskoye rast_e_niye
alpine

суккулент
sukkul_e_nt
succulent

кактус
k_a_ktus
cactus

растение в кадке
rast_e_niye v k_a_dke
potted plant

тенелюбивое растение
tenelyubivoye rast_e_niye
shade plant

вьющееся
растение
v'y_u_shcheyesya
rast_e_niye
climber

цветущий
кустарник
tsvet_u_shchiy
kust_a_rnik
flowering shrub

почвопокровное
растение
pochvopokr_o_vnoye
rast_e_niye
ground cover

ползучее растение
polz_u_cheye rast_e_niye
creeper

декоративное (растение)
dekorat_i_vnoye (rast_e_niye)
ornamental

трава
tra_v_a
grass

садовые инструменты sad<u>o</u>viye instrum<u>e</u>nty • **garden tools**

веерные грабли
veyernyye gr<u>a</u>bli
lawn rake

компост
komp<u>o</u>st
compost

семена
sem<u>e</u>na
seeds

костная мука
k<u>o</u>stnaya muk<u>a</u>
bone meal

лопата
lop<u>a</u>ta
spade

вилы
v<u>i</u>ly
fork

газонные ножницы
gaz<u>o</u>nniye n<u>o</u>zhnitsy
long-handled shears

грабли
gr<u>a</u>bli
rake

мотыга
mot<u>y</u>ga
hoe

гравий
gr<u>a</u>viy
gravel

мешок для сбора травы
mesh<u>o</u>k dlya sb<u>o</u>ra trav<u>y</u>
grass bag

**ручка/
рукоятка**
r<u>u</u>chka/
rukoy<u>a</u>tka
handle

мотор
mot<u>o</u>r
motor

садовая корзинка из шпона
sad<u>o</u>vaya korz<u>i</u>nka iz shp<u>o</u>na
trug

**опорная
стойка**
op<u>o</u>rnaya
st<u>o</u>yka
stand

защитный кожух
zashch<u>i</u>tniy kozh<u>u</u>kh
shield

триммер
tr<u>i</u>mmer
trimmer

газонокосилка
gaz<u>o</u>nokos<u>i</u>lka
lawnmower

тачка
t<u>a</u>chka
wheelbarrow

вилка для прополки
vilka dlya propolki
hand fork

садовый совок
sadoviy sovok
trowel

лезвие
lezviye
blade

садовые ножницы
sadoviye nozhnitsy
shears

ручная пила
ruchnaya pila
handsaw

секатор
sekator
secateurs

ящик для рассады
yashchik dlya rassady
seed tray

пестицид
pestitsid
pesticide

садовые перчатки
sadoviye perchatki
gardening gloves

бечёвка
bechovka
twine

ярлыки
yarlyki
labels

проволочки для подвязки растений
provolochki dlya podvyazki rasteniy
twist ties

кольца для подвязки растений
kol'tsa dlya podvyazki rasteniy
ring ties

опоры для подвязывания
opory dlya podvyazyvaniya
canes

сито
sito
sieve

цветочный горшок
tsvetochniy gorshok
plant pot

резиновые сапоги
rezinoviye sapogi
rubber boots

полив poliv • watering

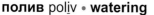

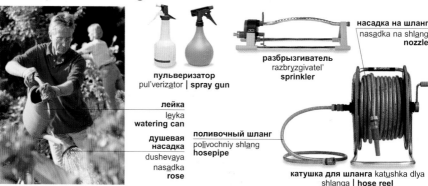

пульверизатор
pul'verizator | **spray gun**

лейка
leyka
watering can

душевая насадка
dushevaya nasadka
rose

поливочный шланг
polivochniy shlang
hosepipe

разбрызгиватель
razbryzgivatel'
sprinkler

насадка на шланг
nasadka na shlang
nozzle

катушка для шланга katushka dlya shlanga | **hose reel**

уход за садом ukhod za sadom • gardening

газон,
лужайка
gazon,
luzhayka
lawn

клумба
klumba
flowerbed

газонокосилка
gazonokosilka
lawnmower

живая
изгородь
zhivaya
izgorod'
hedge

колышек
kolyshek
stake

стричь газон strich' gazon | **mow (v)**

дерновать
dernovat'
turf (v)

прокалывать
prokalyvat'
spike (v)

сгребать
sgrebat'
rake (v)

стричь
strich
trim (v)

копать
kopat'
dig (v)

сеять
seyat'
sow (v)

подкармливать
podkarmlivat'
top dress (v)

поливать
polivat'
water (v)

направлять рост
napravlyat' rost
train (v)

обрывать увядшие соцветия
obryvat' uvyadshiye sotsvetiya
deadhead (v)

опрыскивать
opryskivat'
spray (v)

колышек
kolyshek
cane

прививать
privivat'
graft (v)

черенок
cherenok
cutting

разводить черенкованием
razvodit' cherenkovaniyem
propagate (v)

обрезать
obrezat'
prune (v)

подвязывать
podvyazyvat'
stake (v)

пересаживать
peresazhivat'
transplant (v)

полоть
polot'
weed (v)

мульчировать
mul'chirovat'
mulch (v)

собирать урожай
sobirat' urozhay
harvest (v)

словарь slovar' • vocabulary

выращивать vyrashchivat' **cultivate (v)**	**благоустраивать (участок)** blagoustraivat' (uchastok) **landscape (v)**	**удобрять** udobryat' **fertilize (v)**	**просеивать** proseivat' **sieve (v)**	**органический** organicheskiy **organic**	**сеянец, саженец** seyanets, sazhenets **seedling**	**подпочва** podpochva **subsoil**
ухаживать ukhazhivat' **tend (v)**	**сажать** sazhat' **pot up (v)**	**собирать** sobirat' **pick (v)**	**проветривать** provetrivat' **aerate (v)**	**дренаж** drenazh **drainage**	**удобрение** udobreniye **fertilizer**	**гербицид** gerbitsid **weedkiller**

службы sluzhby
services

экстренные службы ekstrenniye sluzhby • emergency services

скорая помощь skoraya pomoshch' • ambulance

автомобиль скорой помощи
avtomobil' skoroy pomoshchi | **ambulance**

носилки
nosilki
stretcher

парамедик paramedik | **paramedic**

полиция politsiya • police

**жетон
(нагрудный
знак)**
zheton
(nagrudniy
znak)
badge

форма
forma
uniform

сирена
sirena
siren

**проблесковый
маячок**
probleskoviy
mayachok
lights

пистолет
pistolet
gun

дубинка
dubinka
truncheon

наручники
naruchniki
handcuffs

полицейский автомобиль
politseyskiy avtomobil'
police car

полицейский участок
politseyskiy uchastok
police station

полицейский politseyskiy | **police officer**

словарь slovar' • vocabulary

инспектор inspektor **inspector**	**подозре-ваемый** podozrevayemiy **suspect**	**жалоба** zhaloba **complaint**	**арест** arest **arrest**
преступление prestupleniye **crime**	**нападение** napadeniye **assault**	**расследо-вание** rassledovaniye **investigation**	**полицейская камера** politseyskaya kamera **police cell**
детектив, сыщик detektiv, syshchik **detective**	**отпечаток пальца** otpechatok pal'tsa **fingerprint**	**кража со взломом** krazha so vzlomom **burglary**	**обвинение** obvineniye **charge**

пожарная бригада pozharnaya brigada · fire brigade

дым
dym
smoke

шлем
shlem
helmet

пожарный рукав
pozharniy rukav
hose

пожарные
pozharniye
firefighters

спасательная люлька
spasatel'naya lyul'ka
cradle

струя воды
struya vody
water jet

кабина
kabina
cab

вылет лестницы
vylet lesnitsy
boom

лестница
lesnitsa
ladder

пожар pozhar | fire

пожарная часть
pozharnaya chast'
fire station

пожарный выход, пожарная лестница
pozharniy vykhod, pozharnaya lesnitsa
fire escape

пожарный автомобиль
pozharniy avtomobil'
fire engine

дымовой извещатель
dymovoy izveshchatel'
smoke alarm

пожарная сигнализация
pozharnaya signalizatsiya
fire alarm

топор
topor
axe

огнетушитель
ognetushitel'
fire extinguisher

гидрант
gidrant
hydrant

мне нужна полиция/пожарная бригада/скорая помощь. mne nuzhna politsiya/pozharnaya brigada/skoraya pomoshch' **I need the police/fire brigade/ambulance.**	**Пожар по адресу...** pozhar po adresu... **There's a fire at …**	**Произошёл несчастный случай.** proizoshol neschasniy sluchay **There's been an accident.**	**Вызовите полицию!** vyzovite politsiyu! **Call the police!**

банк bank · **bank**

клиент
kliyent
customer

окно
okno
window

кассир
kassir
cashier

рекламные листовки
reklamniye listovki
leaflets

стойка
stoyka
counter

бланки квитанций о внесении на счёт
blanki kvitantsiy o vneseniyi na shchot
paying-in slips

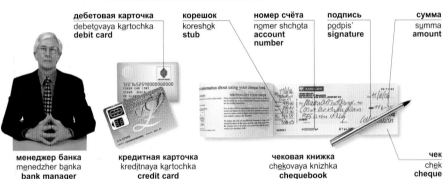

дебетовая карточка
debetovaya kartochka
debit card

корешок
koreshok
stub

номер счёта
nomer shchota
account number

подпись
podpis'
signature

сумма
summa
amount

менеджер банка
menedzher banka
bank manager

кредитная карточка
kreditnaya kartochka
credit card

чековая книжка
chekovaya knizhka
chequebook

чек
chek
cheque

словарь slovar' · **vocabulary**

сбережения sberezheniya **savings**	**ипотека** ipoteka **mortgage**	**платёж, взнос** platyozh, vznos **payment**	**внести деньги на счёт** vnesti den'gi na shchot **pay in (v)**	**текущий счёт** tekushchiy shchot **current account**
налог nalog **tax**	**овердрафт** overdraft **overdraft**	**прямое дебетование** pryamoye debetovaniye **direct debit**	**банковская комиссия** bankovskaya komissiya **bank charge**	**сберегательный счёт** sberegatel'niy shchot **savings account**
заём zayom **loan**	**процентная ставка** protsentnaya stavka **interest rate**	**квитанция о снятии денег с депозита** kvitantsiya o snyatiyi deneg s depozita **withdrawal slip**	**банковский перевод** bankovskiy perevod **bank transfer**	**ПИН-код** pin-kod **PIN**

монета
moneta
coin

банкнота
banknota
note

деньги den'gi | money

экран
ekran
screen

клавиатура
klaviatura
keypad

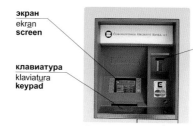

щель для карты
shchel' dlya karty
card slot

банкомат bankomat | ATM

валюта valyuta • foreign currency

обменный пункт
obmenniy punkt
bureau de change

тревел-чеки
trevel-cheki
traveller's cheque

обменный курс
obmenniy kurs
exchange rate

финансы finansy • finance

курс акций
kurs aktsiy
share price

брокер
broker
stockbroker

финансовый консультант
finansoviy konsul'tant
financial advisor

фондовая биржа fondovaya
birzha | **stock exchange**

словарь slovar' • vocabulary

обналичить
obnalichit'
cash (v)

номинал (валюты)
nominal (valyuty)
denomination

комиссия
komissiya
commission

инвестиция
investitsiya
investment

ценные бумаги
tsenniye bumagi
stocks

акции
aktsii
shares

дивиденды
dividendy
dividends

бухгалтер
bukhgalter
accountant

портфель (ценных бумаг)
portfel' (tsennykh bumag)
portfolio

акции; собственный капитал
aktsii; sobstvenniy kapital
equity

Можно это поменять?
mozhno eto pomenyat'?
Can I change this please?

Какой сегодня курс обмена?
kakoy sevodnya kurs obmena?
What's today's exchange rate?

связь svyaz' • communications

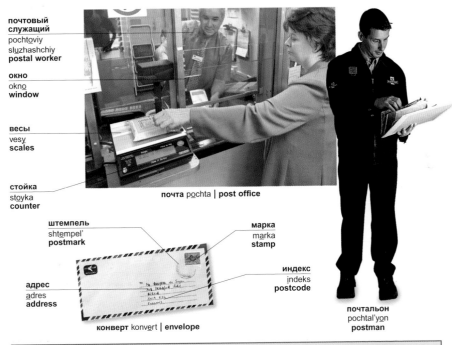

почтовый служащий
pochtoviy sluzhashchiy
postal worker

окно
okno
window

весы
vesy
scales

стойка
stoyka
counter

почта pochta | post office

штемпель
shtempel'
postmark

марка
marka
stamp

индекс
indeks
postcode

адрес
adres
address

конверт konvert | envelope

почтальон
pochtal'yon
postman

словарь slovar' • vocabulary

письмо
pis'mo
letter

авиа
avia
by airmail

заказная почта
zakaznaya pochta
registered post

обратный адрес
obratniy adres
return address

подпись
podpis'
signature

получение (на почте)
pollucheniye (na pochte)
collection

доставка
dostavka
delivery

почтовый денежный перевод
pochtoviy denezhniy perevod
postal order

почтовые расходы
pochtoviye raskhody
postage

хрупкое/ «осторожно!»
khrupkoye/ «ostorozhno!»
fragile

сумка почтальона
sumka pochtal'yona
mailbag

телеграмма
telegramma
telegram

не сгибать
ne sgibat'
do not bend (v)

верх
verkh
this way up

почтовый ящик
pochtoviy yashchik
postbox

почтовый ящик (для писем)
pochtoviy yashchik (dlya pisem)
letterbox

посылка
posylka
parcel

курьер
kur'yer
courier

телефон telefon • telephone

телефонная трубка
telefonnaya trubka
handset

база
baza
base station

беспроводной телефон
besprovodnoy telefon
cordless phone

автоответчик
avtootvetchik
answering machine

видеофон
videofon
video phone

телефонная будка
telefonnaya budka
telephone box

смартфон
smartfon
smartphone

клавиатура
klaviatura
keypad

мобильный телефон
mobil'niy telefon
mobile phone

трубка
trubka
receiver

возврат монет
vozvrat monet
coin return

таксофон
taksofon
payphone

словарь slovar' • vocabulary

справочное бюро
spravochnoye byuro
directory enquiries

приложение
prilozheniye
app

отвечать
otvechat'
answer (v)

обратный звонок
obratn'ye zvonok'
reverse charge call

сообщение (CMC)
soobshcheniye (esemes)
text (SMS)

голосовое сообщение
golosovoye soobshcheniye
voice message

пароль
parol'
passcode

оператор
operator
operator

набирать номер
nabirat' nomer
dial (v)

занято
zanyato
engaged/busy

разъединено
raz-yedineno
disconnected

Можете дать мне номер...?
mozhete dat' mne nomer...?
Can you give me the number for ...?

Какой код...?
kakoy kod...?
What is the dialling code for ...?

Пришлите мне CMC!
prishlite mne esemes!
Text me!

отель otel' · hotel
фойе foye · lobby

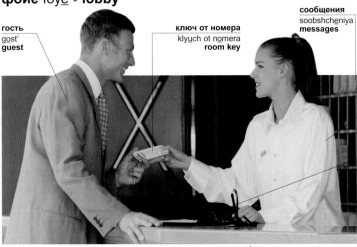

сообщения
soobshcheniya
messages

гость
gost'
guest

ключ от номера
klyuch ot nomera
room key

ячейка для
писем
yacheyka dlya
pisem
pigeonhole

администратор
administrator
receptionist

регистрироваться
registrirovat'sa
register

стойка
stoyka
counter

стойка администратора stoyka administratora | **reception**

багаж
bagazh
luggage

тележка
telezhka
trolley

швейцар shveytsar | **porter**

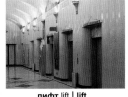

лифт lift | **lift**

номер комнаты
nomer komnaty
room number

номера nomera · rooms

одноместный номер
odnomesniy nomer
single room

**двухместный номер
(номер на двоих)**
dvukhmesniy nomer
(nomer na dvoikh)
double room

**двухместный номер с
двумя кроватями**
dvukhmesniy nomer s
dvumya krovatyami
twin room

отдельная ванная
otdel'naya vannaya
private bathroom

услуги uslugi • services

поднос с завтраком
podnos s zavtrakom
breakfast tray

услуги горничной
uslugi gornichnoy
maid service

услуги прачечной
uslugi prachechnoy
laundry service

доставка еды и напитков в номер dostavka
yedy i napitkov v nomer | **room service**

мини-бар
mini-bar
minibar

ресторан
restoran
restaurant

тренажёрный зал
trenazhorniy zal
gym

бассейн
basseyn
swimming pool

словарь slovar' • vocabulary

ночлег с завтраком
nochleg s zavtrakom
bed and breakfast

полный пансион (комната и трёхразовое питание)
polniy pansion (komnata i tryokhrazovoye pitaniye)
full board

полупансион
polupansion
half board

У вас есть места?
u vas yest' mesta?
Do you have any vacancies?

У меня бронь.
u menya bron'
I have a reservation.

Я бы хотел/хотела одноместный номер.
ya by khotel/khotela odnomesniy nomer
I'd like a single room.

Я бы хотел/хотела номер на три ночи.
ya by khotel/khotela nomer na tri nochi
I'd like a room for three nights.

Сколько стоит одна ночь?
skol'ko stoit odna noch'?
What is the charge per night?

Когда я должен/должна освободить номер?
kogda ya dolzhen/dolzhna osvobodit' nomer?
When do I have to vacate the room?

покупки pokupki
shopping

торговый центр torgoviy tsentr • shopping centre

атриум
atrium
atrium

вывеска
vyveska
sign

лифт
lift
lift

третий этаж
tretiy etazh
second floor

второй этаж
vtoroy etazh
first floor

эскалатор
eskalator
escalator

первый этаж
perviy etazh
ground floor

**посетитель,
покупатель**
posetitel',
pokupatel'
customer

словарь slovar' • vocabulary

**отдел товаров для
детей**
otdel tovarov dlya detey
children's department

отдел багажа
otdel bagazha
luggage department

обувной отдел
obuvnoy otdel
shoe department

указатель магазинов
ukazatel' magazinov
store directory

продавец-консультант
prodavets-konsul'tant
sales assistant

**отдел по работе
с клиентами**
otdel po rabote
s kliyentami
customer services

примерочные
primerochniye
changing rooms

**комната матери
и ребёнка**
komnata materi i rebyonka
baby changing facilities

туалеты
tualety
toilets

Сколько это стоит?
skol'ko eto stoit?
How much is this?

**Можно это
обменять?**
mozhno eto obmenyat'?
May I exchange this?

универмаг univermag • department store

мужская одежда
muzhskaya odezhda
menswear

женская одежда
zhenskaya odezhda
womenswear

женское бельё
zhenskoye bel'yo
lingerie

парфюмерия
parfyumeriya
perfumery

косметика
kosmetika
beauty

постельное и столовое бельё
postel'noye i stolovoye bel'yo
linen

товары для дома
tovary dlya doma
home furnishings

галантерея; швейные принадлежности
galantereya; shveynyye prinadlezhnosti
haberdashery

кухонные принадлежности и посуда
kukhonnyye prinadlezhnosti i posuda
kitchenware

фарфор
farfor
china

электротовары
elektrotovary
electrical goods

светильники
svetil'niki
lighting

спорттовары
sporttovary
sports

игрушки
igrushki
toys

канцтовары
kantstovary
stationery

магазин продуктов
magazin produktov
food hall

супермаркет supermarket • **supermarket**

проход
prokhod
aisle

полка
polka
shelf

конвейерная лента
konveiyernaya lenta
conveyer belt

кассир
kassir
cashier

предложения/ акции
predlozheniya/ aktsii
offers

касса kassa | **checkout**

покупатель
pokupatel'
customer

кассовый аппарат
kassoviy apparat
till

хозяйственная сумка
khozyaystvennaya sumka
shopping bag

продукты (питания)
produkty (pitaniya)
groceries

ручка
ruchka
handle

780863 185779

штрихкод
shtrikhkod
bar code

тележка telezhka | **trolley**

корзинка korzinka | **basket**

сканер skaner | **scanner**

выпечка, хлебобулочные изделия
vypechka, khlebobulochniye izdeliya
bakery

молочные продукты
molochniye produkty
dairy

хлопья для завтрака
khlop'ya dlya zavtraka
breakfast cereals

консервы
konservy
tinned food

кондитерские изделия
konditerskiye izdeliya
confectionery

овощи
ovoshchi
vegetables

фрукты
frukty
fruit

мясо и птица
myaso i ptitsa
meat and poultry

рыба
ryba
fish

деликатесы
delikatesy
deli

замороженные продукты
zamorozhenniye produkty
frozen food

полуфабрикаты
polufabrikaty
convenience food

напитки
napitki
drinks

хозяйственные товары
khozyaystvenniye tovary
household products

косметика для гигиены kosmetika dlya
gigiyeny | **toiletries**

товары для новорождённых
tovary dlya novorozhdyonnykh
baby products

электротовары
elektrotovary
electrical goods

корм для животных
korm dlya zhivotnykh
pet food

журналы zhurnaly | **magazines**

аптека apteka · chemist

уход за зубами
ukhod za zubami
dental care

женская гигиена
zhenskaya
gigiyena
feminine hygiene

дезодоранты
dezodoranty
deodorants

витамины
vitaminy
vitamins

отдел отпуска по рецептам, рецептурный отдел
otdel otpuska po retseptam,
retsepturniy otdel
dispensary

фармацевт
farmatsevt
pharmacist

лекарство от кашля
lekarstvo ot kashlya
cough medicine

растительные лекарственные средства
rastitel'niye
lekarstvenniye
sredstva
herbal remedies

уход за кожей
ukhod za kozhey
skin care

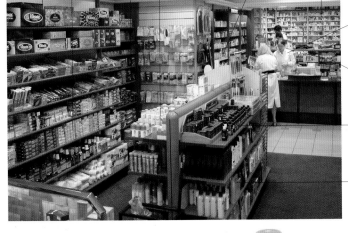

средство после загара
sredstvo posle
zagara
aftersun

солнцезащитный крем
sontsezashchitniy krem
sunscreen

крем-блок от загара
krem-blok ot zagara
sunblock

репеллент
repellent
insect repellent

влажная салфетка
vlazhnaya salfetka
wet wipe

бумажная салфетка
bumazhnaya salfetka
tissue

гигиеническая прокладка
gigiyenicheskaya prokladka
sanitary towel

тампон
tampon
tampon

прокладка на каждый день
prokladka na kazhdiy den'
panty liner

мерная ложка
mernaya lozhka
measuring spoon

инструкция
instruktsiya
instructions

капсула
kapsula
capsule

таблетка
tabletka
pill

сироп
sirop
syrup

ингалятор
ingalyator
inhaler

крем
krem
cream

мазь
maz'
ointment

гель
gel'
gel

свеча, суппозиторий
svecha, suppozitoriy
suppository

пипетка
pipetka
dropper

игла
igla
needle

капли
kapli
drops

шприц
shprits
syringe

спрей
sprey
spray

порошок
poroshok
powder

словарь slovar' · vocabulary

железо zhelezo **iron**	**инсулин** insulin **insulin**	**одноразовый** odnorazoviy **disposable**	**лекарство** lekarstvo **medicine**	**обезболивающее** obezbolivayushcheye **painkiller**
кальций kal'tsiy **calcium**	**побочные эффекты** pobochniye efekty **side effects**	**растворимый** rastvorimiy **soluble**	**слабительное** slabitel'noye **laxative**	**успокоительное** uspokoitel'noye **sedative**
магний magniy **magnesium**	**дата окончания срока годности** data okonchaniya sroka godnosti **expiry date**	**дозировка** dozirovka **dosage**	**диарея; понос** diareya; ponos **diarrhoea**	**снотворное** snotvornoye **sleeping pill**
мультивитамины mul'tivitaminy **multivitamins**	**таблетки от укачивания** tabletki ot ukachivaniya **travel-sickness pills**	**медикаментозное лечение** medikamentoznoye lecheniye **medication**	**пастилки от кашля или боли в горле** pastilki ot kashlya ili boli v gorle **throat lozenge**	**противовоспалительное** protivovospalitel'noye **anti-inflammatory**

цветочный магазин tsvetochniy magazin · **florist**

цветы
tsvety
flowers

гладиолус
gladiolus
gladiolus

ирис
iris
iris

лилия
liliya
lily

ромашка
romashka
daisy

акация
akatsiya
acacia

хризантема
khrizantema
chrysanthemum

гвоздика
gvozdika
carnation

гипсофила
gipsofila
gypsophila

**растение
в горшке**
rasteniye
v gorshke
pot plant

левкой
levkoy
stocks

гербера
gerbera
gerbera

лиственные растения
listvenniye rasteniya
foliage

роза
roza
rose

фрезия
freziya
freesia

ваза
vaza
vase

орхидея
orkhideya
orchid

пион
pion
peony

букет
buket
bunch

стебель
stebel'
stem

нарцисс
nartsis
daffodil

бутон
buton
bud

обёртка
obyortka
wrapping

тюльпан tyul'pan | **tulip**

композиции kompozitsiyi • arrangements

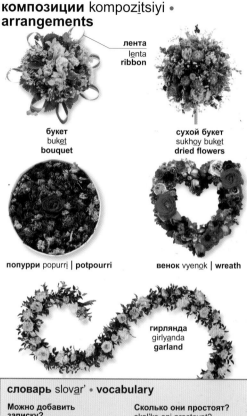

лента
lenta
ribbon

букет
buket
bouquet

сухой букет
sukhoy buket
dried flowers

попурри popurri | **potpourri**

венок vyenok | **wreath**

гирлянда
girlyanda
garland

словарь slovar' • vocabulary

Можно добавить записку?
mozhno dobavit' zapisku?
Can I attach a message?

Можно их завернуть?
mozhno ikh zavernut'?
Can I have them wrapped?

Можно отправить их по адресу…?
mozhno otpravit' ikh po adresu…?
Can you send them to …?

Сколько они простоят?
skol'ko oni prostoyat?
How long will these last?

Они душистые?
oni dushistiye?
Are they fragrant?

Можно мне букет из …?
mozhno mne buket iz…?
Can I have a bunch of … please?

газетный киоск gazetniy kiosk · **newsagent**

сигареты
sigarety
cigarettes

пачка сигарет
pachka sigaret
packet of cigarettes

марки
marki
stamps

открытка
otkrytka
postcard

комикс
komiks
comic

журнал
zhurnal
magazine

газета
gazeta
newspaper

курение kureniye · **smoking**

табак
tabak
tobacco

зажигалка
zazhigalka
lighter

чубук
chubuk
stem

чаша
chasha
bowl

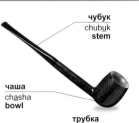

трубка
trubka
pipe

сигара
sigara
cigar

кондитерская konditerskaya • **confectioner**

коробка шоколадных конфет
korobka shokoladnykh konfet
box of chocolates

энергетический батончик
energeticheskiy batonchik
snack bar

чипсы
chipsy
crisps

кондитерская konditerskaya | **sweet shop**

словарь slovar' • **vocabulary**

молочный шоколад
molochniy shokolad
milk chocolate

карамель
karamel'
caramel

тёмный шоколад
tyomniy shokolad
plain chocolate

трюфель
tryufel'
truffle

белый шоколад
beliy shokolad
white chocolate

печенье
pechen'ye
biscuit

выбор сладостей на развес
vybor sladostey na razves
pick and mix

леденцы
ledentsy
boiled sweets

сладости sladosti • **confectionery**

шоколад
shokolad
chocolate

шоколадка
shokoladka
chocolate bar

конфеты
konfety
sweets

леденец на палочке
ledenets na palochke
lollipop

ириска iriska | **toffee**

нуга nuga | **nougat**

воздушный зефир
vozdushniy zefir
marshmallow

мятная конфета
myatnaya konfeta
mint

жевательная резинка
zhevatel'naya rezinka
chewing gum

мармелад джелли бин
marmelad dzhelli bin
jellybean

желатинка
zhelatinka
fruit gum

лакрица
lakritsa
liquorice

другие магазины drugiye magaziny • other shops

булочная
bulochnaya
baker's

кондитерская
konditerskaya
cake shop

мясная лавка
myasnaya lavka
butcher's

рыбный магазин
rybniy magazin
fishmonger's

овощной магазин
ovoshchnoy magazin
greengrocer's

бакалея
bakaleya
grocer's

обувной магазин
obuvnoy magazin
shoe shop

хозтовары
khoztovary
hardware shop

магазин антиквариата
magazin antikvariata
antique shop

магазин подарков
magazin podarkov
gift shop

бюро путешествий
byuro puteshestviy
travel agent's

ювелирный магазин
yuvelirniy magazin
jeweller's

книжный магазин
knizhniy magazin
book shop

магазин звукозаписи
magazin zvukozapisi
record shop

**винно-водочный
магазин**
vinno-vodochniy magazin
off licence

зоомагазин
zoomagazin
pet shop

мебельный магазин
mebel'niy magazin
furniture shop

бутик
butik
boutique

словарь slovar' • vocabulary

агентство
недвижимости
agentstvo
nedvizhimosti
estate agent's

садовый центр
sadoviy tsentr
garden centre

химчистка
khimchistka
dry cleaner's

прачечная
prachechnaya
launderette

фотомагазин
fotomagazin
camera shop

магазин здорового
питания
magazin zdorovova
pitaniya
health food shop

арт-галерея
art-galereya
art shop

секонд-хенд
sekond-khend
second-hand shop

швейное ателье
shveynoye atel'ye
tailor's

парикмахерская
parikmakherskaya
hairdresser's

рынок rynok | **market**

еда yed<u>a</u>
food

мясо myaso · meat

баранина
baranina
lamb

мясник
myasnik
butcher

крюк для туш
kryuk dlya tush
meat hook

весы
vesy
scales

ножеточка
nozhetochka
knife sharpener

бекон
bekon
bacon

сосиски
sosiski
sausages

печень
pechen'
liver

словарь slovar' · vocabulary

свинина svinina **pork**	оленина olenina **venison**	требуха, субпродукты trebukha, subprodukty **offal**	свободного содержания/вольного выгула svobodnogo soderzhaniya/ vol'nogo vygula **free range**	мясо после тепловой обработки myaso posle teplovoy obrabotki **cooked meat**
говядина govyadina **beef**	крольчатина krol'chatina **rabbit**	солёный solyoniy **cured**	органическое organicheskoye **organic**	белое мясо beloye myaso **white meat**
телятина telyatina **veal**	язык yazyk **tongue**	копченый kopchyoniy **smoked**	постное мясо postnoye myaso **lean meat**	красное мясо krasnoye myaso **red meat**

разделка мяса razdelka myasa • **cuts**

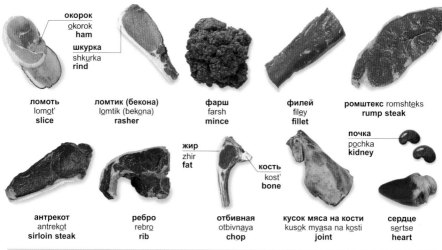

ломоть
lomot'
slice

окорок
okorok
ham

шкурка
shkurka
rind

ломтик (бекона)
lomtik (bekona)
rasher

фарш
farsh
mince

филей
filey
fillet

ромштекс romshteks
rump steak

антрекот
antrekot
sirloin steak

ребро
rebro
rib

жир
zhir
fat

кость
kost'
bone

отбивная
otbivnaya
chop

кусок мяса на кости
kusok myasa na kosti
joint

почка
pochka
kidney

сердце
sertse
heart

птица ptitsa • **poultry**

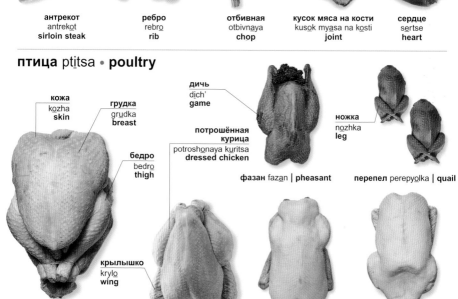

кожа
kozha
skin

грудка
grudka
breast

бедро
bedro
thigh

крылышко
krylo
wing

индейка
indeyka
turkey

дичь
dich'
game

потрошённая курица
potroshonaya kuritsa
dressed chicken

фазан fazan | **pheasant**

курица kuritsa | **chicken**

ножка
nozhka
leg

перепел perepyolka | **quail**

утка utka | **duck**

гусь gus' | **goose**

рыба ryba • fish

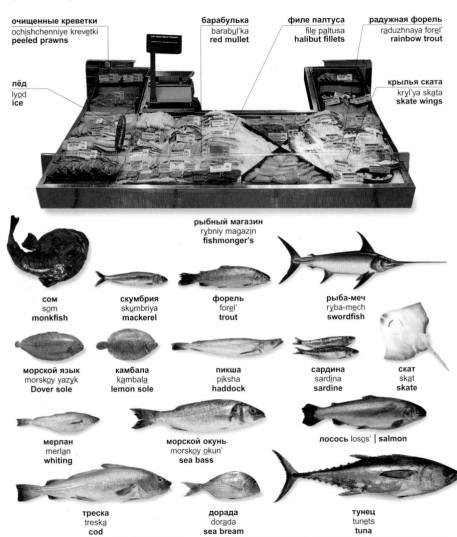

очищенные креветки
ochishchenniye krevetki
peeled prawns

барабулька
barabul'ka
red mullet

филе палтуса
file paltusa
halibut fillets

радужная форель
raduzhnaya forel'
rainbow trout

лёд
lyod
ice

крылья ската
kryl'ya skata
skate wings

рыбный магазин
rybniy magazin
fishmonger's

сом
som
monkfish

скумбрия
skumbriya
mackerel

форель
forel'
trout

рыба-меч
ryba-mech
swordfish

морской язык
morskoy yazyk
Dover sole

камбала
kambala
lemon sole

пикша
piksha
haddock

сардина
sardina
sardine

скат
skat
skate

мерлан
merlan
whiting

морской окунь
morskoy okun'
sea bass

лосось losos' | **salmon**

треска
treska
cod

дорада
dorada
sea bream

тунец
tunets
tuna

морепродукты moreprodukty • seafood

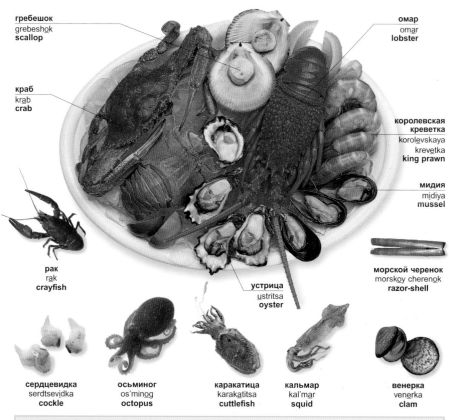

гребешок
grebeshok
scallop

краб
krab
crab

омар
omar
lobster

королевская креветка
korolevskaya krevetka
king prawn

мидия
midiya
mussel

рак
rak
crayfish

устрица
ustritsa
oyster

морской черенок
morskoy cherenok
razor-shell

сердцевидка
serdtsevidka
cockle

осьминог
os'minog
octopus

каракатица
karakatitsa
cuttlefish

кальмар
kal'mar
squid

венерка
venerka
clam

словарь slovar' • vocabulary

замороженный zamorozhenniy **frozen**	**солёный** solyoniy **salted**	**очищенный от костей** ochishchenniy ot kostey **boned**	**разделанный на филе** razdelanniy na file **filleted**	**стейк** steyk **steak**	**спинка** spinka **loin**
свежий svezhiy **fresh**	**очищенный от кожи** ochishchenniy ot kozhi **skinned**	**очищенный от чешуи** ochishchenniy ot cheshui **descaled**	**чешуя** cheshuya **scale**	**филе** file **fillet**	**кость** kost' **bone**
очищенный ochishchenniy **cleaned**	**копчёный** kopchyoniy **smoked**				**хвост** khvost **tail**

Пожалуйста, вы можете очистит это для меня?
pozhaluista, vy mozhete ochistit eto dlya menya?
Will you clean it for me?

овощи 1 ovoshchi • vegetables 1

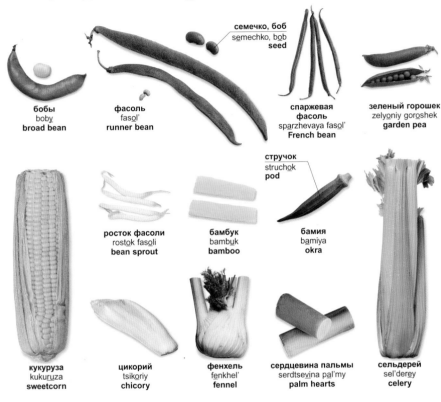

семечко, боб
semechko, bob
seed

бобы
boby
broad bean

фасоль
fasol'
runner bean

спаржевая
фасоль
sparzhevaya fasol'
French bean

зеленый горошек
zelyoniy goroshek
garden pea

стручок
struchok
pod

росток фасоли
rostok fasoli
bean sprout

бамбук
bambuk
bamboo

бамия
bamiya
okra

кукуруза
kukuruza
sweetcorn

цикорий
tsikoriy
chicory

фенхель
fenkhel'
fennel

сердцевина пальмы
serdtsevina pal'my
palm hearts

сельдерей
sel'derey
celery

словарь slovar' • vocabulary

лист list **leaf**	соцветие sotsvetiye **floret**	верхушка verkhushka **tip**	органический organicheskiy **organic**	У вас есть органические овощи? u vas yest' organicheskiye ovoshchi? **Do you sell organic vegetables?**
стебель, черешок stebel', chereshok **stalk**	орешек, ядро oreshek, yadro **kernel**	сердцевина serdtsevina **heart**	пластиковый пакет plastikoviy paket **plastic bag**	Это местная продукция? eto mestnaya produktsiya? **Are these grown locally?**

рукола
rukola
rocket

водяной кресс-салат
vodyanoy kres-salat
watercress

**тревизский цикорий,
радиккио**
trevizskiy tsikoriy, radikkio
radicchio

брюссельская капуста
bryusel'skaya kapusta
Brussels sprout

листовая свёкла
listovaya svyokla
Swiss chard

катран
katran
kale

щавель
shchavel'
sorrel

эндивий; цикорий салатный
endiviy; tsikoriy salatniy
endive

одуванчик
oduvanchik
dandelion

шпинат
shpinat
spinach

кольраби
kol'rabi
kohlrabi

пекинская капуста
pekinskaya kapusta
pak-choi

салат-латук
salat-latuk
lettuce

брокколи
brokkoli
broccoli

капуста
kapusta
cabbage

ранняя зелень
rannyaya zelen'
spring greens

овощи 2 <u>o</u>voshchi • vegetables 2

репа
r<u>e</u>pa
turnip

редис
red<u>i</u>s
radish

артишок
artish<u>o</u>k
artichoke

цветная капуста
tsvetn<u>a</u>ya kap<u>u</u>sta
cauliflower

спаржа
sp<u>a</u>rzha
asparagus

картофель
kart<u>o</u>fel'
potato

**кабачок/
тыква
кустовая**
kabach<u>o</u>k/
t<u>y</u>kva kustov<u>a</u>ya
marrow

лук
luk
onion

сладкий перец
sl<u>a</u>dkiy p<u>e</u>rets
pepper

перец чили
p<u>e</u>rets chili
chilli

сахарная кукуруза
s<u>a</u>kharnaya kukur<u>u</u>za
sweetcorn

словарь slov<u>ar</u>' • vocabulary

помидор черри
pomid<u>o</u>r ch<u>e</u>rri
cherry tomato

морковь
mork<u>o</u>v'
carrot

**плод хлебного
дерева**
pl<u>o</u>d khl<u>e</u>bnogo
d<u>e</u>reva
breadfruit

**молодой
картофель**
molod<u>o</u>y kart<u>o</u>fel'
new potato

**клубневой
сельдерей**
klubnev<u>o</u>y
sel'der<u>e</u>y
celeriac

корень таро
k<u>o</u>ren' t<u>a</u>ro
taro root

маниок
mani<u>o</u>k
cassava

водяной орех
vodyan<u>o</u>y or<u>e</u>kh
water chestnut

замороженный
zamor<u>o</u>zhenniy
frozen

сырой
syr<u>o</u>y
raw

**пряный
(острый)**
pr<u>ya</u>ny (<u>o</u>stry)
hot (spicy)

сладкий
sl<u>a</u>dkiy
sweet

горький
g<u>o</u>r'kiy
bitter

упругий
upr<u>u</u>giy
firm

мякоть
my<u>a</u>kot'
flesh

**корень,
корнеплод**
k<u>o</u>ren',
korn<u>e</u>pl<u>o</u>d
root

**Один килограмм картошки,
пожалуйста?**
<u>o</u>din kilogr<u>a</u>m kart<u>o</u>shki,
pozh<u>a</u>lusta?
**Can I have one kilo of
potatoes please?**

**Сколько стоит килограмм?/
Почём килограмм?**
sk<u>o</u>l'ko st<u>o</u>it kilogr<u>a</u>m?/
poch<u>yo</u>m kilogr<u>a</u>m?
What's the price per kilo?

Как это называется?
K<u>a</u>k <u>e</u>to nazyv<u>a</u>yetsya?
What are those called?

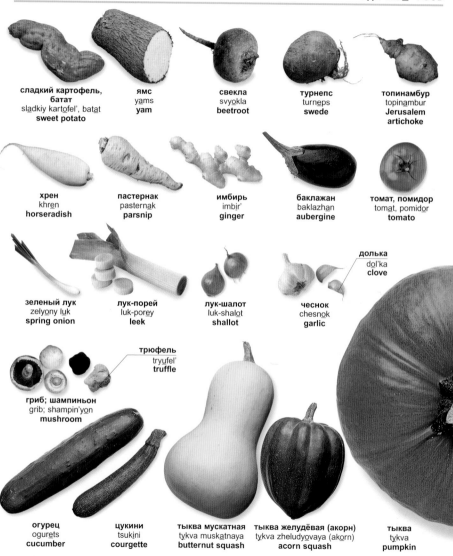

сладкий картофель, батат
sladkiy kartofel', batat
sweet potato

ямс
yams
yam

свекла
svyokla
beetroot

турнепс
turneps
swede

топинамбур
topinambur
Jerusalem artichoke

хрен
khren
horseradish

пастернак
pasternak
parsnip

имбирь
imbir'
ginger

баклажан
baklazhan
aubergine

томат, помидор
tomat, pomidor
tomato

зеленый лук
zelyony luk
spring onion

лук-порей
luk-porey
leek

лук-шалот
luk-shalot
shallot

чеснок
chesnok
garlic

долька
dol'ka
clove

трюфель
tryufel'
truffle

гриб; шампиньон
grib; shampin'yon
mushroom

огурец
ogurets
cucumber

цукини
tsukini
courgette

тыква мускатная
tykva muskatnaya
butternut squash

тыква желудёвая (акорн)
tykva zheludyovaya (akorn)
acorn squash

тыква
tykva
pumpkin

фрукты 1 frukty • fruit 1

цитрусовые tsitrusoviye • citrus fruit

апельсин
apel'sin
orange

клементин
klementin
clementine

агли
agli
ugli fruit

белая часть
кожуры
belaya
chast'
kozhury
pith

грейпфрут
greypfrut
grapefruit

долька
dol'ka
segment

мандарин
mandarin
tangerine

мандарин уншиу
mandarin unshiu
satsuma

цедра
tsedra
zest

лайм
laim
lime

лимон
limon
lemon

кумкват
kumkvat
kumquat

косточковые kostochkoviye • stone fruit

персик
persik
peach

нектарин
nektarin
nectarine

абрикос
abrikos
apricot

слива
sliva
plum

вишня
vishnya
cherry

яблоко
yabloko
apple

груша
grusha
pear

корзинка с фруктами korzinka s fruktami
basket of fruit

ягоды и бахчевые yagody i bakhcheviye • **berries and melons**

клубника
klubnika
strawberry

малина
malina
raspberry

дыня
dynya
melon

виноград
vinograd
grapes

ежевика
yezhevika
blackberry

красная смородина
krasnaya smorodina
redcurrant

клюква
klyukva
cranberry

чёрная смородина
chyornaya smorodina
blackcurrant

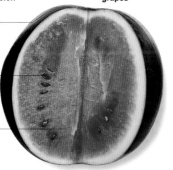

кожура

kozhura
rind

семечко

semechko
seed

мякоть

myakot'
flesh

черника
chernika
blueberry

белая смородина
belaya smorodina
white currant

арбуз
arbuz
watermelon

ягода Логана
yagoda logana
loganberry

крыжовник
kryzhovnik
gooseberry

словарь slovar' • **vocabulary**

ревень reven' **rhubarb**	**кислый** kisliy **sour**	**хрустящий** khrustyashchiy **crisp**	**сок** sok **juice**	**Они спелые?** oni speliye? **Are they ripe?**
клетчатка kletchatka **fibre**	**свежий** svezhiy **fresh**	**гнилой** gniloy **rotten**	**сердцевина** serdtsevina **core**	**Можно попробовать?** mozhno poprobovat'? **Can I try one?**
сладкий sladkiy **sweet**	**сочный** sochniy **juicy**	**мякоть** myakot' **pulp**	**без косточек** bez kostochek **seedless**	**Сколько времени они хранятся?** skol'ko vremeni oni khranyatsya? **How long will they keep?**

фрукты 2 frukty • fruit 2

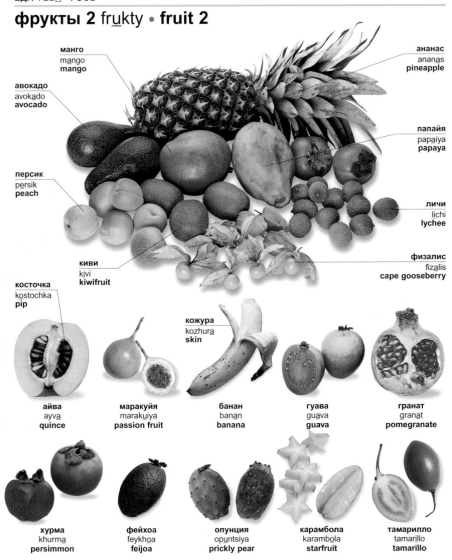

манго
mango
mango

авокадо
avokado
avocado

персик
persik
peach

киви
kivi
kiwifruit

косточка
kostochka
pip

ананас
ananas
pineapple

папайя
papaiya
papaya

личи
lichi
lychee

физалис
fizalis
cape gooseberry

кожура
kozhura
skin

айва
ayva
quince

маракуйя
marakuiya
passion fruit

банан
banan
banana

гуава
guava
guava

гранат
granat
pomegranate

хурма
khurma
persimmon

фейхоа
feykhoa
feijoa

опунция
opuntsiya
prickly pear

карамбола
karambola
starfruit

тамарилло
tamarillo
tamarillo

Орехи и сухофрукты orekhi i sukhofrukty •
nuts and dried fruit

кедровые орешки kedroviye oreshki **pine nut**	**фисташки** fistashki **pistachio**	**кешью** kesh'yu **cashew nut**	**арахис** arakhis **peanut**	**фундук** funduk **hazelnut**

бразильский орех brazil'skiy orekh **brazil nut**	**орех-пекан** orekh-pekan **pecan**	**миндаль** mindal' **almond**	**грецкий орех** gretskiy orekh **walnut**	**каштан** kashtan **chestnut**

скорлупа
skorlupa
shell

макадамия makadamiya **macadamia**	**инжир** inzhir **fig**	**финик** finik **date**	**чернослив** chernosliv **prune**

мякоть
myakot'
flesh

изюм; кишмиш izyum; kishmish **sultana**	**изюм** izyum **raisin**	**коринка** korinka **currant**	**кокос** kokos **coconut**

словарь slovar' • vocabulary

зеленый, **незрелый** zeleniy, nezreliy **green**	**твёрдый** tvyordiy **hard**	**орешек, ядро** oreshek, yadro **kernel**	**солёный** soloniy **salted**	**жареный** zhareniy **roasted**	**очищенный** ochishchenniy **shelled**	**цукаты** tsukaty **candied fruit**
зрелый zreliy **ripe**	**мягкий** myahkiy **soft**	**сушёный** sushoniy **desiccated**	**сырой** syroy **raw**	**сезонный** sezonniy **seasonal**	**целый** tseliy **whole**	**тропические** **фрукты** tropicheskiye frukty **tropical fruit**

злаки и зернобобовые zlaki i zernoboboviye • grains and pulses

злаки zlaki • grains

пшеница
pshenitsa
wheat

овёс
ovyos
oats

ячмень
yachmen'
barley

просо, пшено
proso, psheno
millet

кукуруза
kukuruza
corn

киноа
kinoa
quinoa

словарь slovar' • vocabulary

зерно zerno **seed**	**душистый** dushistyy **fragranced**	**пропаренный** proparenniy **easy cook**
шелуха shelukha **husk**	**крупа; хлопья** krupa; khlop'ya **cereal**	**длинно-зёрный** dlinnozyorniy **long-grain**
ядро yadro **kernel**	**цельнозерновой** tsel'nozernovoy **wholegrain**	**коротко-зёрный** korotkozyorniy **short-grain**
сухой sukhoy **dry**	**замачивать** zamachivat' **soak (v)**	
свежий svezhiy **fresh**		

рис ris • rice

белый рис
beliy ris
white rice

коричневый рис
korichneviy ris
brown rice

дикий рис
dikiy ris
wild rice

рис для пудинга
ris dlya pudinga
pudding rice

крупы krupy • processed grains

кускус
kuskus
couscous

крупа из плющеной пшеницы
krupa iz plyushchenoy pshenitsy
cracked wheat

манная крупа
mannaya krupa
semolina

отруби
otrubi
bran

бобовые boboviye • **pulses**

белая фасоль лима
belaya fasol' lima
butter beans

белая фасоль неви
belaya fasol' nevi
haricot beans

красная фасоль
krasnaya fasol'
red kidney beans

адзуки
adzuki
adzuki beans

бобы
boby
broad beans

соевые бобы
soyeviye boby
soya beans

вигна черноглазка
vigna chernoglazka
black-eyed beans

пёстрая фасоль пинто
pyostraya fasol' pinto
pinto beans

маш
mash
mung beans

флажолет
flazholet
flageolet beans

коричневая чечевица
korichnevaya
chechevitsa
brown lentils

красная чечевица
krasnaya chechevitsa
red lentils

зелёный горошек
zelyoniy goroshek
green peas

нут; турецкий горох
nut; turetskiy gorokh
chickpeas

дроблёный горох
droblyoniy gorokh
split peas

семена semena • **seeds**

**тыквенные
семечки**
tykvenniye
semechki
pumpkin seed

семена горчицы
semena gorchitsy
mustard seed

тмин
tmin
caraway

кунжут
kunzhut
sesame seed

семечки подсолнуха
semechki podsolnukha
sunflower seed

травы и пряности travy i pryanosti • herbs and spices

пряности pryanosti • spices

ваниль vanil' | **vanilla**

мускатный орех
muskatniy orekh
nutmeg

мускатный цвет
muskatniy tsvet
mace

куркума
kurkuma
turmeric

зира
zira
cumin

букет приправ
buket priprav
bouquet garni

душистый перец
dushistiy perets
allspice

перец
perets
peppercorn

шамбала, пажитник
shambala, pazhitnik
fenugreek

чили
chili
chilli

цельный
tsel'niy
whole

дроблёный
droblyoniy
crushed

шафран
shafran
saffron

кардамон
kardamon
cardamom

карри
karri
curry powder

молотый
molotiy
ground

паприка
paprika
paprika

хлопья
khlop'ya
flakes

чеснок
chesnok
garlic

пряные травы pryaniye travy • herbs

палочки
palochki
sticks

семена фенхеля
semena fenkhelya
fennel seeds

фенхель
fenkhel'
fennel

лавровый лист
lavroviy list
bay leaf

петрушка
petrushka
parsley

корица
koritsa
cinnamon

сорго лимонное
sorgo limonnoye
lemon grass

гвоздика
gvozdika
cloves

шнитт-лук
shnit-luk
chives

мята
myata
mint

тимьян
tim'yan
thyme

шалфей
shalfey
sage

бадьян
bad'yan
star anise

эстрагон
estragon
tarragon

майоран
mayoran
marjoram

базилик
bazilik
basil

имбирь
imbir'
ginger

душица
dushitsa
oregano

кориандр
koriandr
coriander

укроп
ukrop
dill

розмарин
rozmarin
rosemary

бутилированные продукты
butilirovanniye produkty • bottled foods

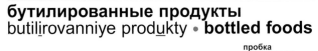

масло грецкого ореха
maslo gretskava orekha
walnut oil

масло из виноградных косточек
maslo iz vinogradnykh kostochek
grapeseed oil

пробка
probka
cork

подсолнечное масло
podsolnechnoye maslo
sunflower oil

миндальное масло
mindal'noye maslo
almond oil

кунжутное масло
kunzhutnoye maslo
sesame seed oil

масло лесного ореха
maslo lesnova orekha
hazelnut oil

оливковое масло
olivkovoye maslo
olive oil

пряные травы
pryanyye travy
herbs

ароматизированное масло
aromatizirovannoye maslo
flavoured oil

масла
masla
oils

сладкие пасты sladkiye pasty •
sweet spreads

банка
banka
jar

медовые соты
medoviye soty
honeycomb

кристаллизованный мёд
kristalizovanniy myod
set honey

лимонный крем
limonniy krem
lemon curd

малиновое варенье
malinovoye varen'ye
raspberry jam

мармелад
marmelad
marmalade

прозрачный мёд
prozrachniy myod
clear honey

кленовый сироп
klenoviy sirop
maple syrup

соусы и заправки sousye i zapravki • sauces and condiments

яблочный уксус
yablochniy uksus
cider vinegar

бальзамический уксус
bal'zamicheskiy uksus
balsamic vinegar

бутылка
butylka
bottle

майонез
mayonez
mayonnaise

чатни
chatni
chutney

солодовый уксус
solodoviy uksus
malt vinegar

винный уксус
vinniy uksus
wine vinegar

уксус
uksus
vinegar

кетчуп
ketchup
ketchup

английская горчица
angliyskaya gorchitsa
English mustard

французская горчица
frantsuskaya gorchitsa
French mustard

соус
sous
sauce

зерновая горчица
zernovaya gorchitsa
wholegrain mustard

запечатанная банка
zapechatannaya banka
preserving jar

арахисовое масло
arakhisovoye maslo
peanut butter

шоколадная паста
shokoladnaya pasta
chocolate spread

консервированные фрукты
konservirovannyye frukty
preserved fruit

словарь slovar' • vocabulary

кукурузное масло
kukuruznoye maslo
corn oil

масло из арахиса
maslo iz arakhisa
groundnut oil

растительное масло
rastitelnoye maslo
vegetable oil

рапсовое масло
rapsovoye maslo
rapeseed oil

масло холодного отжима
maslo kholodnava otzhima
cold-pressed oil

молочные продукты molochniye produkty • dairy produce

сыр syr • cheese

тёртый сыр
tyortiy syr
grated cheese

корка
korka
rind

полутвёрдый сыр
polutvyordiy syr
semi-hard cheese

твёрдый сыр
tvyordiy syr
hard cheese

полумягкий сыр
polumyakhkiy syr
semi-soft cheese

творог
tvorog
cottage cheese

сливочный сыр
slivochniy syr
cream cheese

голубой сыр (с плесенью)
goluboy syr (s plesen'yu)
blue cheese

мягкий сыр
myakhkiy syr
soft cheese

свежий сыр svezhiy syr | **fresh cheese**

молоко moloko • milk

цельное молоко
tselnoye moloko
whole milk

полужирное молоко
poluzhirnoye moloko
semi-skimmed milk

снятое (обезжиренное) молоко
snyatoye (obezzhirennoye) moloko
skimmed milk

пакет молока
paket moloka
milk carton

козье молоко
kozye moloko
goat's milk

сгущённое молоко
sguschyonoye moloko
condensed milk

коровье молоко korovye moloko | **cow's milk**

масло
maslo
butter

маргарин
margarin
margarine

сливки
slivki
cream

сливки к кофе
slivki k kofe
single cream

двойные сливки
dvoyniye slivki
double cream

взбитые сливки
vzbitiye slivki
whipped cream

сметана
smetana
sour cream

йогурт
yogurt
yoghurt

мороженое
morozhenoye
ice cream

яйца yaytsa • eggs

белок
belok
egg white

желток
zheltok
yolk

скорлупа
skorlupa
shell

**подставка
для яйца**
podstavka
dlya yaytsa
egg cup

варёное яйцо varyonoye yaytso
boiled egg

куриное яйцо
kurinoye yaytso
hen's egg

утиное яйцо
utinoye yaytso
duck egg

гусиное яйцо
gusinoye yaytso
goose egg

перепелиное яйцо
perepelinoye yaytso
quail egg

словарь slovar' • vocabulary

пастеризованный pasterizovanniy **pasteurized**	**овечье молоко** ovech'ye moloko **sheep's milk**	**солёный** solyoniy **salted**	**лактоза** laktoza **lactose**	**гомогенизированный** gomogenizirovanniy **homogenized**
непастеризованный nepasterizovanniy **unpasteurized**	**пахта** pakhta **buttermilk**	**несолёный** nesolyoniy **unsalted**	**обезжиренный** obezzhirenniy **fat free**	**порошковое молоко** poroshkovoye moloko **powdered milk**
молочный коктейль molochniy kokteyl' **milkshake**	**замороженный йогурт** zamorozhenniy yogurt **frozen yogurt**			

хлеб и мука khleb i muka • breads and flours

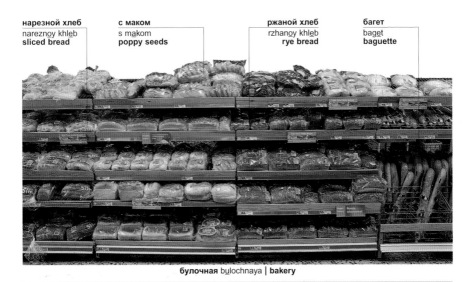

нарезной хлеб	с маком	ржаной хлеб	багет
nareznoy khleb	s makom	rzhanoy khleb	baget
sliced bread	**poppy seeds**	**rye bread**	**baguette**

булочная bulochnaya | **bakery**

хлебопечение khlebopecheniye • making bread

белая мука	обдирная мука	цельнозерновая мука	дрожжи
belaya muka	obdirnaya muka	tselnozernovaya muka	drozzhi
white flour	**brown flour**	**wholemeal flour**	**yeast**

тесто
tyesto
dough

просеивать proseivat'
sift (v)

смешивать smeshivat'
mix (v)

месить mesit' | **knead (v)**

печь pech | **bake (v)**

корочка
korochka
crust

белый хлеб
beliy khleb
white bread

тёмный хлеб с отрубями
tyomniy khleb s otrubyami
brown bread

буханка
bukhanka
loaf

цельнозерновой хлеб
tsel'nozernovoy khleb
wholemeal bread

ломтик
lomtik
slice

хлеб с зёрнами
khleb s zyornami
granary bread

кукурузный хлеб
kukuruzniy khleb
corn bread

хлеб на соде
khleb na sode
soda bread

хлеб на закваске
khleb na zakvaske
sourdough bread

лепёшка
lepyoshka
flatbread

бублик
bublik
bagel

булочка
bulochka | **bap**

булочка
bulochka | **roll**

хлеб с сухофруктами
khleb s sukhofruktami
fruit bread

хлеб с семечками
khleb s semechkami
seeded bread

наан
naan
naan bread

пита
pita
pitta bread

хрустящие хлебцы
khrustyashchiye khlebtsy
crispbread

словарь slovar' • vocabulary

сильная мука (с высоким содержанием клейковины)
sil'naya muka (s vysokim soderzhaniyem kleykoviny)
strong flour

мука с разрыхлителем
muka s razrykhlitelem
self-raising flour

подходить
podkhodit'
rise (v)

мука без разрыхлителя
muka bez razrykhlitelya
plain flour

подходить, расстаиваться
podkhodit', rasstaivat'sya
prove (v)

глазировать
glazirovat'
glaze (v)

хлебные крошки
khlebnyye kroshki
breadcrumbs

бороздка
borozdka
flute

хлеборезка
khleborezka
slicer

пекарь
pekar'
baker

пирожные и десерты pirozhniye i deserty · cakes and desserts

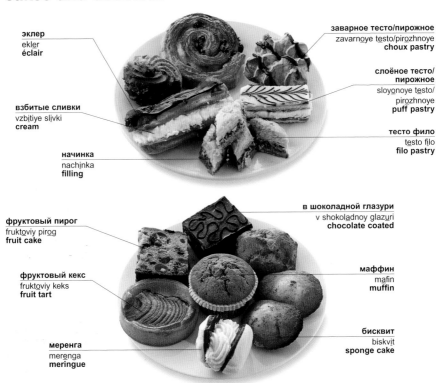

эклер
ekler
éclair

заварное тесто/пирожное
zavarnoye testo/pirozhnoye
choux pastry

слоёное тесто/пирожное
sloyonoye testo/pirozhnoye
puff pastry

взбитые сливки
vzbitiye slivki
cream

тесто фило
testo filo
filo pastry

начинка
nachinka
filling

фруктовый пирог
fruktoviy pirog
fruit cake

в шоколадной глазури
v shokoladnoy glazuri
chocolate coated

фруктовый кекс
fruktoviy keks
fruit tart

маффин
mafin
muffin

меренга
merenga
meringue

бисквит
biskvit
sponge cake

пирожные pirozhniye | **cakes**

словарь slovar' · vocabulary

пирожное с кремом pirozhnoye s kremom **crème pâtissière**	сдобная булочка sdobnaya bulochka **bun**	пирожное; сладкая выпечка pirozhnoye; sladkaya vypechka **pastry**	рисовый пудинг risoviy puding **rice pudding**	Можно мне кусочек? Mozhno mne kusochek? **May I have a slice please?**
шоколадный торт shokoladniy tort **chocolate cake**	заварной крем zavarnoy krem **custard**	кусок kusok **slice**	праздник praznik **celebration**	

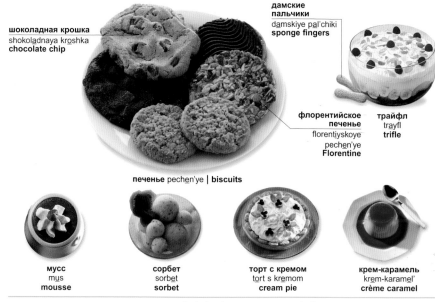

шоколадная крошка
shokoladnaya kroshka
chocolate chip

дамские пальчики
damskiye pal'chiki
sponge fingers

флорентийское печенье
florentiyskoye pechen'ye
Florentine

трайфл
trayfl
trifle

печенье pechen'ye | **biscuits**

мусс
mus
mousse

сорбет
sorbet
sorbet

торт с кремом
tort s kremom
cream pie

крем-карамель
krem-karamel'
crème caramel

праздничные торты prazdnichniye torty • celebration cakes

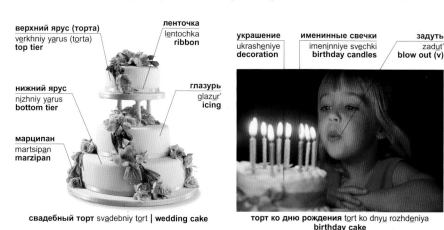

верхний ярус (торта)
verkhniy yarus (torta)
top tier

ленточка
lentochka
ribbon

нижний ярус
nizhniy yarus
bottom tier

глазурь
glazur'
icing

марципан
martsipan
marzipan

свадебный торт svadebniy tort | **wedding cake**

украшение
ukrasheniye
decoration

именинные свечки
imeninniye svechki
birthday candles

задуть
zadut'
blow out (v)

торт ко дню рождения tort ko dnyu rozhdeniya
birthday cake

деликатесы delikatesy • delicatessen

пикантная колбаса
pikantnaya kolbasa
spicy sausage

масло
maslo
oil

флан; открытый пирог
flan; otkrytiy pirog
flan

уксус
uksus
vinegar

сырое мясо
syroye myaso
uncooked meat

прилавок
prilavok
counter

салями
salyami
salami

пеперони; острая копчёная колбаса
peperoni; ostraya kopchonaya kolbasa
pepperoni

паштет
pashtet
pâté

моцарелла
motsarella
mozzarella

бри
bri
Brie

козий сыр
koziy syr
goat's cheese

чеддер
chedder
cheddar

пармезан
parmezan
Parmesan

камамбер
kamamber
Camembert

корка
korka
rind

эдам
edam
Edam

манчего
manchego
Manchego

пироги с начинкой
pirogi s nachinkoy
pies

черная оливка, маслина
chyornaya olivka, maslina
black olive

чили
chili
chilli

соус
sous
sauce

булочка
bulochka
bread roll

варёное мясо
varyonoye myaso
cooked meat

зелёная оливка
zelyonaya olivka
green olive

витрина с бутербродами vitrina s buterbrodami
sandwich counter

ветчина
vetchina
ham

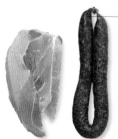

копчёная рыба
kopchonaya ryba
smoked fish

каперсы
kapersy
capers

чоризо
chorizo
chorizo

прошутто
proshutto
prosciutto

фаршированная оливка
farshirovannaya olivka
stuffed olive

словарь slovar' • vocabulary

в масле v masle **in oil**	**маринованный** marinovanny **marinated**	**копчёный** kopchoniy **smoked**
в рассоле v rassole **in brine**	**солёный** solyoniy **salted**	**вяленый** vyaleniy **cured**

Пожалуйста, возьмите талон с номером очереди.
pozhaluysta, voz'mite talon s nomerom ocheredi
Take a number please.

Можно это попробовать?
mozhno eto poprobovat'?
Can I try some of that please?

Можно мне шесть ломтиков этого?
mozhno mne shest' lomtikov etova?
May I have six slices of that please?

напитки napitki • drinks

вода voda • water

вода в бутылках
voda v butylkakh
bottled water

газированная
gazirovannaya
sparkling

негазированная
negazirovannaya
still

вода из-под крана
voda iz-pod krana
tap water

тоник
tonik
tonic water

минеральная вода
mineral'naya voda | **mineral water**

содовая
sodovaya
soda water

горячие напитки goryachiye napitki • hot drinks

пакетик чая
paketik chaya
teabag

рассыпной
листовой чай
rassypnoy listovoy
chay
loose leaf tea

чай
chay
tea

зёрна
zyorna
beans

молотый кофе
molotiy kofe
ground coffee

кофе
kofe
coffee

горячий шоколад
goryachiy shokolad
hot chocolate

ячменный кофе
yachmenniy kofe
malted drink

безалкогольные напитки bezalkogol'nyye napitki • soft drinks

соломинка
solominka
straw

томатный сок
tomatny sok
tomato juice

виноградный сок
vinogradny sok
grape juice

лимонад
limonad
lemonade

оранжад
oranzhad
orangeade

кола
kola
cola

алкогольные напитки alkogol'niye napitki • alcoholic drinks

джин
dzhin | **gin**

пиво
pivo
beer

банка
banka
can

сидр
sidr
cider

биттер
bitter
bitter

стаут; крепкий портер
staut; krepkiy porter
stout

водка
vodka | **vodka**

виски viski | **whisky**

ром
rom
rum

бренди
brendi
brandy

портвейн
portveyn
port

сухой
sukhoy
dry

херес
kheres
sherry

кампари
kampari
Campari

розовое
rozovoye
rosé

белое
beloye
white

красное
krasnoye
red

ликёр
likyor
liqueur

текила
tekila
tequila

шампанское
shampanskoye
champagne

вино vino | **wine**

питание вне дома pit*a*niye vne d*o*ma
eating out

кафе kafe · café

навес; маркиза
naves; markiza
awning

меню
menyu
menu

зонтик
zontik
umbrella

кафе на террасе
kafe na terrase
terrace café

официант
ofitsiant
waiter

кофемашина
kofemashina
coffee machine

столик
stolik
table

уличное кафе ulichnoye kafe | **pavement café**

снек-бар; закусочная snek-bar; zakusochnaya
snack bar

кофе kofe · coffee

кофе с молоком
kofe s molokom
white coffee

чёрный кофе
chorniy kofe
black coffee

какао-порошок
kakao-poroshok
cocoa powder

пенка
penka
froth

фильтрованный кофе
fil'trovanniy kofe
filter coffee

эспрессо
espresso
espresso

капучино
kapuchino
cappuccino

холодный кофе
kholodniy kofe
iced coffee

чай chay • tea

травяной чай
travyanoy chay
herbal tea

ромашковый чай
romashkoviy chay
camomile tea

зеленый чай
zelyoniy chay
green tea

чай с молоком
chay s molokom
tea with milk

черный чай
chorniy chay
black tea

чай с лимоном
chay s limonom
tea with lemon

мятный чай
myatniy chay
mint tea

холодный чай
kholodniy chay
iced tea

соки и молочные коктейли soki i molochnyye kokteyli • juices and milkshakes

шоколадный коктейль
shokoladniy kokteyl'
chocolate milkshake

клубничный коктейль
klubnichniy kokteyl'
strawberry milkshake

молочный коктейль с кофе
molochniy kokteyl' s kofe
coffee milkshake

апельсиновый сок
apel'sinoviy sok
orange juice

яблочный сок
yablochniy sok
apple juice

ананасный сок
ananasniy sok
pineapple juice

томатный сок
tomatniy sok
tomato juice

еда yeda • food

чёрный хлеб
chorniy khleb
brown bread

шарик
sharik
scoop

тост-сэндвич
tost-sendvich
toasted sandwich

салат
salat
salad

мороженое
morozhenoye
ice cream

сладкая выпечка
sladkaya vypechka
pastry

бар bar · **bar**

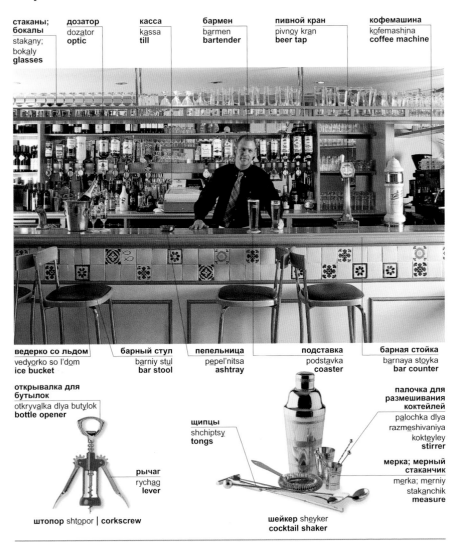

стаканы;
бокалы
stakany;
bokaly
glasses

дозатор
dozator
optic

касса
kassa
till

бармен
barmen
bartender

пивной кран
pivnoy kran
beer tap

кофемашина
kofemashina
coffee machine

ведерко со льдом
vedyorko so l'dom
ice bucket

барный стул
barniy stul
bar stool

пепельница
pepel'nitsa
ashtray

подставка
podstavka
coaster

барная стойка
barnaya stoyka
bar counter

открывалка для
бутылок
otkryvalka dlya butylok
bottle opener

щипцы
shchiptsy
tongs

палочка для
размешивания
коктейлей
palochka dlya
razmeshivaniya
kokteyley
stirrer

рычаг
rychag
lever

мерка; мерный
стаканчик
merka; merniy
stakanchik
measure

штопор shtopor | **corkscrew**

шейкер sheyker
cocktail shaker

кувшин
kuvshin
pitcher

кубик льда
kubik l'da
ice cube

джин с тоником
dzhin s tonikom
gin and tonic

скотч с водой
skotch s vodoy
scotch and water

ром с колой
rom s koloy
rum and cola

водка с апельсиновым соком
vodka s apel'sinovym sokom
vodka and orange

мартини
martini
martini

коктейль
kokteyl'
cocktail

вино
vino
wine

пиво pivo | **beer**

двойной
dvoynoy
double

одинарный
odinarniy
single

лёд и лимон
lyod i limon
ice and lemon

порция (спиртного)
portsiya (spirtnova)
a shot

мерка
merka
measure

без льда
bez l'da
without ice

со льдом
so l'dom
with ice

барные закуски barniye zakuski • **bar snacks**

кешью
kesh'ju
cashew nuts

арахис
arakhis
peanuts

миндаль
mindal'
almonds

чипсы chipsy | **crisps**

орешки oreshki | **nuts**

оливки olivki | **olives**

ресторан restoran • restaurant

сервировка стола
servirovka stola
table setting

помощник повара
pomoshchnik povara
commis chef

шеф-повар
shef-povar
chef

бокал
bokal
glass

поднос
podnos
tray

кухня kukhnya | **kitchen**

официант ofitsiant | **waiter**

словарь slovar' • vocabulary

вечернее меню vecherneye menyu **evening menu**	**фирменные блюда** firmenniye blyuda **specials**	**цена** tsena **price**	**чаевые** chayeviye **tip**	**буфет** bufet **buffet**	**соль** sol' **salt**
винная карта vinnaya karta **wine list**	**а-ля карт** a-lya kart **à la carte**	**счёт** schyot **bill**	**обслуживание включено** obsluzhivaniye vklyucheno **service included**	**бар** bar **bar**	**перец** perets **pepper**
обеденное меню obedennoye menyu **lunch menu**	**тележка с десертами** telezhka s desertami **sweet trolley**	**чек** chek **receipt**	**обслуживание не включено** obsluzhivaniye ne vklyucheno **service not included**	**клиент** kliyent **customer**	

меню
menyu
menu

блюдо из детского меню
blyudo iz detskogo menyu
child's meal

заказ zakaz | **order (v)**

(за)платить (za)platit' | **pay (v)**

смена блюд smena blyud • **courses**

аперитив
aperitiv
apéritif

закуска
zakuska
starter

суп
sup
soup

основное блюдо
osnovnoye blyudo
main course

гарнир
garnir
side order

десерт desert | **dessert**

кофе kofe | **coffee**

Столик на двоих, пожалуйста.
stolik na dvoikh, pozhalusta.
A table for two please.

Можно посмотреть меню/винную карту?
mozhno posmotret' menyu/vinnuyu kartu?
Can I see the menu/wine list please?

У вас есть меню по фиксированной цене/комплексное меню с выбором блюд?
u vas yest' menyu po fiksirovannoy tsene/kompleksnoye menyu s vyborom blyud?
Is there a fixed price menu?

У вас есть вегетарианские блюда?
u vas yest' vegetarianskiye blyuda?
Do you have any vegetarian dishes?

Можно счёт/чек, пожалуйста?
mozhno schyot/chek, pozhalusta?
Could I have the bill/a receipt please?

Можно нам заплатить раздельно?
mozhno nam zaplatit' razdel'no?
Can we pay separately?

Простите, где здесь туалет?
prostite, gde zdes' tualet?
Where are the toilets, please?

фастфуд fastfud • **fast food**

соломинка
solominka
straw

бургер
burger
burger

безалкогольные напитки
bezalkogol'niye napitki
soft drink

картофель фри
kartofel' fri
French fries

бумажная салфетка
bumazhnaya salfetka
paper napkin

поднос
podnos
tray

бургер-комплекс burger-kompleks | **burger meal**

пицца
pitsa
pizza

прейскурант
preyskurant
price list

напиток в банке
napitok v banke
canned drink

доставка на дом dostavka na dom
home delivery

уличный киоск ulichniy kiosk
street stall

булочка
bulochka
bun

горчица
gorchitsa
mustard

сосиска
sosiska
sausage

гамбургер
gamburger
hamburger

чикенбургер
chikenburger
chicken burger

вегетарианский бургер
vegetarianskiy burger
veggie burger

хот-дог khot-dog | **hot dog**

начинка
nachinka
filling

сэндвич
sendvich
sandwich

клубный сэндвич
klubniy sendvich
club sandwich

открытый бутерброд
otkrytiy buterbrod
open sandwich

ролл в лаваше
roll v lavashe
wrap

соус
sous
sauce

несладкий
nesladkiy
savoury

сладкий
sladkiy
sweet

начинка
nachinka
topping

кебаб
kebab
kebab

куриные наггетсы
kuriniye nagetsy
chicken nuggets

блинчики blinchiki | **crêpes**

рыба с жареной картошкой
ryba s zharenoy kartoshkoy
fish and chips

рёбрышки
ryobryshki
ribs

жареная курица
zharenaya kuritsa
fried chicken

пицца
pitsa
pizza

завтрак zavtrak • breakfast

молоко
moloko
milk

хлопья; сухой завтрак
khlop'ya; sukhoy zavtrak
cereal

сухофрукты
sukhofrukty
dried fruit

ветчина
vetchina
ham

сыр
syr
cheese

хлебцы
khlebtsy
crispbread

завтрак-буфет
zavtrak-bufet
breakfast buffet

мармелад
marmelad
marmalade

варенье, джем
varen'ye, dzhem
jam

паштет
pashtet
pâté

масло
maslo
butter

фруктовый сок
fruktoviy sok
fruit juice

кофе
kofe
coffee

горячий шоколад
goryachiy shokolad
hot chocolate

круассан
kruasan
croissant

чай
chay
tea

стол для завтрака stol dlya zavtraka | **breakfast table**

напитки napitki | **drinks**

бриошь
briosh
brioche

хлеб
khleb
bread

помидор, томат
pomidor, tomat
tomato

кровяная колбаса
krovyanaya kolbasa
black pudding

тост
tost
toast

яичница
yaichnitsa
fried egg

сосиска
sosiska
sausage

бекон
bekon
bacon

английский завтрак
angliyskiy zavtrak
English breakfast

копчёная рыба
kopchonaya ryba
kippers

французский тост
frantsuskiy tost
French toast

желток
zheltok
yolk

варёное яйцо
varyonoye yaytso
boiled egg

яичница-болтунья
yaichnitsa-boltun'ya
scrambled eggs

сливки
slivki
cream

фруктовый йогурт
fruktoviy yogurt
fruit yoghurt

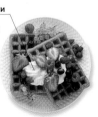

блинчики
blinchiki
pancakes

вафли
vafli
waffles

овсянка; каша
ovsyanka; kasha
porridge

свежие фрукты
svezhiye frukty
fresh fruit

обед ob<u>e</u>d · **dinner**

суп sup | **soup**

бульон bul'y<u>o</u>n | **broth**

рагу rag<u>u</u> | **stew**

карри k<u>a</u>rri | **curry**

жаркое zhark<u>o</u>ye | **roast**

пирог с начинкой pir<u>o</u>g s nach<u>i</u>nkoy | **pie**

суфле sufl<u>e</u> | **soufflé**

кебаб keb<u>a</u>b | **kebab**

лапша
lapsh<u>a</u>
noodles

фрикадельки frikad<u>e</u>l'ki **meatballs**

омлет oml<u>e</u>t | **omelette**

жареное блюдо zh<u>a</u>renoye bly<u>u</u>do | **stir-fry**

паста; макароны p<u>a</u>sta; makar<u>o</u>ny | **pasta**

рис ris | **rice**

салат sal<u>a</u>t **mixed salad**

зелёный салат zely<u>o</u>niy sal<u>a</u>t | **green salad**

заправка; салатный соус zapr<u>a</u>vka; sal<u>a</u>tny s<u>o</u>us | **dressing**

способы приготовления sposoby prigotovleniya • **techniques**

фаршированный
farshirovanniy | **stuffed**

в соусе v souse
in sauce

жареный на гриле
zhareniy na grile | **grilled**

маринованный
marinovanniy | **marinated**

пашот pashot | **poached**

пюре
pyure | **mashed**

запечённый
zapechyonniy | **baked**

жаренный целиком
zhareniy tselikom | **pan fried**

жареный zhareniy | **fried**

маринованный
marinovanniy | **pickled**

копченый kopchyoniy
smoked

жаренный во фритюре
zhareniy vo frityure
deep-fried

в сиропе v sirope
in syrup

заправленный
zapravlenniy | **dressed**

приготовленный на пару
prigotovlenniy na paru
steamed

вяленый vyaleniy
cured

учёба uchyoba
study

школа shkola · **school**

маркерная доска
markernaya doska
whiteboard

учитель
uchitel'
teacher

ученик
uchenik
pupil

парта
parta
desk

класс klas | **classroom**

ранец
ranets
school bag

школьница
shkol'nitsa
schoolgirl

школьник
shkol'nik
schoolboy

словарь slovar' · **vocabulary**

история istoriya **history**	естествознание yestestvoznaniye **science**	физика fizika **physics**
языки yazyki **languages**	изобразительное искусство izobrazitel'noye iskustvo	химия khimiya **chemistry**
литература literatura **literature**	**art** музыка muzyka	биология biologiya **biology**
география geografiya **geography**	**music** математика matematika **maths**	физкультура fizkul'tura **physical education**

занятия zanyatiya · **activities**

читать chitat' | **read (v)**

писать pisat' | **write (v)**

писать по буквам pisat'
po bukvam | **spell (v)**

рисовать risovat'
draw (v)

цифровой проектор
tsifrovoy proyektor
digital projector

перо
pero
nib

ручка
ruchka
pen

цветной карандаш
tsvetnoy karandash
colouring pencil

точилка
tochilka
pencil sharpener

карандаш
karandash
pencil

ластик
lastik
rubber

тетрадь
tetrad'
notebook

учебник uchebnik | **textbook**

пенал penal | **pencil case**

линейка lineyka | **ruler**

спрашивать sprashivat'
question (v)

отвечать otvechat'
answer (v)

обсуждать obsuzhdat'
discuss (v)

учиться uchit'sya
learn (v)

словарь slovar' • **vocabulary**

директор школы direktor shkoly **head teacher**	**ответ** otvet **answer**	**отметка** otmetka **grade**
урок urok **lesson**	**домашнее задание** domashneye zadaniye **homework**	**год** god **year**
вопрос vopros **question**	**экзамен** ekzamen **examination**	**словарь** slovar' **dictionary**
конспектировать konspektirovat' **take notes (v)**	**сочинение** sochineniye **essay**	**энциклопедия** entsiklopediya **encyclopedia**

математика matematika · **maths**

геометрические фигуры geometricheskiye figury · **shapes**

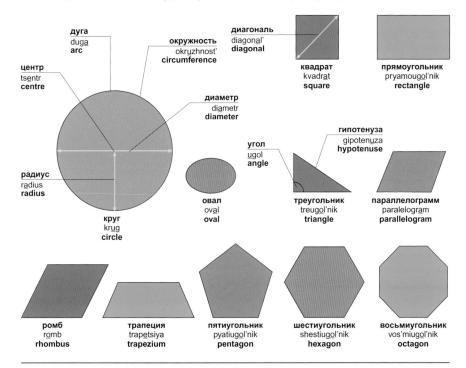

дуга
duga
arc

окружность
okruzhnost'
circumference

диагональ
diagonal'
diagonal

квадрат
kvadrat
square

прямоугольник
pryamougol'nik
rectangle

центр
tsentr
centre

диаметр
diametr
diameter

радиус
radius
radius

угол
ugol
angle

гипотенуза
gipotenuza
hypotenuse

овал
oval
oval

круг
krug
circle

треугольник
treugol'nik
triangle

параллелограмм
paralelogram
parallelogram

ромб
romb
rhombus

трапеция
trapetsiya
trapezium

пятиугольник
pyatiugol'nik
pentagon

шестиугольник
shestiugol'nik
hexagon

восьмиугольник
vos'miugol'nik
octagon

геометрические тела geometricheskiye tela · **solids**

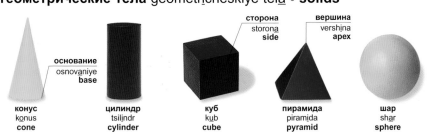

сторона
storona
side

вершина
vershina
apex

основание
osnovaniye
base

конус
konus
cone

цилиндр
tsilindr
cylinder

куб
kub
cube

пирамида
piramida
pyramid

шар
shar
sphere

линии linii • lines

прямая	**параллельная**	**перпендикулярная**	**кривая**
pryamaya	paralel'naya	perpendikulyarnaya	krivaya
straight	**parallel**	**perpendicular**	**curved**

измерения izmereniya • **measurements**

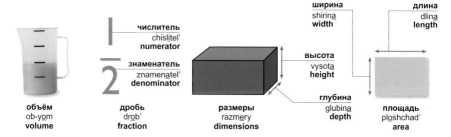

числитель
chislitel'
numerator

знаменатель
znamenatel'
denominator

ширина
shirina
width

длина
dlina
length

высота
vysota
height

глубина
glubina
depth

объём	**дробь**	**размеры**		**площадь**
ob-yom	drob'	**razmery**		ploshchad'
volume	**fraction**	**dimensions**		**area**

принадлежности prinadlezhnosti • **equipment**

угольник	**транспортир**	**линейка**	**циркуль**	**калькулятор**
ugol'nik	transportir	lineyka	tsirkul'	kal'kulyator
set square	**protractor**	**ruler**	**compass**	**calculator**

словарь slovar' • **vocabulary**

геометрия	**плюс**	**умножать**	**равно**	**складывать**	**умножать**	**уравнение**
geometriya	plyus	umnozhat'	ravno	skladyvat'	umnozhat'	uravneniye
geometry	**plus**	**times**	**equals**	**add (v)**	**multiply (v)**	**equation**
арифметика	**минус**	**делить на**	**считать**	**вычитать**	**делить**	**процент**
arifmetika	minus	delit' na	schitat'	vychitat'	delit'	protsent
arithmetic	**minus**	**divided by**	**count (v)**	**subtract (v)**	**divide (v)**	**percentage**

естественные науки yestestvenniye nauki • science

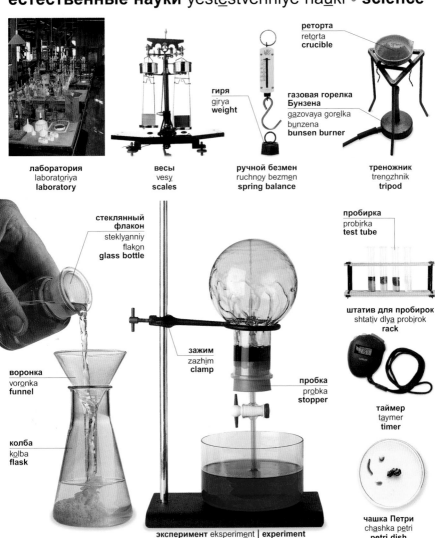

лаборатория
laboratoriya
laboratory

весы
vesy
scales

гиря
girya
weight

ручной безмен
ruchnoy bezmen
spring balance

реторта
retorta
crucible

газовая горелка Бунзена
gazovaya gorelka bunzena
bunsen burner

треножник
trenozhnik
tripod

стеклянный флакон
steklyanniy flakon
glass bottle

воронка
voronka
funnel

колба
kolba
flask

зажим
zazhim
clamp

пробка
probka
stopper

пробирка
probirka
test tube

штатив для пробирок
shtativ dlya probirok
rack

таймер
taymer
timer

чашка Петри
chashka petri
petri dish

эксперимент eksperiment | **experiment**

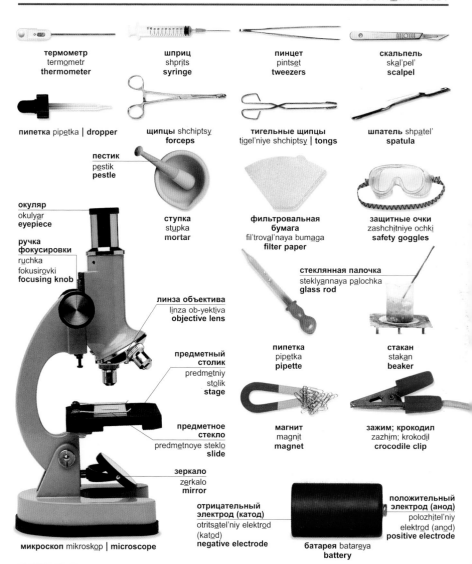

термометр
termometr
thermometer

шприц
shprits
syringe

пинцет
pintset
tweezers

скальпель
skal'pel'
scalpel

пипетка pipetka | **dropper**

щипцы shchiptsy
forceps

тигельные щипцы
tigel'niye shchiptsy | **tongs**

шпатель shpatel'
spatula

пестик
pestik
pestle

ступка
stupka
mortar

**фильтровальная
бумага**
fil'troval'naya bumaga
filter paper

защитные очки
zashchitniye ochki
safety goggles

окуляр
okulyar
eyepiece

**ручка
фокусировки**
ruchka
fokusirovki
focusing knob

линза объектива
linza ob-yektiva
objective lens

стеклянная палочка
steklyannaya palochka
glass rod

**предметный
столик**
predmetniy
stolik
stage

пипетка
pipetka
pipette

стакан
stakan
beaker

**предметное
стекло**
predmetnoye steklo
slide

магнит
magnit
magnet

зажим; крокодил
zazhim; krokodil
crocodile clip

зеркало
zerkalo
mirror

микроскоп mikroskop | **microscope**

**отрицательный
электрод (катод)**
otritsatel'niy elektrod
(katod)
negative electrode

батарея batareya
battery

**положительный
электрод (анод)**
polozhitel'niy
elektrod (anod)
positive electrode

колледж koledzh • college

приёмная комиссия
priyomnaya komisiya
admissions

столовая
stolovaya
refectory

спортивно-оздоровительный комплекс
sportivno-ozdorovitel'niy kompleks
health centre

спортивная площадка
sportivnaya ploshchadka
sports field

общежитие
obshchezhitiye
hall of residence

библиотекарь
bibliotekar'
librarian

кампус kampus | campus

словарь slovar' • vocabulary

читательский билет chitatel'skiy bilet **library card**	**справочный отдел** spravochniy otdel **enquiries**	**абонемент** abonement **loan**
читальный зал chital'niy zal **reading room**	**брать в библиотеке** brat' v biblioteke **borrow (v)**	**книга** kniga **book**
список книг для чтения spisok knig dlya chteniya **reading list**	**резервировать** rezervirovat' **reserve (v)**	**название** nazvaniye **title**
дата возврата data vozvrata **return date**	**продлевать** prodlevat' **renew (v)**	**проход** prokhod **aisle**

периодический
periodicheskyi
periodical

абонементный стол
abonementniy stol
loans desk

книжная полка
knizhnaya polka
bookshelf

журнал
zhurnal
journal

библиотека biblioteka | library

студент
student
undergraduate

лектор
lektor
lecturer

выпускник
vypusknik
graduate

мантия
mantiya
robe

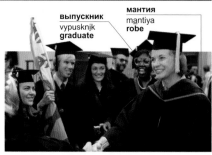

лекционный зал lektsionniy zal | **lecture theatre**

выпускная церемония/вручение дипломов
vypusknaya tseremoniya/vrucheniye diplomov
graduation ceremony

школы shkoly • schools

модель
model'
model

колледж искусств
koledzh iskustv
art college

музыкальная школа
muzykal'naya shkola
music school

танцевальная академия
tantseval'naya akademiya
dance academy

словарь slovar' • vocabulary

стипендия
stipendiya
scholarship

диплом
diplom
diploma

степень
stepen'
degree

аспирант
aspirant
postgraduate

исследовательская работа
issledovatel'skaya rabota
research

степень магистра
stepen' magistra
master's

докторская степень
doktorskaya stepen'
doctorate

диссертация
disertatsiya
thesis

диссертация
disertatsiya
dissertation

факультет
fakul'tet
department

право
pravo
law

технические науки
tekhnicheskiye nauki
engineering

медицина
meditsina
medicine

зоология
zoologiya
zoology

физика
fizika
physics

политика
politika
politics

философия
filosofiya
philosophy

литература
literatura
literature

история искусств
istoriya iskustv
history of art

экономика
ekonomika
economics

работа rab<u>o</u>ta
work

офис 1 <u>o</u>fis • office 1

монитор
monitor
monitor

входящая корреспонденция
vkhod<u>ya</u>shchaya korespond<u>e</u>ntsiya
in-tray

настольный органайзер
nast<u>o</u>l'niy organ<u>a</u>yzer
desktop organizer

блокнот
blokn<u>o</u>t
notebook

ноутбук
noutb<u>u</u>k
laptop

исходящая корреспонденция
iskhod<u>ya</u>shchaya korespond<u>e</u>ntsiya
out-tray

выдвижной ящик
vydvizhn<u>o</u>y <u>ya</u>shchik
drawer

письменный стол
pis'm<u>e</u>nniy st<u>o</u>l
desk

офисное кресло
<u>o</u>fisnoye kr<u>e</u>slo
swivel chair

корзина для мусора
korz<u>i</u>na dl<u>ya</u> m<u>u</u>sora
wastebasket

шкаф для документов
shk<u>a</u>f dl<u>ya</u> dokum<u>e</u>ntov
filing cabinet

офисное оборудование <u>o</u>fisnoye obor<u>u</u>dovaniye • **office equipment**

лоток для бумаги
lot<u>o</u>k dl<u>ya</u> bum<u>a</u>gi
paper tray

принтер pr<u>i</u>nter | **printer**

бумагорезка bum<u>a</u>gorezka
shredder

словарь slov<u>a</u>r' • **vocabulary**

печатать
pech<u>a</u>tat'
print (v)

увеличивать
uvel<u>i</u>chivat'
enlarge (v)

копировать
kop<u>i</u>rovat'
copy (v)

уменьшать
umen'sh<u>a</u>t'
reduce (v)

Мне нужно сделать несколько копий.
Mn<u>e</u> n<u>u</u>zhno sd<u>e</u>lat' n<u>e</u>skol'ko k<u>o</u>piy
I need to make some copies.

офисные принадлежности ofisniye prinadlezhnosti • office supplies

бланк с логотипом
blank s logotipom
letterhead

сопроводительная карточка
soprovoditel'naya kartochka
compliments slip

конверт
konvert
envelope

папка-регистратор
papka-registrator
box file

планшетка с зажимом
planshetka s zazhimom
clipboard

блокнот
bloknot
note pad

крепёж
krepyozh
tab

подвесная папка
podvesnaya papka
hanging file

разделитель
razdelitel'
divider

классификатор
klasifikator
concertina file

папка с арочным прижимом
papka s arochnym prizhimom
lever arch file

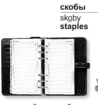

личный органайзер
lichniy organayzer
personal organizer

скобы
skoby
staples

степлер
stepler
stapler

скотч; клейкая лента
skoch; kleykaya lenta
sticky tape

катушка-диспенсер для клейкой ленты
katushka-dispenser dlya kleykoy lenty
tape dispenser

дырокол
dyrokol
hole punch

чернильная подушечка
chernil'naya podushechka
ink pad

печать
pechat'
rubber stamp

резинка для бумаг
rezinka dlya bumag
rubber band

зажим для бумаг
zazhim dlya bumag
bulldog clip

скрепка
skrepka
paper clip

кнопка
knopka
drawing pin

доска для объявлений doska dlya ob-yavleniy | **notice board**

офис 2 ofis • office 2

флипчарт
flipchart
flip chart

стойка для флипчарта
stoyka dlya flipcharta
easel

менеджер
menedzher
manager

предложение
predlozheniye
proposal

протокол
protokol
minutes

отчёт
otchyot
report

**ответственный
сотрудник**
otvetstvenniy
sotrudnik
executive

заседание, встреча zasedaniye, vstrecha | **meeting**

словарь slovar' • vocabulary

конференц-зал
konferents-zal
meeting room

присутствовать
prisutstvovat'
attend (v)

повестка дня
povestka dnya
agenda

председательствовать
predsedatel'stvovat'
chair (v)

Во сколько начинается встреча?
Vo skol'ko nachinayetsya vstrecha?
What time is the meeting?

В какое время вы в офисе?
V kakoye vremya vy v ofise?
What are your office hours?

докладчик
dokladchik
speaker

презентация prezentatsiya | **presentation**

бизнес b<u>i</u>znes • business

бизнесмен
biznesm<u>e</u>n
businessman

бизнесвумен
biznesv<u>u</u>men
businesswoman

деловой обед del<u>o</u>v<u>o</u>y ob<u>e</u>d | **business lunch**

деловая поездка del<u>o</u>v<u>a</u>ya po<u>e</u>zdka | **business trip**

встреча
vstr<u>e</u>cha
appointment

записная книжка-календарь zapisn<u>a</u>ya kn<u>i</u>zhka-kalend<u>a</u>r' | **diary**

управляющий
директор
upravl<u>ya</u>yushchiy
dir<u>e</u>ktor
**managing
director**

клиент
kli<u>ye</u>nt
client

сделка sd<u>e</u>lka | **business deal**

словарь slov<u>a</u>r' • vocabulary

компания komp<u>a</u>niya **company**	сотрудники sotr<u>u</u>dniki **staff**	бухгалтерский отдел bukhg<u>a</u>lterskiy otd<u>e</u>l **accounts department**	юридический отдел yurid<u>i</u>cheskiy otd<u>e</u>l **legal department**
головной офис golovn<u>o</u>y <u>o</u>fis **head office**	зарплата zarpl<u>a</u>ta **salary**	отдел маркетинга otd<u>e</u>l mark<u>e</u>tinga **marketing department**	отдел по работе с клиентами otd<u>e</u>l po rab<u>o</u>te s kli<u>ye</u>ntami **customer service department**
филиал fil<u>i</u>al **branch**	платёжная ведомость platy<u>o</u>zhnaya v<u>e</u>domost' **payroll**	отдел продаж otd<u>e</u>l prod<u>a</u>zh **sales department**	отдел кадров otd<u>e</u>l k<u>a</u>drov **human resources department**

компьютер komp'yuter • computer

принтер
printer
printer

экран
ekran
screen

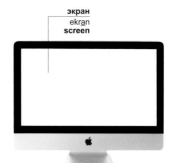

сканер
skaner
scanner

ноутбук
noutbuk | **laptop**

клавиша
klavisha
key

клавиатура
klaviatura
keyboard

компьютерная мышь
komp'yuternaya mysh'
mouse

докладчик
dokladchik
speaker

аппаратное обеспечение
aparatnoye obespecheniye
hardware

словарь slovar' • **vocabulary**

память pamyat' **memory**	**программное обеспечение** programnoye obespecheniye **software**	**сервер** server **server**
RAM, оперативная память ram, operativnaya pamyat' **RAM**	**приложение** prilozheniye **application**	**порт** port **port**
байты bayty **bytes**	**программа** programma **program**	**процессор** protsessor **processor**
система sistema **system**	**сеть** set' **network**	**кабель питания** kabel' pitaniya **power cable**

USB-флеш-накопитель
yu-es-bi-flesh-nakopitel'
memory stick

внешний жёсткий диск
vneshniy zhyostkiy disk
external hard drive

планшет
planshet
tablet

смартфон
smartfon
smartphone

рабочий стол rabochiy stol • desktop

файл
fayl
file

строка меню
stroka menyu
menubar

шрифт
shrift
font

иконка
ikonka
icon

панель инструментов
panel' instrumentov
toolbar

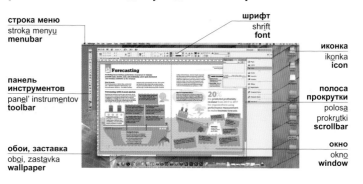

полоса прокрутки
polosa prokrutki
scrollbar

папка
papka
folder

обои, заставка
oboi, zastavka
wallpaper

окно
okno
window

корзина
korzina
trash

интернет internet • internet

браузер
brauzer
browser

входящие
vkhodyashchiye
inbox

веб-сайт
veb-sayt
website

просматривать prosmatrivat' | **browse (v)**

имейл imeyl • email

адрес электронной почты
adres elektronnoy pochty
email address

словарь slovar' • vocabulary

соединять soyedinyat' **connect (v)**	**сервис-провайдер** servis-provayder **service provider**	**входить в систему** vkhodit' v sistemu **log on (v)**	**загружать** zagruzhat' **download (v)**	**отправлять** otpravlyat' **send (v)**	**сохранять** sokhranyat' **save (v)**
устанавливать ustanavlivat' **install (v)**	**аккаунт электронной почты** akaunt elektronnoy pochty **email account**	**онлайн** onlayn **online**	**приложение** prilozheniye **attachment**	**получать** poluchat' **receive (v)**	**искать** iskat' **search (v)**

СМИ smi • media

телестудия telestudiya • television studio

съёмочная площадка
s-yomochnaya
ploshchadka
set

ведущий
vedushchiy
presenter

свет
svet
light

камера
kamera
camera

кран-штатив
kran-shtativ
camera crane

оператор
operator
cameraman

словарь slovar' • vocabulary

канал kanal **channel**	**новости** novosti **news**	**пресса** pressa **press**	**мыльная опера** myl'naya opera **soap**	**мультфильм** mul'tfil'm **cartoon**	**прямая трансляция** pryamaya translyatsiya **live**
программы programmy **programming**	**документальный фильм** dokumental'niy fil'm **documentary**	**телесериал** teleserial **television series**	**игровое шоу; телевикторина** igrovoye shou; televiktorina **game show**	**в записи** v zapisi **prerecorded**	**транслировать** translirovat' **broadcast (v)**

интервьюер interv'yuyer
interviewer

репортёр reportyor
reporter

телесуфлёр telesuflyor
autocue

**ведущий/диктор
новостей** vedushchiy/
diktor novostey
newsreader

актёры aktyory | **actors**

удочка для микрофона
udochka dlya mikrofona
sound boom

хлопушка khlopushka
clapper board

декорации dekoratsii
film set

радио radio • **radio**

звукоинженер
zvukoinzhener
**sound
technician**

микшерный пульт
miksherniy pul't
mixing desk

микрофон
mikrofon
microphone

студия звукозаписи studiya zvukozapisi | **recording studio**

словарь slovar' • **vocabulary**

радиостанция
radiostantsiya
radio station

**трансляция;
вещание**
translyatsiya;
veshchaniye
broadcast

длина волны
dlina volny
wavelength

длинные волны
dlinniye volny
long wave

короткие волны
korotkiye volny
short wave

аналоговое радио
analogovoye radio
analogue

средние волны
sredniye volny
medium wave

частота
chastota
frequency

громкость
gromkost'
volume

настраивать
nastraivat'
tune (v)

диджей
didzhey
DJ

цифровое радио
tsifrovoye radio
digital

правосудие pravos<u>u</u>diye • **law**

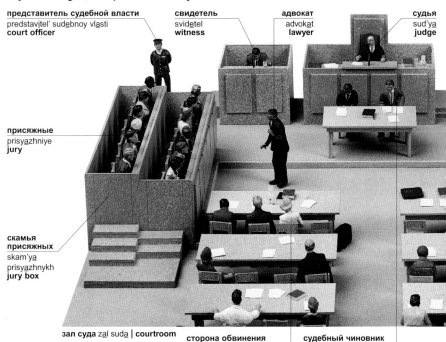

представитель судебной власти
predstav<u>i</u>tel' sud<u>e</u>bnoy vl<u>a</u>sti
court officer

свидетель
svid<u>e</u>tel
witness

адвокат
advok<u>a</u>t
lawyer

судья
sud'<u>ya</u>
judge

присяжные
prisy<u>a</u>zhniye
jury

**скамья
присяжных**
skam'<u>ya</u>
pris<u>ya</u>zhnykh
jury box

зал суда z<u>a</u>l sud<u>a</u> | **courtroom**

сторона обвинения
storon<u>a</u> obvin<u>e</u>niya
prosecution

судебный чиновник
sud<u>e</u>bniy chin<u>o</u>vnik
court official

словарь slov<u>a</u>r' • **vocabulary**

офис адвоката
<u>o</u>fis advok<u>a</u>ta
lawyer's office

консультация юриста
konsul't<u>a</u>tsiya yur<u>i</u>sta
legal advice

клиент
kli<u>e</u>nt
client

вызов в суд; повестка
v<u>y</u>zov v s<u>u</u>d; pov<u>e</u>stka
summons

заявление
zayavl<u>e</u>niye
statement

ордер
<u>o</u>rder
warrant

судебное предписание
sud<u>e</u>bnoye predpis<u>a</u>niye
writ

дата слушаний
d<u>a</u>ta sl<u>u</u>shaniy
court date

заявление ответчика
zayavl<u>e</u>niye otv<u>e</u>tchika
plea

дело
d<u>e</u>lo
court case

обвинение
obvin<u>e</u>niye
charge

обвиняемый
obvin<u>ya</u>yemiy
accused

стенографист
stenografist
stenographer

подозреваемый
podozrevayemiy
suspect

подсудимый; ответчик
podsudimiy; otvetchik
defendant

сторона защиты
storona zashchity
defence

преступник
prestupnik
criminal

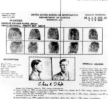

фоторобот
fotorobot | **photofit**

криминальное досье
kriminal'noye dos'ye
criminal record

тюремные охранники
tyuremniye okhranniki | **prison guard**

камера
kamera | **cell**

тюрьма tyur'ma | **prison**

словарь slovar' • vocabulary

улики uliki **evidence**	**виновен** vinoven **guilty**	**залог** zalog **bail**	**Я хочу встретиться с адвокатом.** Ya khochu vstretit'sya s advokatom **I want to see a lawyer.**
вердикт verdikt **verdict**	**оправдан** opravdan **acquitted**	**апелляция** apelyatsiya **appeal**	**Где находится суд?** Gde nakhoditsya sud? **Where is the courthouse?**
невиновен nevinoven **innocent**	**приговор** prigovor **sentence**	**условно-досрочное освобождение** uslovno-dosrochnoye osvobozhdeniye **parole**	**Могу ли я внести залог?** Mogu li ya vnesti zalog? **Can I post bail?**

ферма 1 ferma • farm 1

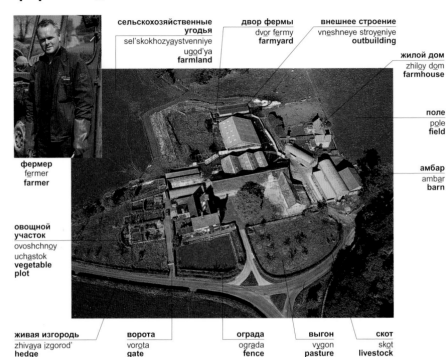

сельскохозяйственные угодья
sel'skokhozyaystvenniye ugod'ya
farmland

двор фермы
dvor fermy
farmyard

внешнее строение
vneshneye stroyeniye
outbuilding

жилой дом
zhiloy dom
farmhouse

поле
pole
field

амбар
ambar
barn

фермер
fermer
farmer

овощной участок
ovoshchnoy uchastok
vegetable plot

живая изгородь
zhivaya izgorod'
hedge

ворота
vorota
gate

ограда
ograda
fence

выгон
vygon
pasture

скот
skot
livestock

культиватор
kul'tivator
cultivator

трактор traktor | **tractor**

(хлебоуборочный) комбайн (khlebouborochniy) kombayn | **combine harvester**

виды фермерских хозяйств vidy f<u>e</u>rmerskikh khoz<u>ya</u>ystv • types of farm

урожай
ur<u>o</u>zhay
crop

стадо овец
st<u>a</u>do ov<u>e</u>ts
flock

земледельческая ферма
zemled<u>e</u>l'cheskaya f<u>e</u>rma
arable farm

молочная ферма
mol<u>o</u>chnaya f<u>e</u>rma
dairy farm

овцеферма
ovtsef<u>e</u>rma
sheep farm

птицеферма ptitsef<u>e</u>rma
poultry farm

виноградная лоза
vinogr<u>a</u>dnaya loz<u>a</u>
vine

свиноферма
svinof<u>e</u>rma
pig farm

рыбоводное хозяйство
rybov<u>o</u>dnoye khoz<u>ya</u>ystvo
fish farm

плодоводческая ферма
plodov<u>o</u>dcheskaya f<u>e</u>rma
fruit farm

виноградник
vinogr<u>a</u>dnik
vineyard

действия d<u>e</u>ystviya • actions

борозда
bor<u>o</u>zda
furrow

пахать
pakh<u>a</u>t'
plough (v)

сеять
s<u>e</u>yat'
sow (v)

доить
do<u>i</u>t'
milk (v)

кормить
korm<u>i</u>t'
feed (v)

поливать poliv<u>a</u>t'
water (v)

собирать урожай sobir<u>a</u>t'
ur<u>o</u>zhay | **harvest (v)**

словарь slov<u>a</u>r' • vocabulary

гербицид gerbits<u>i</u>d **herbicide**	**стадо** st<u>a</u>do **herd**	**кормушка** korm<u>u</u>shka **trough**
пестицид pestits<u>i</u>d **pesticide**	**силос** s<u>i</u>los **silo**	**сажать** sazh<u>a</u>t' **plant (v)**

ферма 2 ferma • farm 2

урожай urozhay • crops

пшеница
pshenitsa
wheat

кукуруза
kukuruza
corn

ячмень
yachmen'
barley

рапс
raps
rapeseed

подсолнух
podsolnukh
sunflower

тюк
tyuk
bale

сено
seno
hay

люцерна
lyutserna
alfalfa

табак
tabak
tobacco

рис
ris
rice

чай
chay
tea

кофе
kofe
coffee

лён
lyon
flax

сахарный тростник
sakharniy trostnik
sugarcane

хлопок
khlopok
cotton

пугало
pugalo
scarecrow

скот sk<u>o</u>t • livestock

поросёнок
porosy<u>o</u>nok
piglet

свинья
svin'y<u>a</u>
pig

телёнок
tely<u>o</u>nok
calf

корова
kor<u>o</u>va
cow

бык
byk
bull

овца
ovts<u>a</u>
sheep

козлёнок
kozly<u>o</u>nok
kid

жеребёнок
zhereby<u>o</u>nok
foal

ягнёнок
yagny<u>o</u>nok
lamb

коза
koz<u>a</u>
goat

лошадь/конь
l<u>o</u>shad'/k<u>o</u>n'
horse

осёл
os<u>yo</u>l
donkey

цыплёнок
tsyply<u>o</u>nok
chick

утёнок
uty<u>o</u>nok
duckling

курица
k<u>u</u>ritsa
chicken

петух
pet<u>u</u>kh
cockerel

индюк
indy<u>u</u>k
turkey

утка
<u>u</u>tka
duck

стойло
st<u>o</u>ylo
stable

загон
zag<u>o</u>n
pen

курятник
kury<u>a</u>tnik
chicken coop

свинарник
svin<u>a</u>rnik
pigsty

строительство stroitel'stvo • construction

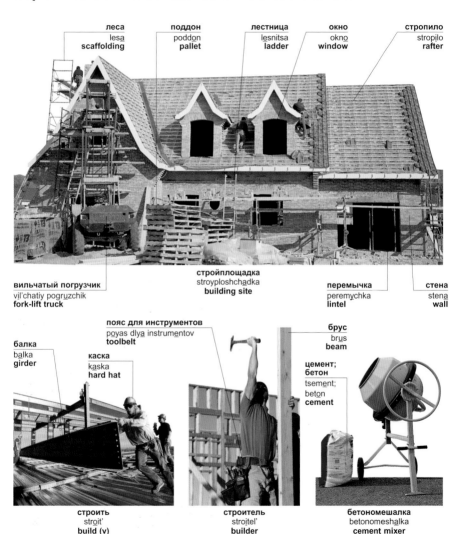

леса
lesa
scaffolding

поддон
poddon
pallet

лестница
lesnitsa
ladder

окно
okno
window

стропило
stropilo
rafter

вильчатый погрузчик
vil'chatiy pogruzchik
fork-lift truck

стройплощадка
stroyploshchadka
building site

перемычка
peremychka
lintel

стена
stena
wall

балка
balka
girder

каска
kaska
hard hat

пояс для инструментов
poyas dlya instrumentov
toolbelt

брус
brus
beam

**цемент;
бетон**
tsement;
beton
cement

строить
stroit'
build (v)

строитель
stroitel'
builder

бетономешалка
betonomeshalka
cement mixer

материалы materialy • **materials**

кирпич
kirpich
brick

дерево
derevo
timber

черепица
cherepitsa
roof tile

бетонные блоки
betonniye bloki
breeze block

инструменты instrumenty • **tools**

строительный раствор
stroitel'niy rastvor
mortar

кельма
kel'ma
trowel

спиртовой уровень
spirtovoy uroven'
spirit level

рукоятка
rukoyatka
handle

кувалда
kuvalda
sledgehammer

кирка-мотыга
kirka-motyga
pickaxe

лопата
lopata
shovel

техника tekhnika • **machinery**

каток
katok
roadroller

самосвал
samosval
dumper truck

выносная опора
vynosnaya opora
support

крюк
kryuk
hook

подъёмный кран pod-yomniy kran | **crane**

дорожные работы dorozhniye raboty • **roadworks**

асфальт
asfal't
tarmac

конус
konus
cone

отбойный молоток
otboyniy molotok
pneumatic drill

замена дорожного покрытия
zamena dorozhnogo pokrytiya
resurfacing

экскаватор
ekskavator
mechanical digger

профессии 1 professiy • occupations 1

плотник
plotnik
carpenter

электрик
elektrik
electrician

водопроводчик
vodoprovodchik
plumber

строитель
stroitel'
builder

садовод
sadovod
gardener

пылесос
pylesos
vacuum cleaner

уборщик
uborshchik
cleaner

механик
mekhanik
mechanic

мясник
myasnik
butcher

продавец рыбы
prodavets ryby
fishmonger

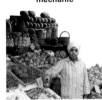

зеленщик
zelenschik
greengrocer

флорист
florist
florist

женский парикмахер
zhenskiy parikmakher
hairdresser

мужской парикмахер
muzhskoy parikmakher
barber

ювелир
yuvelir
jeweller

продавец-консультант
prodavets-konsul'tant
shop assistant

агент по недвижимости
agent po nedvizhimosti
estate agent

окулист
okulist
optician

маска
maska
mask

зубной врач
zubnoy vrach
dentist

врач
vrach
doctor

фармацевт
farmatsevt
pharmacist

медсестра
medsestra
nurse

ветеринар
veterinar
vet

фермер
fermer
farmer

рыбак
rybak
fisherman

автомат
avtomat
**machine
gun**

нагрудный знак
nagrudniy znak
identity badge

охранник
okhrannik
security guard

форма
forma
uniform

моряк
moryak
sailor

солдат
soldat
soldier

полицейский
politseyskiy
policeman

пожарный
pozharniy
fireman

профессии 2 professiy • occupations 2

юрист
yurist
lawyer

бухгалтер
bukhgalter
accountant

макет
maket
model

архитектор arkhitektor | **architect**

учёный
uchyoniy
scientist

учительница
uchitel'nitsa
teacher

библиотекарь
bibliotekar'
librarian

администратор
administrator
receptionist

сумка
почтальона
sumka
pochtalyona
mailbag

почтальон
pochtalyon
postman

водитель автобуса
voditel' avtobusa
bus driver

водитель грузовика
voditel' gruzovika
lorry driver

таксист
taksist
taxi driver

пилот
pilot
pilot

стюардесса
styuardessa
air stewardess

турагент
turagent
travel agent

поварской
колпак
povarskoy
kolpak
chef's hat

шеф-повар
shef-povar
chef

пачка
pachka
tutu

музыкант
muzykant
musician

балерина
balerina
dancer

актриса
aktrisa
actress

певица
pevitsa
singer

официантка
ofitsiantka
waitress

бармен
barmen
bartender

спортсмен
sportsmen
sportsman

скульптор
skul'ptor
sculptor

заметки
zametki
notes

художник
khudozhnik
painter

фотограф
fotograf
photographer

ведущий новостей, диктор
vedushchiy novostey, diktor
newsreader

журналист
zhurnalist
journalist

редактор
redaktor
editor

дизайнер
dizayner
designer

швея
shveya
seamstress

портной
portnoy
tailor

транспорт tr<u>a</u>nsport
transport

дороги dorogi · **roads**

шоссе
shose
motorway

**пункт взимания
дорожных
сборов**
punkt vzimaniya
dorozhnykh
sborov
toll booth

**дорожная
разметка**
dorozhnaya
razmetka
road markings

съезд
s-yezd
slip road

**одностороннее
движение**
odnostoronneye
dvizheniye
one-way street

**направляющий
островок**
napravlyayushchiy
ostrovok
divider

слияние
sliyaniye
junction

светофор
svetofor
traffic light

**внутренняя
полоса движения**
vnutrennyaya
polosa dvizheniya
inside lane

**средняя полоса
движения**
srednyaya polosa
dvizheniya
middle lane

**внешняя
полоса
движения**
vneshnyaya
polosa dvizheniya
outside lane

наклонный съезд
naklonniy s-yezd
exit ramp

движение
dvizheniye
traffic

эстакада
estakada
flyover

обочина
obochina
hard shoulder

**проезд под
путепроводом**
proyezd pod
puteprovodom
underpass

грузовик
gruzovik
lorry

разделительная зона
razdelitel'naya zona
central reservation

**аварийный
телефон**
avariyniy telefon
emergency phone

**парковка для
инвалидов**
parkovka dlya invalidov
disabled parking

пробка
probka
traffic jam

**пешеходный
переход**
peshekhodniy
perekhod
pedestrian crossing

**спутниковый
навигатор**
sputnikoviy navigator
satnav

**счётчик
на стоянке**
schyotchik
na stoyanke
parking meter

**инспектор
дорожного движения**
inspektor dorozhnogo
dvizheniya
traffic policeman

словарь slovar' • **vocabulary**

**кольцевая
развязка**
kol'tsevaya
razvyazka
roundabout

объезд
ob-yezd
diversion

**дорожные
работы**
dorozhniye raboty
roadworks

**аварийное
заграждение**
avariynoye
zagrazhdeniye
crash barrier

автомагистраль
avtomagistral'
dual carriageway

парковаться
parkovatsa
park (v)

вести машину
vesti mashinu
drive (v)

**давать задний
ход**
davat' zadniy khod
reverse (v)

обгонять
obgonyat'
overtake (v)

буксировать
buksirovat'
tow away (v)

Это дорога на ...?
eto doroga na ...?
Is this the road to ...?

**Где можно
припарковаться?**
gde mozhno
priparkovatsa?
Where can I park?

дорожные знаки dorozhniye znaki • **road signs**

**въезд
запрещён**
v-yezd
zapreshchyon
no entry

**ограничение
скорости**
ogranicheniye
skorosti
speed limit

опасность
opasnost'
hazard

**остановка
запрещена**
ostanovka
zapreshchena
no stopping

**поворот направо
запрещён**
povorot napravo
zapreshchyon
no right turn

автобус avt<u>o</u>bus · **bus**

сиденье водителя
siden'ye voditelya
driver's seat

поручень
por<u>u</u>chen'
handrail

автоматическая дверь
avtomat<u>i</u>cheskaya dv<u>e</u>r'
automatic door

переднее колесо
per<u>e</u>dneye koles<u>o</u>
front wheel

багажный отсек
bag<u>a</u>zhniy ots<u>e</u>k
luggage hold

дверь dv<u>e</u>r' | **door**

междугородный автобус mezhdugor<u>o</u>dniy avt<u>o</u>bus | **coach**

виды автобусов v<u>i</u>dy avt<u>o</u>busov · **types of buses**

номер маршрута
n<u>o</u>mer
marshr<u>u</u>ta
route number

водитель
vodit<u>e</u>l'
driver

двухэтажный автобус
dvukhet<u>a</u>zhniy avt<u>o</u>bus
double-decker bus

трамвай
tramv<u>a</u>y
tram

троллейбус
troll<u>e</u>ybus
trolley bus

школьный автобус shk<u>o</u>l'niy avt<u>o</u>bus | **school bus**

кнопка остановки
knopka ostanovki
stop button

окно
okno
window

заднее колесо
zadneye koleso
rear wheel

автобусный билет
avtobusniy bilet
bus ticket

звонок
zvonok
bell

автобусная станция
avtobusnaya stantsiya
bus station

**автобусная
остановка**
avtobusnaya
ostanovka
bus stop

словарь slovar' • vocabulary

плата за проезд
plata za proyezd
fare

расписание
raspisaniye
timetable

**доступ для инвалидов-
колясочников**
dostup dlya invalidov-
kolyasochnikov
wheelchair access

крытая автобусная остановка
krytaya avtobusnaya ostanovka
bus shelter

**Есть ли остановка
на…?**
yest' li ostanovka na…?
Do you stop at …?

Какой автобус идёт на…?
kakoy avtobus idyot na…?
Which bus goes to …?

мини-автобус
mini-avtobus
minibus

экскурсионный автобус ekskursionniy avtobus | **tourist bus**

маршрутное такси
marshrutnoye taksi | **shuttle bus**

автомобиль 1 avtomobil' · **car 1**

вид снаружи vid snaruzhi · **exterior**

лобовое стекло
lobovoye steklo
windscreen

стеклоочиститель
stekloochistitel'
windscreen wiper

зеркало заднего вида
zerkalo zadneva vida
rear-view mirror

боковое зеркало заднего вида
bokovoye zerkalo zadneva vida
wing mirror

дверь
dver'
door

багажник
bagazhnik
boot

капот
kapot
bonnet

индикатор
indikator
indicator

номерной знак
nomernoy znak
licence plate

бампер
bamper
bumper

фара
fara
headlight

колесо
koleso
wheel

шина
shina
tyre

багаж
bagazh
luggage

багажник на крыше
bagazhnik na kryshe
roof rack

задняя дверь
zadnyaya dver'
tailgate

ремень безопасности
remen' bezopasnosti
seat belt

детское сиденье
detskoye siden'ye
child seat

виды vidy • types

электромобиль
elektromobil'
electric car

хетчбэк
khetchbek
hatchback

седан
sedan
saloon

универсал
universal
estate

автомобиль с откидным верхом
avtomobil' s otkidnym verkhom
convertible

спортивный автомобиль
sportivniy avtomobil'
sports car

пассажирский автомобиль
passazhirskiy avtomobil'
people carrier

полный привод
polniy privod
four-wheel drive

ретроавтомобиль,
retroavtomobil'
vintage

лимузин
limuzin
limousine

заправочная станция
zapravochnaya stantsiya •
petrol station

бензонасос
benzonasos
petrol pump

цена
tsena
price

заправочная площадка
zapravochnaya ploshchadka
forecourt

словарь slovar' • vocabulary

масло
maslo
oil

бензин
benzin
petrol

этилированный
etilirovanniy
leaded

неэтилированный
neetilirovanniy
unleaded

гараж
garazh
garage

автомойка
avtomoyka
car wash

антифриз
antifriz
antifreeze

стеклоомыватель
stekloomyvatel'
screenwash

дизель
dizel'
diesel

Пожалуйста, заполните бензобак.
pozhaluysta, zapolnite benzobak
Fill the tank, please.

автомобиль 2 avtomobil' · **car 2**

салон sal<u>o</u>n · **interior**

заднее сиденье
z<u>a</u>dneye sid<u>e</u>n'ye
back seat

подлокотник
podlok<u>o</u>tnik
armrest

подголовник
podgol<u>o</u>vnik
headrest

дверной замок
dvern<u>o</u>y zam<u>o</u>k
door lock

ручка
r<u>u</u>chka
handle

словарь slov<u>a</u>r' · **vocabulary**

двухдверный dvukhdv<u>e</u>rniy **two-door**	**четырёхдверный** chetyryokhdv<u>e</u>rniy **four-door**	**автоматический** avtomat<u>i</u>cheskiy **automatic**	**тормоз** t<u>o</u>rmoz **brake**	**акселератор** akseler<u>a</u>tor **accelerator**
трёхдверный tryokhdv<u>e</u>rniy **three-door**	**ручной** ruchn<u>o</u>y **manual**	**зажигание** zazhig<u>a</u>niye **ignition**	**сцепление** stsepl<u>e</u>niye **clutch**	**кондиционер** kondition<u>e</u>r **air conditioning**

Как проехать…?
kak proy<u>e</u>khat'…?
Can you tell me the way to …?

Где находится автостоянка?
gde nakh<u>o</u>ditsya avtostoy<u>a</u>nka?
Where is the car park?

Можно ли здесь припарковаться?
m<u>o</u>zhno li zd<u>e</u>s' priparkov<u>a</u>t'sya?
Can I park here?

управление upravlyeniye • **controls**

руль
rul'
steering wheel

звуковой сигнал
zvukovoy signal
horn

приборная панель
pribornaya panel'
dashboard

аварийная сигнализация
avariynaya signalizatsiya
hazard lights

спутниковая навигация
sputnikovaya navigatsiya
satellite navigation

леворульный автомобиль levorul'niy avtomobil' | **left-hand drive**

датчик температуры
datchik temperatury
temperature gauge

тахометр
takhometr
rev counter

спидометр
spidometr
speedometer

индикатор уровня топлива
indikator urovnya topliva
fuel gauge

автомагнитола
avtomagnitola
car stereo

переключатель освещения
pereklyuchatel' osveshcheniya
lights switch

управление обогревателем
upravleniye obogrevatelem
heater controls

одометр
odometr
odometer

ручка КПП
ruchka ka-pe-pe
gearstick

подушка безопасности
podushka bezopasnosti
air bag

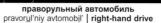

праворульный автомобиль
pravorul'niy avtomobil' | **right-hand drive**

автомобиль 3 avtomobil' • car 3

механика mekhanika • mechanics

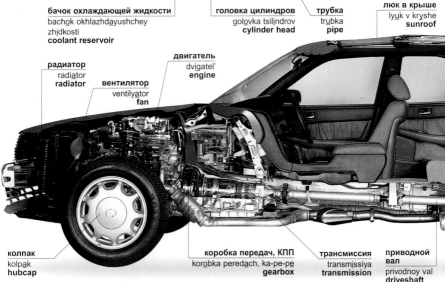

бачок омывателя
bachok omyvatelya
screen wash reservoir

щуп (масломерный)
shchup (maslomerniy)
dipstick

воздушный фильтр
vozdushniy fil'tr
air filter

бачок тормозной жидкости
bachok tormoznoy zhidkosti
brake fluid reservoir

аккумулятор
akkumulyator
battery

кузовные работы
kuzovniye raboty
bodywork

бачок охлаждающей жидкости
bachok okhlazhdayushchey zhidkosti
coolant reservoir

головка цилиндров
golovka tsilindrov
cylinder head

трубка
trubka
pipe

люк в крыше
lyuk v kryshe
sunroof

радиатор
radiator
radiator

вентилятор
ventilyator
fan

двигатель
dvigatel'
engine

колпак
kolpak
hubcap

коробка передач, КПП
korobka peredach, ka-pe-pe
gearbox

трансмиссия
transmissiya
transmission

приводной вал
privodnoy val
driveshaft

прокол prok<u>o</u>l • **puncture**

запасная шина
zapasn<u>a</u>ya sh<u>i</u>na
spare tyre

гаечный ключ
g<u>a</u>yechniy kly<u>u</u>ch
wrench

колёсные гайки
kol<u>yo</u>sniye g<u>a</u>yki
wheel nuts

домкрат
domkr<u>a</u>t
jack

менять колесо
meny<u>a</u>t' koles<u>o</u>
change a wheel (v)

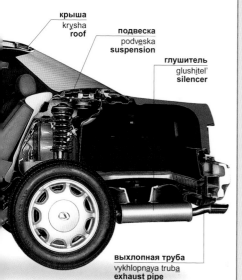

крыша
kr<u>y</u>sha
roof

подвеска
podv<u>e</u>ska
suspension

глушитель
glush<u>i</u>tel'
silencer

выхлопная труба
vykhlopn<u>a</u>ya trub<u>a</u>
exhaust pipe

словарь slov<u>a</u>r' • **vocabulary**

ДТП
de-te-p<u>e</u>
car accident

поломка
pol<u>o</u>mka
breakdown

страховка
strakh<u>o</u>vka
insurance

эвакуатор
evaku<u>a</u>tor
tow truck

механик
mekh<u>a</u>nik
mechanic

давление в шине
davl<u>e</u>niye v sh<u>i</u>ne
tyre pressure

**блок
предохранителей**
bl<u>o</u>k predokhran<u>i</u>teley
fuse box

свеча зажигания
svech<u>a</u> zazhig<u>a</u>niya
spark plug

ремень вентилятора
rem<u>e</u>n' ventily<u>a</u>tora
fan belt

бензобак
benzob<u>a</u>k
petrol tank

момент зажигания
mom<u>e</u>nt zazhig<u>a</u>niya
timing

турбина
turb<u>i</u>na
turbocharger

**распределитель
зажигания**
raspredel<u>i</u>tel' zazhig<u>a</u>niya
distributor

шасси
shass<u>i</u>
chassis

ручной тормоз
ruchn<u>o</u>y t<u>o</u>rmoz
handbrake

генератор
gener<u>a</u>tor
alternator

ремень грм
rem<u>e</u>n' ge-er-<u>e</u>m
cam belt

....

**Моя машина
сломалась.**
mo<u>ya</u> mash<u>i</u>na slom<u>a</u>las'
I've broken down.

**Моя машина не
заводится.**
mo<u>ya</u> mash<u>i</u>na ne
zav<u>o</u>ditsa
My car won't start.

мотоцикл mototsikl • motorbike

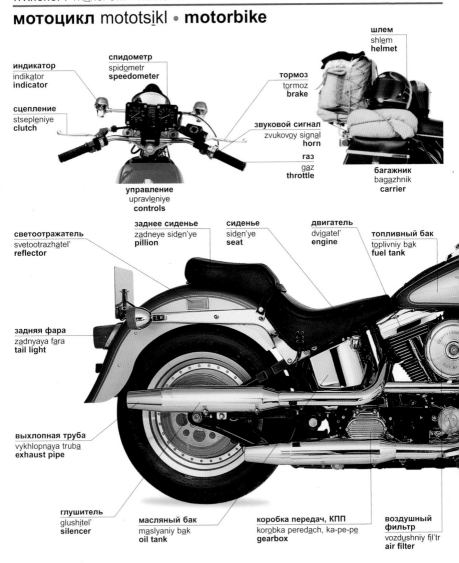

индикатор
indikator
indicator

сцепление
stsepleniye
clutch

спидометр
spidometr
speedometer

тормоз
tormoz
brake

звуковой сигнал
zvukovoy signal
horn

газ
gaz
throttle

управление
upravleniye
controls

шлем
shlem
helmet

багажник
bagazhnik
carrier

светоотражатель
svetootrazhatel'
reflector

заднее сиденье
zadneye siden'ye
pillion

сиденье
siden'ye
seat

двигатель
dvigatel'
engine

топливный бак
toplivniy bak
fuel tank

задняя фара
zadnyaya fara
tail light

выхлопная труба
vykhlopnaya truba
exhaust pipe

глушитель
glushitel'
silencer

масляный бак
maslyaniy bak
oil tank

коробка передач, КПП
korobka peredach, ka-pe-pe
gearbox

воздушный фильтр
vozdushniy fil'tr
air filter

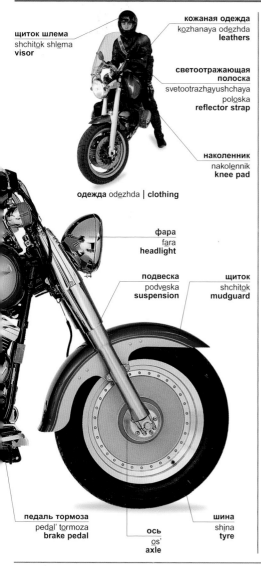

щиток шлема
shchitok shlema
visor

кожаная одежда
kozhanaya odezhda
leathers

**светоотражающая
полоска**
svetootrazhayushchaya
poloska
reflector strap

наколенник
nakolennik
knee pad

одежда odezhda | **clothing**

фара
fara
headlight

подвеска
podveska
suspension

щиток
shchitok
mudguard

педаль тормоза
pedal' tormoza
brake pedal

ось
os'
axle

шина
shina
tyre

виды vidy • types

гоночный мотоцикл
gonochniy mototsikl | **racing bike**

ветровое стекло
vetrovoye steklo
windshield

дорожный мотоцикл
dorozhniy mototsikl | **tourer**

кроссовый мотоцикл
krossoviy mototsikl | **dirt bike**

стойка
stoyka
stand

скутер skuter | **scooter**

велосипед velosip<u>e</u>d · **bicycle**

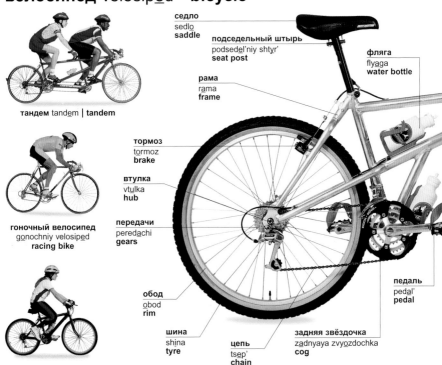

седло
sedl<u>o</u>
saddle

подседельный штырь
podsed<u>e</u>l'niy sht<u>y</u>r'
seat post

фляга
fly<u>a</u>ga
water bottle

рама
r<u>a</u>ma
frame

тормоз
t<u>o</u>rmoz
brake

втулка
vt<u>u</u>lka
hub

передачи
pered<u>a</u>chi
gears

обод
<u>o</u>bod
rim

шина
sh<u>i</u>na
tyre

цепь
tsep'
chain

задняя звёздочка
z<u>a</u>dnyaya zvy<u>o</u>zdochka
cog

педаль
ped<u>a</u>l'
pedal

тандем tand<u>e</u>m | **tandem**

гоночный велосипед
g<u>o</u>nochniy velosip<u>e</u>d
racing bike

горный велосипед
g<u>o</u>rniy velosip<u>e</u>d
mountain bike

туристский велосипед
tur<u>i</u>stskiy velosip<u>e</u>d
touring bike

шлем
shl<u>e</u>m
helmet

дорожный велосипед
dor<u>o</u>zhniy velosip<u>e</u>d
road bike

велосипедная дорожка
velosip<u>e</u>dnaya dor<u>o</u>zhka | **cycle lane**

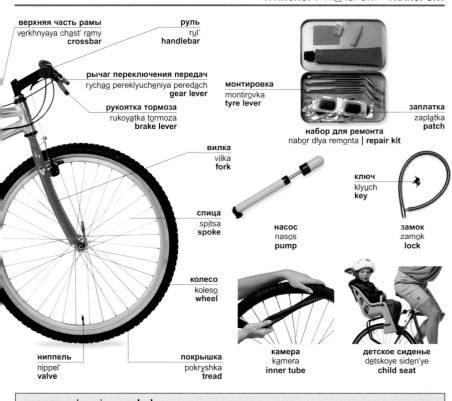

верхняя часть рамы
verkhnyaya chast' ramy
crossbar

руль
rul'
handlebar

рычаг переключения передач
rychag pereklyucheniya peredach
gear lever

рукоятка тормоза
rukoyatka tormoza
brake lever

монтировка
montirovka
tyre lever

набор для ремонта
nabor dlya remonta | **repair kit**

заплатка
zaplatka
patch

вилка
vilka
fork

ключ
klyuch
key

спица
spitsa
spoke

насос
nasos
pump

замок
zamok
lock

колесо
koleso
wheel

ниппель
nippel'
valve

покрышка
pokryshka
tread

камера
kamera
inner tube

детское сиденье
detskoye siden'ye
child seat

словарь slovar' • vocabulary

лампа lampa **lamp**	**откидная подножка** otkidnaya podnozhka **kickstand**	**тормозная колодка** tormoznaya kolodka **brake block**	**корзинка** korzinka **basket**	**туклипс** tuklips **toe clip**	**тормозить** tormozit' **brake (v)**
задняя фара zadnyaya fara **rear light**	**автомобильный багажник для велосипеда** avtomobil'niy bagazhnik dlya velosipeda **bike rack**	**тросик** trosik **cable**	**динамо** dinamo **dynamo**	**ремешок педали** remeshok pedali **toe strap**	**ехать на велосипеде** yekhat' na velosipede **cycle (v)**
отражатель otrazhatel' **reflector**	**стабилизаторы** stabilizatory **stabilisers**	**звёздочка** zvyozdochka **sprocket**	**прокол** prokol **puncture**	**крутить педали** krutit' pedali **pedal (v)**	**переключать передачу** pereklyuchat' peredachu **change gear (v)**

поезд poyezd • train

вагон
vagon
carriage

номер
платформы
nomer platformy
platform number

платформа
platforma
platform

пассажир
pasazhir
commuter

тележка
telezhka
trolley

вокзал vokzal | train station

виды поездов vidy poyezdov • types of train

локомотив
lokomotiv
engine

кабина машиниста
kabina mashinista
driver's cab

рельс
rel's
rail

паровоз
parovoz
steam train

дизельный поезд dizel'niy poyezd | diesel train

электро поезд
elektro poyezd
electric train

скоростной поезд
skorostnoy poyezd
high-speed train

монорельс
monorel's
monorail

поезд метро
poyezd metro
underground train

трамвай
tramvay
tram

грузовой поезд
gruzovoy poyezd
freight train

багажная полка
bagazhnaya polka
luggage rack

окно
okno
window

путь
put'
track

дверь
dver'
door

место
mesto
seat

турникет turniket | **ticket barrier**

купе
kupe | **compartment**

система оповещения пассажиров
sistema opoveshcheniya pasazhirov
public address system

расписание
raspisaniye
timetable

билет
bilet
ticket

вагон-ресторан
vagon-restoran | **dining car**

спальное купе
spal'noye kupe
sleeping compartment

центральный зал вокзала tsentral'niy zal vokzala | **concourse**

словарь slovar' · vocabulary

железнодорожная сеть
zheleznodorozhnaya set'
rail network

междугородный поезд
mezhdugorodniy poyezd
inter-city train

час пик
chas pik
rush hour

карта метро
karta metro
underground map

опоздание
opozdaniye
delay

плата за проезд
plata za proyezd
fare

билетная касса
biletnaya kassa
ticket office

контролёр
kontrolyor
ticket inspector

делать пересадку
delat' peresadku
change (v)

контактный рельс
kontaktniy rel's
live rail

сигнал
signal
signal

стоп-кран
stop-kran
emergency lever

воздушные суда vozdushniye suda · **aircraft**

авиалайнер avialayner · **airliner**

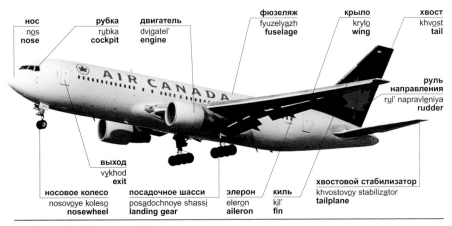

нос
nos
nose

рубка
rubka
cockpit

двигатель
dvigatel'
engine

фюзеляж
fyuzelyazh
fuselage

крыло
krylo
wing

хвост
khvost
tail

руль направления
rul' napravleniya
rudder

выход
vykhod
exit

носовое колесо
nosovoye koleso
nosewheel

посадочное шасси
posadochnoye shassi
landing gear

элерон
eleron
aileron

киль
kil'
fin

хвостовой стабилизатор
khvostovoy stabilizator
tailplane

кабина kabina · **cabin**

аварийный выход
avariyniy vykhod
emergency exit

бортпроводник
bortprovodnik
flight attendant

багажная полка
bagazhnaya polka
overhead locker

вентиляция
ventilyatsiya
air vent

окно
okno
window

индивидуальное освещение
individual'noye osveshcheniye
reading light

место
mesto
seat

ряд
ryad
row

откидной столик
otkidnoy stolik
tray-table

подлокотник
podlokotnik
armrest

проход
prokhod
aisle

спинка сидения
spinka sideniya
seat back

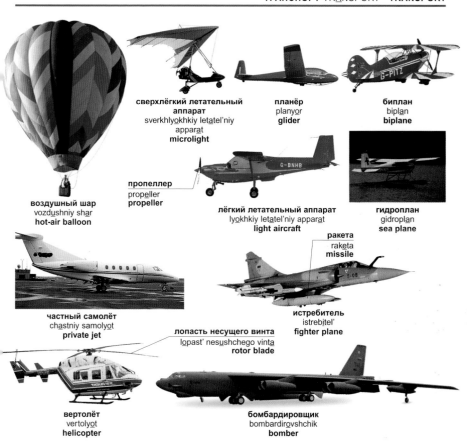

сверхлёгкий летательный аппарат
sverkhlyokhkiy letatel'niy apparat
microlight

планёр
planyor
glider

биплан
biplan
biplane

воздушный шар
vozdushniy shar
hot-air balloon

пропеллер
propeller
propeller

лёгкий летательный аппарат
lyokhkiy letatel'niy apparat
light aircraft

гидроплан
gidroplan
sea plane

ракета
raketa
missile

частный самолёт
chastniy samolyot
private jet

истребитель
istrebitel'
fighter plane

лопасть несущего винта
lopast' nesushchego vinta
rotor blade

вертолёт
vertolyot
helicopter

бомбардировщик
bombardirovshchik
bomber

словарь slovar' • vocabulary

пилот pilot **pilot**	**взлетать** vzletat' **take off (v)**	**приземляться** prizemlyat'sa **land (v)**	**экономкласс** ekonomklass **economy class**	**ручная кладь** ruchnaya klad' **hand luggage**
второй пилот vtoroy pilot **co-pilot**	**летать** letat' **fly (v)**	**высота** vysota **altitude**	**бизнес-класс** biznes-klass **business class**	**ремень безопасности** remen' bezopasnosti **seat belt**

аэропорт aeroport • **airport**

стоянка самолётов
stoyanka samolyotov
apron

багажный тягач
bagazhniy tyagach
baggage trailer

терминал
terminal
terminal

служебный автомобиль
sluzhebniy avtomobil'
service vehicle

телетрап
teletrap
jetway

авиалайнер avialayner | **airliner**

словарь slovar' • **vocabulary**

взлётно-посадочная
полоса, ВПП
vzlyotno-posadochnaya
polosa, ve-pe-pe
runway

международный
рейс
mezhdunarodniy reys
international flight

внутренний рейс
vnutrenniy reys
domestic flight

стыковка рейсов
stykovka reysov
connection

номер рейса
nomer reysa
flight number

иммиграционный
контроль
immigratsionniy
kontrol'
immigration

таможенный
контроль
tamozhenniy kontrol'
customs

перевес багажа
pereves bagazha
excess baggage

багажная карусель,
bagazhnaya karusel'
carousel

охрана
okhrana
security

рентгеновский аппарат
(для осмотра багажа)
rentgenovskiy apparat (dlya
osmotra bagazha)
x-ray machine

туристическая брошюра
turisticheskaya broshyura
holiday brochure

отпуск
otpusk
holiday

регистрироваться
registrirovat'sya
check in (v)

диспетчерская вышка
dispetcherskaya vyshka
control tower

бронировать
авиабилет
bronirovat' aviabilet
book a flight (v)

виза
viza
visa

ручная кладь
ruchnaya klad'
hand luggage

багаж
bagazh
luggage

тележка
telezhka
trolley

паспорт pasport | **passport**

посадочный талон
posadochniy talon
boarding pass

стойка регистрации
stoyka registratsii
check-in desk

паспортный контроль
pasportniy kontrol'
passport control

билет
bilet
ticket

**номер выхода на
посадку**
nomer vykhoda na
posadku
gate number

вылет
vylet
departures

зал вылета
zal vyleta
departure lounge

пункт назначения
punkt naznacheniya
destination

прилёт
prilyot
arrivals

информационное табло
informatsionnoye tablo
information screen

**магазин беспошлинной
торговли**
magazin besposhlinnoy
torgovli
duty-free shop

получение багажа
polucheniye bagazha
baggage reclaim

стоянка такси
stoyanka taksi
taxi rank

аренда автомобилей
arenda avtomobiley
car hire

корабль korabl' · **ship**

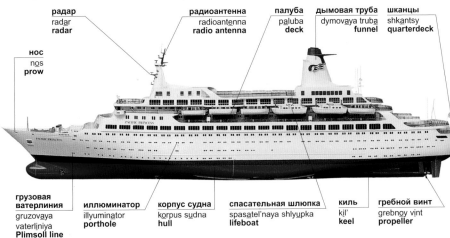

радар
radar
radar

радиоантенна
radioantenna
radio antenna

палуба
paluba
deck

дымовая труба
dymovaya truba
funnel

шканцы
shkantsy
quarterdeck

нос
nos
prow

грузовая
ватерлиния
gruzovaya
vaterliniya
Plimsoll line

иллюминатор
illyuminator
porthole

корпус судна
korpus sudna
hull

спасательная шлюпка
spasatel'naya shlyupka
lifeboat

киль
kil'
keel

гребной винт
grebnoy vint
propeller

океанский лайнер okeanskiy layner | **ocean liner**

мостик
mostik
bridge

машинное отделение
mashinnoye otdeleniye
engine room

каюта
kayuta
cabin

камбуз
kambuz
galley

словарь slovar' · **vocabulary**

док
dok
dock

порт
port
port

сходня
skhodnya
gangway

якорь
yakor'
anchor

швартовая труба
shvartovaya truba
bollard

брашпиль
brashpil'
windlass

капитан
kapitan
captain

быстроходный
катер
bystrokhodniy
kater
speedboat

гребное судно
grebnoye sudno
rowing boat

каноэ
kanoe
canoe

другие суда drugiye suda • **other ships**

паром
parom
ferry

подвесной мотор
podvesnoy motor
outboard motor

надувная лодка
naduvnaya lodka
inflatable dinghy

СПК
es-pe-ka
hydrofoil

яхта
yakhta
yacht

катамаран
katamaran
catamaran

буксирный катер
buksirniy kater
tug boat

судно на воздушной подушке
sudno na vozdushnoy podushke
hovercraft

контейнеровоз
konteynerovoz
container ship

оснастка
osnastka
rigging

парусное судно
parusnoye sudno
sailing boat

трюм
tryum
hold

грузовое судно
gruzovoye sudno
freighter

нефтетанкер
neftetanker
oil tanker

авианосец
avianosets
aircraft carrier

линейный корабль
lineyniy korabl'
battleship

боевая рубка
boyevaya rubka
conning tower

подводная лодка
podvodnaya lodka
submarine

порт p<u>o</u>rt · **port**

склад | подъёмный кран | вилочный погрузчик | подъездная дорога | таможня
skl<u>a</u>d | pod-yomniy | vilochniy pogr<u>u</u>zchik | pod-yezdn<u>a</u>ya dor<u>o</u>ga | tam<u>o</u>zhnya
warehouse | kr<u>a</u>n **crane** | **fork-lift truck** | **access road** | **customs house**

док | контейнер | причал | груз
d<u>o</u>k | kont<u>e</u>yner | prich<u>a</u>l | gr<u>u</u>z
dock | **container** | **quay** | **cargo**

терминал парома | паром
termin<u>a</u>l par<u>o</u>ma | par<u>o</u>m
ferry terminal | **ferry**

билетная касса | пассажир
bil<u>e</u>tnaya k<u>a</u>ssa | passazhir
ticket office | **passenger**

контейнерный порт kont<u>e</u>ynerniy p<u>o</u>rt | **container port**

пассажирский порт
passazh<u>i</u>rskiy p<u>o</u>rt | **passenger port**

сеть
set'
net

рыболовное судно
rybolovnoye sudno
fishing boat

швартовка
shvartovka
mooring

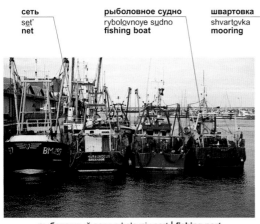

яхтенный причал
yakhtenniy prichal | **marina**

рыболовный порт rybolovniy port | **fishing port**

гавань gavan' | **harbour**

пирс pirs **I pier**

мол
mol
jetty

верфь
verf'
shipyard

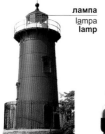

лампа
lampa
lamp

маяк
mayak
lighthouse

буй
buy
buoy

словарь slovar' • vocabulary

береговая охрана
beregovaya
okhrana
coastguard

капитан порта
kapitan porta
harbour master

бросать якорь
brosat' yakor'
drop anchor (v)

сухой док
sukhoy dok
dry dock

пришвартовываться
prishvartovyvatsa
moor (v)

вводить в док
vvodit' v dok
dock (v)

**садиться на
корабль**
saditsa na korabl'
board (v)

**сходить на
берег**
skhodit' na bereg
disembark (v)

**отправляться в
плавание**
otpravlyatsa v
plavaniye
set sail (v)

спорт sport
sports

американский футбол amerikanskiy futbol • American football

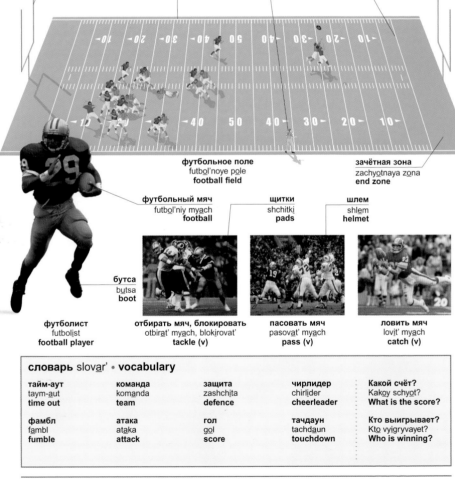

штанга
shtanga
goalpost

боковая линия
bokovaya liniya
sideline

судья на линии
sud'ya na linii
referee

линия ворот
liniya vorot
goal line

футбольное поле
futbol'noye pole
football field

зачётная зона
zachyotnaya zona
end zone

футбольный мяч
futbol'niy myach
football

щитки
shchitki
pads

шлем
shlem
helmet

бутса
butsa
boot

футболист
futbolist
football player

отбирать мяч, блокировать
otbirat' myach, blokirovat'
tackle (v)

пасовать мяч
pasovat' myach
pass (v)

ловить мяч
lovit' myach
catch (v)

словарь slovar' • vocabulary

тайм-аут taym-aut **time out**	**команда** komanda **team**	**защита** zashchita **defence**	**чирлидер** chirlider **cheerleader**	**Какой счёт?** Kakoy schyot? **What is the score?**
фамбл fambl **fumble**	**атака** ataka **attack**	**гол** gol **score**	**тачдаун** tachdaun **touchdown**	**Кто выигрывает?** Kto vyigryvayet? **Who is winning?**

регби regbi • rugby

площадь ворот
ploshchad' vorot
in-goal area

боковая линия поля
bokovaya liniya polya
touch line

флажок
flazhok
flag

линия мёртвого мяча
liniya myortvogo myacha
dead ball line

ворота
vorota
goal

поле для регби pole dlya regbi | **rugby pitch**

мяч
myach
ball

регбийная полоска
regbiynaya poloska
rugby strip

бросать
brosat'
throw (v)

бить по мячу
bit' po myachu
kick (v)

передавать мяч
peredavat' myach
pass (v)

производить захват
proizvodit' zakhvat
tackle (v)

попытка
popytka
try

игрок
igrok
player

рак rak | **ruck**

схватка skhvatka | **scrum**

футбол futbol • soccer

футбол
futbol
football

нападающий
napadayushchiy
forward

судья
sud'ya
referee

центральный круг
tsentral'niy krug
centre circle

вратарь
vratar'
goalkeeper

**футбольная
полоска**
futbol'naya
poloska
football strip

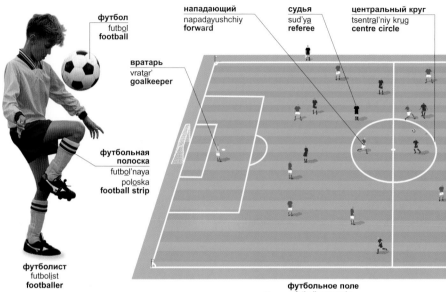

футболист
futbolist
footballer

футбольное поле
futbol'noye pole
football pitch

штанга	**сетка**	**перекладина**
shtanga	setka	perekladina
goalpost	**net**	**crossbar**

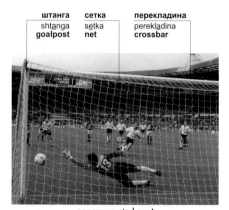

ворота vorota | **goal**

вести мяч vesti myach
dribble (v)

ударить по мячу головой
udarit' po myachu golovoy
head (v)

стенка
stenka
wall

штрафной удар
shtrafnoy udar | **free kick**

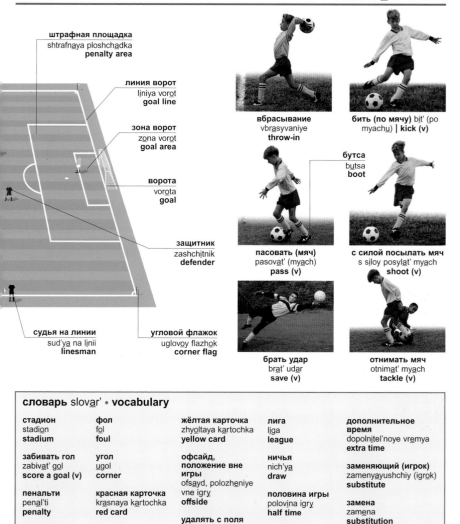

штрафная площадка
shtrafnaya ploshchadka
penalty area

линия ворот
liniya vorot
goal line

зона ворот
zona vorot
goal area

ворота
vorota
goal

защитник
zashchitnik
defender

судья на линии
sud'ya na linii
linesman

угловой флажок
uglovoy flazhok
corner flag

вбрасывание
vbrasyvaniye
throw-in

бить (по мячу) bit' (po
myachu) | **kick (v)**

бутса
butsa
boot

пасовать (мяч)
pasovat' (myach)
pass (v)

с силой посылать мяч
s siloy posylat' myach
shoot (v)

брать удар
brat' udar
save (v)

отнимать мяч
otnimat' myach
tackle (v)

словарь slovar' • vocabulary

стадион stadion **stadium**	**фол** fol **foul**	**жёлтая карточка** zhyoltaya kartochka **yellow card**	**лига** liga **league**	**дополнительное время** dopolnitel'noye vremya **extra time**
забивать гол zabivat' gol **score a goal (v)**	**угол** ugol **corner**	**офсайд, положение вне игры** ofsayd, polozheniye vne igry **offside**	**ничья** nich'ya **draw**	**заменяющий (игрок)** zamenyayushchiy (igrok) **substitute**
пенальти penal'ti **penalty**	**красная карточка** krasnaya kartochka **red card**		**половина игры** polovina igry **half time**	**замена** zamena **substitution**
		удалять с поля udalyat' s polya **send off**		

хоккей khokey • hockey

хоккей на льду khokey na l'du • ice hockey

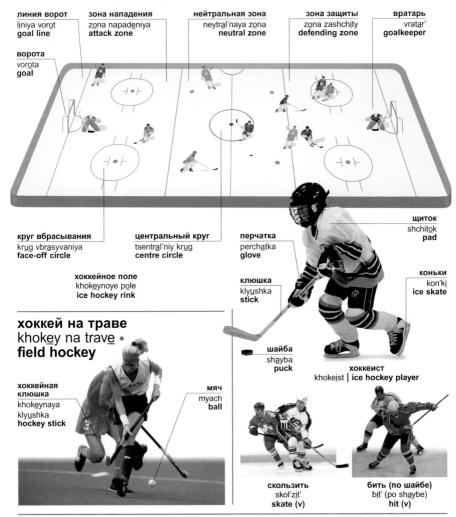

линия ворот
liniya vorot
goal line

зона нападения
zona napadeniya
attack zone

нейтральная зона
neytral'naya zona
neutral zone

зона защиты
zona zashchity
defending zone

вратарь
vratar'
goalkeeper

ворота
vorota
goal

круг вбрасывания
krug vbrasyvaniya
face-off circle

центральный круг
tsentral'niy krug
centre circle

хоккейное поле
khokeynoye pole
ice hockey rink

щиток
shchitok
pad

коньки
kon'ki
ice skate

перчатка
perchatka
glove

клюшка
klyushka
stick

шайба
shayba
puck

хоккеист khokeist | **ice hockey player**

хоккей на траве
khokey na trave •
field hockey

**хоккейная
клюшка**
khokeynaya
klyushka
hockey stick

мяч
myach
ball

скользить
skol'zit'
skate (v)

бить (по шайбе)
bit' (po shaybe)
hit (v)

крикет kri<u>k</u>et • **cricket**

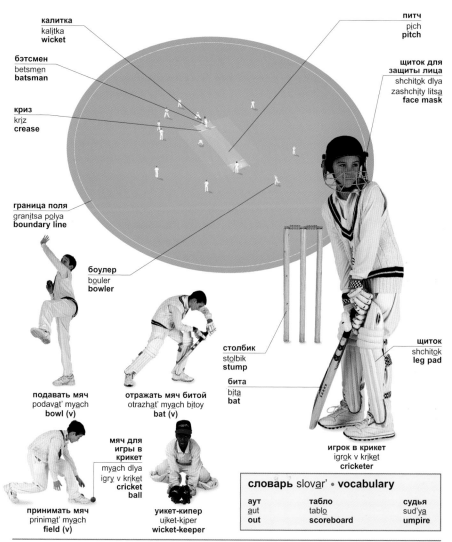

калитка
kali<u>t</u>ka
wicket

бэтсмен
betsm<u>e</u>n
batsman

криз
kr<u>i</u>z
crease

граница поля
granitsa p<u>o</u>lya
boundary line

боулер
b<u>o</u>uler
bowler

питч
pi<u>ch</u>
pitch

щиток для
защиты лица
shchit<u>o</u>k dlya
zashchity lits<u>a</u>
face mask

столбик
st<u>o</u>lbik
stump

бита
b<u>i</u>ta
bat

щиток
shchit<u>o</u>k
leg pad

подавать мяч
podav<u>a</u>t' my<u>a</u>ch
bowl (v)

отражать мяч битой
otrazh<u>a</u>t' my<u>a</u>ch bitoy
bat (v)

принимать мяч
prinim<u>a</u>t' my<u>a</u>ch
field (v)

мяч для
игры в
крикет
my<u>a</u>ch dlya
igry v kri<u>k</u>et
**cricket
ball**

уикет-кипер
uiket-k<u>i</u>per
wicket-keeper

игрок в крикет
igr<u>o</u>k v kri<u>k</u>et
cricketer

словарь slov<u>a</u>r' • **vocabulary**		
аут <u>a</u>ut **out**	табло tabl<u>o</u> **scoreboard**	судья sud'y<u>a</u> **umpire**

баскетбол basketbol · **basketball**

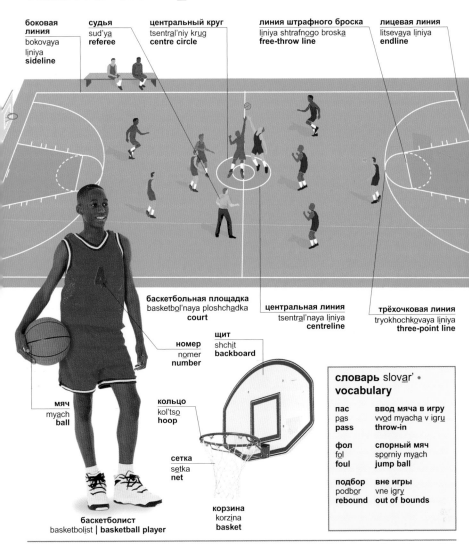

боковая линия
bokovaya liniya
sideline

судья
sud'ya
referee

центральный круг
tsentral'niy krug
centre circle

линия штрафного броска
liniya shtrafnogo broska
free-throw line

лицевая линия
litsevaya liniya
endline

баскетбольная площадка
basketbol'naya ploshchadka
court

центральная линия
tsentral'naya liniya
centreline

трёхочковая линия
tryokhochkovaya liniya
three-point line

номер
nomer
number

щит
shchit
backboard

мяч
myach
ball

кольцо
kol'tso
hoop

сетка
setka
net

корзина
korzina
basket

баскетболист
basketbolist | **basketball player**

словарь slovar' · **vocabulary**

пас pas **pass**	**ввод мяча в игру** vvod myacha v igru **throw-in**
фол fol **foul**	**спорный мяч** sporniy myach **jump ball**
подбор podbor **rebound**	**вне игры** vne igry **out of bounds**

действия d<u>e</u>ystviya • **actions**

бросать	ловить	с силой посылать мяч	прыгать
bros<u>a</u>t'	lov<u>i</u>t'	s s<u>i</u>loy pos<u>y</u>lat' my<u>a</u>ch	pr<u>y</u>gat'
throw (v)	**catch (v)**	**shoot (v)**	**jump (v)**

персонально опекать	блокировать	вести мяч	слем-данк
person<u>a</u>l'no opek<u>a</u>t'	blokirov<u>a</u>t'	vest<u>i</u> my<u>a</u>ch	slem-d<u>a</u>nk
mark (v)	**block (v)**	**bounce (v)**	**dunk (v)**

волейбол voleyb<u>o</u>l • **volleyball**

блокировать
blokirov<u>a</u>t'
block (v)

сетка
s<u>e</u>tka
net

принимать
мяч снизу
prinim<u>a</u>t'
my<u>a</u>ch sn<u>i</u>zu
dig (v)

судья
sud'y<u>a</u>
referee

наколенник
nakol<u>e</u>nnik
knee support

площадка ploshch<u>a</u>dka | **court**

бейсбол beysbol · **baseball**

поле pole · **field**

левая сторона поля
levaya storona polya
left field

внутреннее поле
vnutrenneye pole
infield

центр поля
tsentr polya
centre field

бита
bita
bat

шлем
shlem
helmet

бейсмен
beysmen
baseman

круг подачи
krug podachi
pitcher's mound

дом; домашняя база
dom; domashnyaya baza
home plate

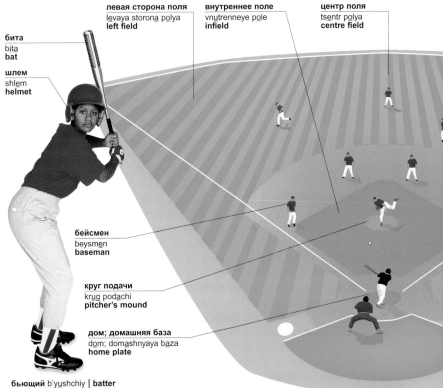

бьющий b'yushchiy | **batter**

словарь slovar' · **vocabulary**

иннинг	сейф	фол-бол
inning	seyf	fol-bol
inning	**safe**	**foul ball**
ран	аут	страйк
ran	aut	strayk
run	**out**	**strike**

рукавица
rukavitsa
mitt

мяч
myach
ball

бейсбольная маска
beysbol'naya maska
mask

действия d<u>e</u>ystviya • **actions**

внешнее поле
vn<u>e</u>shneye p<u>o</u>le
outfield

правая
сторона поля
pr<u>a</u>vaya
storon<u>a</u> pol<u>ya</u>
right field

линия фола
liniya f<u>o</u>la
foul line

команда
kom<u>a</u>nda
team

места для игроков
mest<u>a</u> dlya igrok<u>o</u>v
dugout

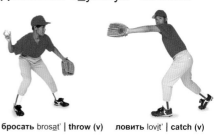

бросать bros<u>a</u>t' | **throw (v)**

ловить lov<u>i</u>t' | **catch (v)**

бежать
bezh<u>a</u>t'
run (v)

принимать мяч
prinim<u>a</u>t' my<u>a</u>ch | **field (v)**

скользить
skol'z<u>i</u>t'
slide (v)

касаться
kas<u>a</u>t'sya
tag (v)

подавать
podav<u>a</u>t'
pitch (v)

бить битой
bit' bit<u>o</u>y
bat (v)

судья
sud'y<u>a</u>
umpire

разыгрывать мяч raz<u>y</u>gryvat' my<u>a</u>ch | **play (v)**

кетчер k<u>e</u>cher | **catcher**

питчер p<u>i</u>cher | **pitcher**

теннис tenis • tennis

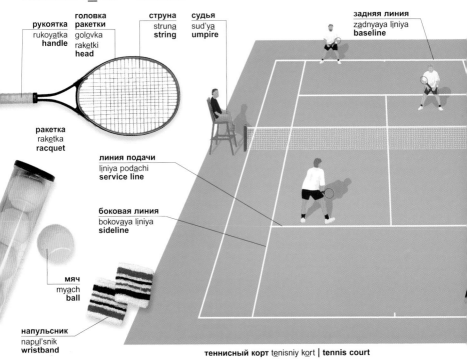

рукоятка
rukoyatka
handle

**головка
ракетки**
golovka
raketki
head

струна
struna
string

судья
sud'ya
umpire

задняя линия
zadnyaya liniya
baseline

ракетка
raketka
racquet

линия подачи
liniya podachi
service line

боковая линия
bokovaya liniya
sideline

мяч
myach
ball

напульсник
napul'snik
wristband

теннисный корт tenisniy kort | **tennis court**

словарь slovar' • vocabulary

одиночная игра odinochnaya igra **singles**	**сет** set **set**	**ноль** nol' **love**	**ошибка** oshibka **fault**	**резаный удар** rezaniy udar **slice**	**судья на линии** sud'ya na linii **linesman**
парная игра parnaya igra **doubles**	**матч** mach **match**	**ровно** rovno **deuce**	**эйс** eys **ace**	**обмен ударами** obmen udaram **rally**	**чемпионат** chempionat **championship**
гейм geym **game**	**тай-брейк** tay-breyk **tiebreak**	**больше** bol'she **advantage**	**укороченный удар** ukorochenniy udar **dropshot**	**два мяча!** dva myacha! **let!**	**вращение (мяча)** vrashcheniye (myacha) **spin**

удары udary • strokes

сетка
setka
net

смеш
smesh
smash

подающий мячи
podayushchiy
myachi
ball boy

подавать (мяч)
podavat' (myach)
serve (v)

**теннисные
туфли**
tenisniye tufli
tennis shoes

игрок igrok | **player**

подача
podacha
serve

удар с лёта
udar s lyota
volley

приём подачи
priyom podachi
return

свеча
svecha
lob

удар справа
udar sprava
forehand

удар слева
udar sleva
backhand

игры с ракеткой igry s raketkoy • racquet games

волан
volan
shuttlecock

ракетка
raketka
bat

бадминтон
badminton
badminton

настольный теннис
nastol'niy tenis
table tennis

сквош
skvosh
squash

ракетбол
raketbol
racquetball

гольф golf • golf

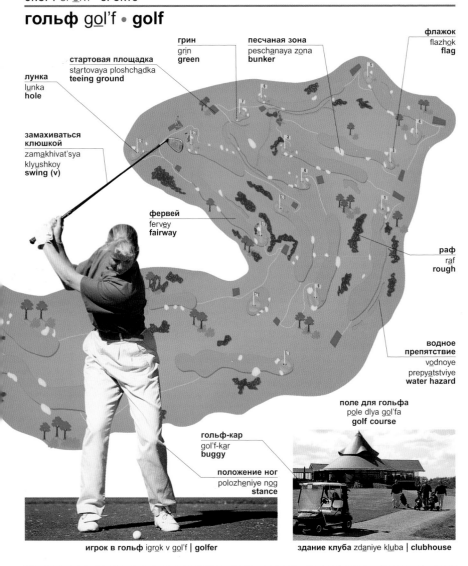

грин
grin
green

песчаная зона
peschanaya zona
bunker

флажок
flazhok
flag

стартовая площадка
startovaya ploshchadka
teeing ground

лунка
lunka
hole

замахиваться клюшкой
zamakhivat'sya klyushkoy
swing (v)

фервей
fervey
fairway

раф
raf
rough

водное препятствие
vodnoye prepyatstviye
water hazard

поле для гольфа
pole dlya gol'fa
golf course

гольф-кар
gol'f-kar
buggy

положение ног
polozheniye nog
stance

игрок в гольф igrok v gol'f | **golfer**

здание клуба zdaniye kluba | **clubhouse**

снаряжение snaryazheniye • **equipment**

клюшки для гольфа klyushki dlya gol'fa • **golf clubs**

мячик для гольфа
myachik dlya gol'fa
golf ball

колышек для мяча
kolyshek dlya myacha
tee

сумка для гольф-клюшек
sumka dlya gol'f-klyushek
golf bag

шипы
shipy
spikes

перчатка
perchatka
glove

тележка для гольфа
telezhka dlya gol'fa
golf trolley

ботинки для игры в гольф
botinki dlya igry v gol'f
golf shoe

вуд
vud
wood

паттер
patter
putter

айрон
ayron
iron

веджи
vedzhi
wedge

действия deystviya • **actions**

первый удар
perviy udar
tee-off (v)

драйв
drayv
drive (v)

патт, катящий удар
patt, katyashchiy udar
putt (v)

чип
chip
chip (v)

словарь slovar' • **vocabulary**

лунка за раз lunka za raz **hole in one**	**пар** par **par**	**гандикап** gandikap **handicap**	**кедди** keddi **caddy**	**замах назад** zamakh nazad **backswing**	**удар** udar **stroke**
меньше, чем пар men'she, chem par **under par**	**больше, чем пар** bol'she, chem par **over par**	**турнир** turnir **tournament**	**зрители** zriteli **spectators**	**тренировочный свинг** trenirovochniy sving **practice swing**	**линия игры** liniya igry **line of play**

лёгкая атлетика lyohkaya atletika • athletics

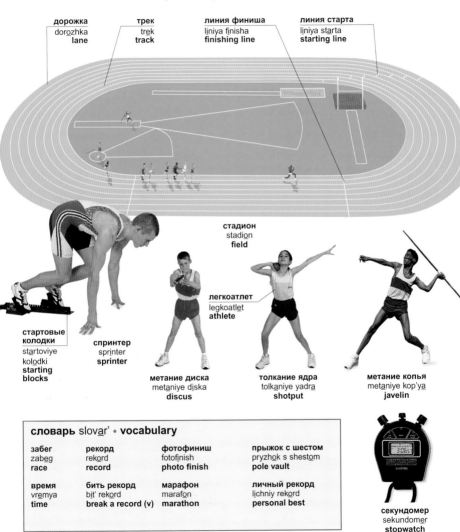

| дорожка dorozhka **lane** | трек trek **track** | линия финиша liniya finisha **finishing line** | линия старта liniya starta **starting line** |

стадион
stadion
field

легкоатлет
legkoatlet
athlete

стартовые колодки
startoviye kolodki
starting blocks

спринтер
sprinter
sprinter

метание диска
metaniye diska
discus

толкание ядра
tolkaniye yadra
shotput

метание копья
metaniye kop'ya
javelin

словарь slovar' • vocabulary

забег zabeg **race**	рекорд rekord **record**	фотофиниш fotofinish **photo finish**	прыжок с шестом pryzhok s shestom **pole vault**
время vremya **time**	бить рекорд bit' rekord **break a record (v)**	марафон marafon **marathon**	личный рекорд lichniy rekord **personal best**

секундомер
sekundomer
stopwatch

эстафетная палочка
estafetnaya palochka
baton

перекладина
perekladina
crossbar

эстафета
estafeta
relay race

прыжок в высоту
pryzhok v vysotu
high jump

прыжок в длину
pryzhok v dlinu
long jump

препятствия
prepyatstviya
hurdles

гимнастика gimnastika • **gymnastics**

гимнастический мостик
gimnasticheskiy mostik
springboard

гимнастка
gimnastka
gymnast

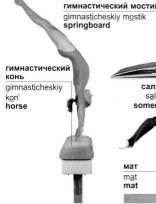
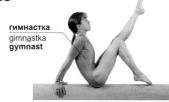

гимнастический конь
gimnasticheskiy kon'
horse

сальто
sal'to
somersault

бревно brevno | **beam**

лента
lenta
ribbon

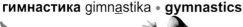

мат
mat
mat

опорный прыжок
oporniy pryzhok
vault

вольные упражнения
vol'niye uprazhneniya
floor exercises

акробатический прыжок
akrobaticheskiy pryzhok
cartwheel

ритмическая гимнастика
ritmicheskaya gimnastika
rhythmic gymnastics

словарь slovar' • **vocabulary**

перекладина perekladina **horizontal bar**	**гимнастический конь** gimnasticheskiy kon' **pommel horse**	**кольца** kol'tsa **rings**	**медали** medali **medals**	**серебро** serebro **silver**
параллельные брусья paralel'niye brus'ya **parallel bars**	**разновысокие брусья** raznovysokiye brus'ya **asymmetric bars**	**подиум** podium **podium**	**золото** zoloto **gold**	**бронза** bronza **bronze**

спортивные единоборства sportivniye yedinob<u>o</u>rstva • **combat sports**

противник
prot<u>i</u>vnik
opponent

защитный шлем
zashch<u>i</u>tniy shl<u>e</u>m
guard

перчатка
perch<u>a</u>tka
glove

пояс
p<u>o</u>yas
belt

тхэквондо tkhekvond<u>o</u> | **tae-kwon-do**

карате karat<u>e</u> | **karate**

дзюдо dzyud<u>o</u> | **judo**

айкидо aykid<u>o</u> | **aikido**

маска
m<u>a</u>ska
mask

меч
m<u>e</u>ch
sword

кендо kend<u>o</u> | **kendo**

кунг-фу kun-fu | **kung fu**

кикбоксинг
kikb<u>o</u>ksing | **kickboxing**

борьба bor'b<u>a</u> | **wrestling**

бокс b<u>o</u>ks | **boxing**

действия deystviya • actions

падение padeniye | **fall**

захват zakhvat | **hold**

бросок brosok | **throw**

удержание
uderzhaniye | **pin**

удар ногой
udar nogoy | **kick**

удар кулаком
udar kulakom | **punch**

удар udar | **strike**

рубящий удар
rubyashchiy udar | **chop**

прыжок pryzhok | **jump**

блок blok | **block**

словарь slovar' • vocabulary

боксёрский ринг boksyorskiy ring **boxing ring**	**раунд** raund **round**	**кулак** kulak **fist**	**чёрный пояс** chyorniy poyas **black belt**	**капоэйра** kapoeyra **capoeira**
боксёрские перчатки boksyorskiye perchatki **boxing gloves**	**поединок** poyedinok **bout**	**нокаут** nokaut **knock out**	**самозащита** samozashchita **self-defence**	**борьба сумо** bor'ba sumo **sumo wrestling**
капа kapa **mouth guard**	**спарринг** sparring **sparring**	**боксёрская груша** boksyorskaya grusha **punchbag**	**боевые искусства** boyeviye iskustva **martial arts**	**тайцзицюань** taytszitsyuan' **Tai Chi**

плавание plavaniye · **swimming**

спортивный инвентарь sportivniy inventar' · **equipment**

носовой зажим
nosovoy zazhim
nose clip

нарукавник для плавания
narukavnik dlya plavaniya
armband

очки для плавания
ochki dlya plavaniya | **goggles**

плавательная доска
plavatel'naya doska
float

купальник
kupal'nik
swimsuit

дорожка
dorozhka
lane

вода
voda
water

стартовая тумба
startovaya tumba
starting block

шапочка
shapochka
cap

плавки
plavki
trunks

плавательный бассейн plavatel'niy baseyn | **swimming pool**

трамплин
tramplin
springboard

ныряльщик
nyryal'shchik
diver

пловец plovets | **swimmer**

нырять nyryat' | **dive (v)**

плавать plavat' | **swim (v)**

поворот povorot | **turn**

стили плавания stili plavaniya • styles

кроль на груди krol' na grudi | **front crawl**

брасс bras | **breaststroke**

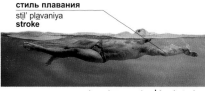

стиль плавания
stil' plavaniya
stroke

плавание на спине plavaniye na spine | **backstroke**

удары ног
udary nog
kick

баттерфляй baterflyay | **butterfly**

дайвинг с аквалангом dayving s akvalangom • scuba diving

гидрокостюм
gidrokostyum
wetsuit

ласт
last
flipper

грузовой пояс
gruzovoy poyas
weight belt

баллон акваланга
balon akvalanga
air cylinder

маска
maska
mask

регулятор
regulyator
regulator

дыхательная трубка
dykhatel'naya trubka
snorkel

словарь slovar' • vocabulary

прыжок в воду pryzhok v vodu **dive**	**плыть стоя** plyt' stoya **tread water (v)**	**шкафчики для одежды** shkafchiki dlya odezhdy **lockers**	**водное поло** vodnoye polo **water polo**	**мелкая часть** melkaya chast' **shallow end**	**судорога** sudoroga **cramp**
прыжок с трамплина pryzhok s tramplina **high dive**	**стартовый прыжок** startoviy pryzhok **racing dive**	**спасатель** spasatel' **lifeguard**	**глубина** glubina **deep end**	**синхронное плавание** sinkhronnoye plavaniye **synchronized swimming**	**тонуть** tonut' **drown (v)**

парусный спорт p<u>a</u>rusniy sp<u>o</u>rt • **sailing**

компас
kompas
compass

якорь
yakor'
anchor

передний парус
peredniy p<u>a</u>rus
headsail

стопор
stopor
cleat

потопчина
potopchina
sidedeck

форштевень
forsht<u>e</u>ven'
bow

румпель
rumpel'
tiller

корпус
korpus
hull

управлять судном upravlyat' s<u>u</u>dnom
navigate (v)

мачта
m<u>a</u>chta
mast

такелаж
takel<u>a</u>zh
rigging

грот
grot
mainsail

гик
gik
boom

корма
korma
stern

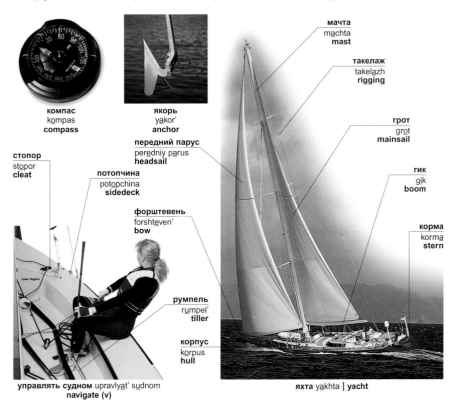

яхта y<u>a</u>khta | **yacht**

безопасность bezop<u>a</u>snost' • **safety**

фальшфейер
fal'shf<u>e</u>iyer
flare

спасательный круг
spas<u>a</u>tel'niy kr<u>u</u>g
lifebuoy

спасательный жилет
spas<u>a</u>tel'niy zhil<u>e</u>t
life jacket

спасательный плот
spas<u>a</u>tel'niy pl<u>o</u>t
life raft

водные виды спорта vodniye vidy sporta • **watersports**

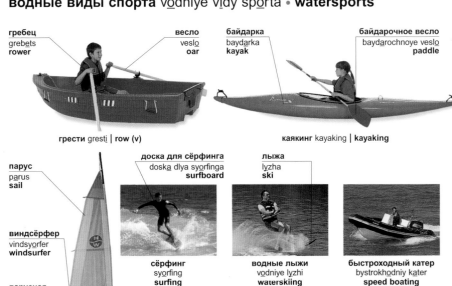

гребец
grebets
rower

весло
veslo
oar

байдарка
baydarka
kayak

байдарочное весло
baydarochnoye veslo
paddle

грести gresti | **row (v)**

каякинг kayaking | **kayaking**

парус
parus
sail

доска для сёрфинга
doska dlya syorfinga
surfboard

лыжа
lyzha
ski

виндсёрфер
vindsyorfer
windsurfer

**парусная
доска**
parusnaya
doska
board

петля для ноги
petlya dlya nogi
footstrap

сёрфинг
syorfing
surfing

водные лыжи
vodniye lyzhi
waterskiing

быстроходный катер
bystrokhodniy kater
speed boating

рафтинг
rafting
rafting

катание на гидроцикле
kataniye na gidrotsikle
jet skiing

виндсёрфинг vindsyorfing | **windsurfing**

словарь slovar' • **vocabulary**

воднолыжник vodnolyzhnik **waterskier**	**команда, экипаж** komanda, ekipazh **crew**	**ветер** veter **wind**	**прибой** priboy **surf**	**шкот** shkot **sheet**	**опускной киль** opusknoy kil' **centreboard**
сёрфер syorfer **surfer**	**делать поворот** delat' povorot **tack (v)**	**волна** volna **wave**	**пороги реки** porogi reki **rapids**	**руль судна** rul' sudna **rudder**	**опрокидываться** oprokidyvat'sya **capsize (v)**

верховая езда verkhovaya yezda • horse riding

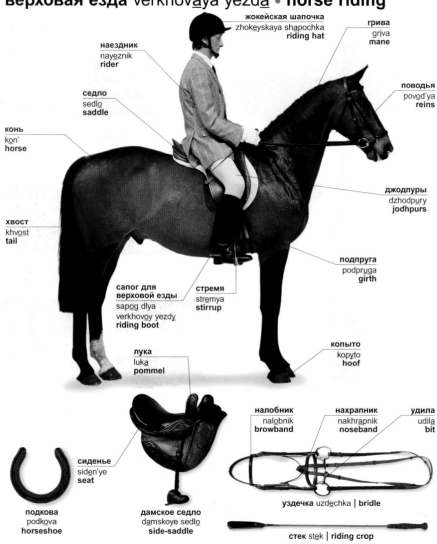

жокейская шапочка
zhokeyskaya shapochka
riding hat

грива
griva
mane

наездник
nayeznik
rider

поводья
povod'ya
reins

седло
sedlo
saddle

конь
kon'
horse

джодпуры
dzhodpury
jodhpurs

хвост
khvost
tail

подпруга
podpruga
girth

сапог для верховой езды
sapog dlya verkhovoy yezdy
riding boot

стремя
stremya
stirrup

копыто
kopyto
hoof

лука
luka
pommel

налобник
nalobnik
browband

нахрапник
nakhrapnik
noseband

удила
udila
bit

сиденье
siden'ye
seat

подкова
podkova
horseshoe

дамское седло
damskoye sedlo
side-saddle

уздечка uzdechka | **bridle**

стек stek | **riding crop**

виды соревнований vidy sorevnovaniy • events

скаковая лошадь
skakovaya loshad'
racehorse

изгородь
izgorod'
fence

скачки
skachki
horse race

скачки с препятствиями
skachki s prepyatstviyami
steeplechase

рысистые бега
rysistiye bega
harness race

родео
rodeo
rodeo

конкур
konkur
showjumping

соревнования конных упряжек
sorevnovaniya konnykh upryazhek
carriage race

треккинг на лошадях
treking na loshadyakh | **trekking**

выездка viyezdka | **dressage**

поло polo | **polo**

словарь slovar' • vocabulary

шаг shag **walk**	кентер kenter **canter**	прыжок pryzhok **jump**	недоуздок nedouzdok **halter**	выгул vygul **paddock**	скачки без препятствий skachki bez prepyatstviy **flat race**
рысь rys' **trot**	галоп galop **gallop**	конюх konyukh **groom**	конюшня konyushnya **stable**	арена arena **arena**	ипподром ipodrom **racecourse**

рыбная ловля rybnaya lovlya • fishing

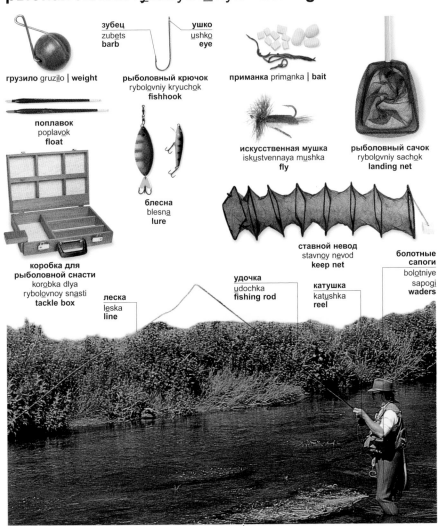

грузило gruzilo | **weight**

зубец
zubets
barb

ушко
ushko
eye

рыболовный крючок
rybolovniy kryuchok
fishhook

приманка primanka | **bait**

поплавок
poplavok
float

блесна
blesna
lure

искусственная мушка
iskustvennaya mushka
fly

рыболовный сачок
rybolovniy sachok
landing net

**коробка для
рыболовной снасти**
korobka dlya
rybolovnoy snasti
tackle box

ставной невод
stavnoy nevod
keep net

**болотные
сапоги**
bolotniye
sapogi
waders

удочка
udochka
fishing rod

катушка
katushka
reel

леска
leska
line

рыболов rybolov | **angler**

виды рыбной ловли vidy rybnoy lovli • types of fishing

речная рыбалка
rechnaya rybalka
freshwater fishing

ловля рыбы нахлыстом
lovlya ryby nakhlystom
fly fishing

спортивное рыболовство
sportivnoye rybolovstvo
sport fishing

глубоководное рыболовство
glubokovodnoye rybolovstvo
deep sea fishing

морская береговая рыбалка
morskaya beregovaya
rybalka | **surfcasting**

действия deystviya • activities

забрасывать удочку
zabrasyvat' udochku
cast (v)

ловить
lovit'
catch (v)

наматывать
namatyvat'
reel in (v)

ловить сетью
lovit' set'yu
net (v)

выпускать
vypuskat'
release (v)

словарь slovar' • vocabulary

приманивать primanivat' **bait (v)**	**рыболовные снасти** rybolovniye snasti **tackle**	**непромокаемая одежда** nepromokayemaya odezhda **waterproofs**	**разрешение на ловлю рыбы** razresheniye na lovlyu ryby **fishing permit**	**верша** versha **creel**
клевать klevat' **bite (v)**	**катушка** katushka **spool**	**шест** shest **pole**	**морское рыболовство** morskoye rybolovstvo **marine fishing**	**подводная охота** podvodnaya okhota **spearfishing**

лыжный спорт lyzhniy sport • skiing

кресельный подъёмник
kresel'niy pod-yomnik
chairlift

горнолыжный склон
gornolyzhniy sklon
ski slope

вагон фуникулёра
vagon funikulyora
cable car

лыжня
lyzhnya
ski run

защитный барьер
zashchitniy bar'yer
safety barrier

перчатка
perchatka
glove

лыжная палка
lyzhnaya palka
ski pole

ребро лыжи
rebro lyzhi
edge

лыжа
lyzha
ski

лыжная куртка
lyzhnaya kurtka
ski jacket

носок лыжи
nosok lyzhi
tip

лыжный ботинок
lyzhniy botinok
ski boot

лыжник
lyzhnik
skier

виды соревнований vidy sorevnovaniy • events

горнолыжный спорт
gornolyzhniy sport
downhill skiing

ворота
vorota
gate

слалом
slalom
slalom

лыжный трамплин
lyzhniy tramplin
ski jump

лыжные гонки
lyzhniye gonki
cross-country skiing

зимние виды спорта zimniye vidy sporta • winter sports

ледолазание
ledolazaniye
ice climbing

конькобежный спорт
kon'kobezhniy sport
ice-skating

защитные лыжные очки
zashchitniye lyzhniye ochki
goggles

конёк
konyok
skate

фигурное катание
figurnoye kataniye
figure skating

сноубординг
snoubording
snowboarding

бобслей
bobsley
bobsleigh

санный спорт
sanniy sport
luge

снегомобиль
snegomobil'
snowmobile

катание на санках
kataniye na sankakh
sledding

словарь slovar' • vocabulary

горнолыжный спорт
gornolyzhniy sport
alpine skiing

гигантский слалом
gigantskiy slalom
giant slalom

вне трасс
vne tras
off-piste

кёрлинг
kyorling
curling

катание на собачьих упряжках
kataniye na sobach'ikh upryazhkakh
dog sledding

скоростной бег на коньках
skorostnoy beg na kon'kakh
speed skating

биатлон
biatlon
biathlon

лавина
lavina
avalanche

другие виды спорта drugiye vidy sporta • other sports

планёр
planyor
glider

дельтаплан
del'taplan
hang-glider

планёрный спорт
planyorniy sport
gliding

дельтапланеризм
del'taplanerizm
hang-gliding

трос
tros
rope

парашют
parashyut
parachute

альпинизм
al'pinizm
rock climbing

парашютный спорт
parashyutniy sport
parachuting

параглайдинг
paraglayding
paragliding

затяжные прыжки с парашютом
zatyazhniye pryzhki s parashyutom
skydiving

дюльфер
dyul'fer
abseiling

банджи-джампинг
bandzhi-dzhamping
bungee jumping

ралли
ralli
rally driving

гонщик
gonshchik
racing driver

автомобильные гонки
avtomobil'niye gonki
motor racing

мотокросс
motokros
motorcross

мотогонки
motogonki
motorbike racing

скейтборд
skeytbord
skateboard

скейтбординг
skeytbording
skateboarding

катание на роликовых коньках
kataniye na rolikovykh kon'kakh
inline skating

стик
stik
stick

лакросс
lakros
lacrosse

маска
maska
mask

рапира
rapira
foil

фехтование
fekhtovaniye
fencing

кегля
keglya
pin

боулинг
bouling
bowling

лук
luk
bow

стрела
strela
arrow

колчан
kolchan
quiver

стрельба из лука
strel'ba iz luka
archery

мишень
mishen'
target

спортивная стрельба
sportivnaya strel'ba
target shooting

шар для боулинга
shar dlya boulinga
bowling ball

пул
pul
pool

снукер
snuker
snooker

фитнес fitnes • fitness

велотренажёр
velotrenazhyor
exercise bike

тренажёрный снаряд
trenazhyorniy snaryad
gym machine

скамейка
skameyka
bench

свободные веса
svobodniye vesa
free weights

штанга
shtanga
bar

тренажёрный зал
trenazhyorniy zal
gym

гребной тренажёр
grebnoy trenazhyor
rowing machine

беговая дорожка
begovaya dorozhka
treadmill

эллипсоид; орбитрек
ellipsoid; orbitrek
cross trainer

персональный тренер
personal'niy trener
personal trainer

степ-тренажёр
step-trenazhyor
step machine

плавательный бассейн
plavatel'niy baseyn
swimming pool

сауна
sauna
sauna

упражнения uprazhneniya · **exercises**

растяжка
rastyazhka
stretch

выпад
vypad
lunge

трико
triko
tights

отжимание
otzhimaniye
press-up

приседание
prisedaniye
squat

подъём туловища
pod-yom tulovishcha
sit-up

гантель
gantel'
dumbbell

подъём на бицепс
pod-yom na bitseps
bicep curl

жим ногами
zhim nogami
leg press

гриф
штанги
grif shtangi
weight bar

кроссовки
krosovki
trainers

жим лёжа
zhim lyozha
chest press

тренинг с отягощениями
trening s otyagoshcheniyami
weight training

бег трусцой
beg trustsoy
jogging

пилатес
pilates
Pilates

словарь slovar' · **vocabulary**

тренироваться
trenirovat'sya
train (v)

разогреваться
razogrevat'sya
warm up (v)

бежать на месте
bezhat' na meste
jog on the spot (v)

сгибать
sgibat'
flex (v)

растягивать
rastyagivat'
extend (v)

подтягиваться
podtyagivat'sya
pull up (v)

**прыжки через
скакалку**
pryzhki cherez
skakalku
skipping

боксерсайз
boksersayz
boxercise

**круговая
тренировка**
krugovaya
trenirovka
circuit training

досуг dos<u>u</u>g
leisure

театр teatr • theatre

занавес
zanaves
curtain

кулисы
kulisy
wings

декорации
dekoratsii
set

зрители
zriteli
audience

оркестр
orkestr
orchestra

сцена stsena | **stage**

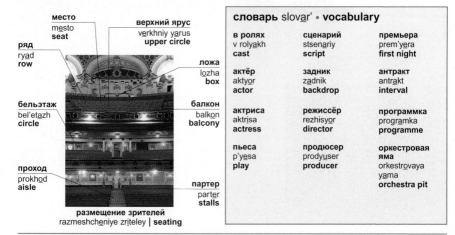

место
mesto
seat

верхний ярус
verkhniy yarus
upper circle

ряд
ryad
row

ложа
lozha
box

бельэтаж
bel'etazh
circle

балкон
balkon
balcony

проход
prokhod
aisle

партер
parter
stalls

размещение зрителей
razmeshcheniye zriteley | **seating**

словарь slovar' • vocabulary

в ролях v rolyakh **cast**	сценарий stsenariy **script**	премьера prem'yera **first night**
актёр aktyor **actor**	задник zadnik **backdrop**	антракт antrakt **interval**
актриса aktrisa **actress**	режиссёр rezhisyor **director**	программка programka **programme**
пьеса p'yesa **play**	продюсер prodyuser **producer**	оркестровая яма orkestrovaya yama **orchestra pit**

концерт kontsert | **concert**

мюзикл myuzikl | **musical**

костюм
kostyum
costume

балет balet | **ballet**

словарь slovar' • vocabulary

капельдинер
kapel'diner
usher

классическая музыка
klasicheskaya muzyka
classical music

музыка к спектаклю;
партитура
muzyka k spektaklyu;
partitura
musical score

фонограмма
fonogramma
soundtrack

аплодировать
aplodirovat'
applaud (v)

(на) бис
(na) bis
encore

Когда он начинается?
Kogda on nachinayetsya?
What time does it start?

Мне два билета на сегодняшний
спектакль.
Mne dva bileta na segodnyashniy
spektakl'
**I'd like two tickets for tonight's
performance.**

опера
opera | **opera**

КИНО kino • cinema

попкорн
popkorn
popcorn

афиша
afisha
poster

билетная касса
biletnaya kassa
box office

вестибюль
vestibyul'
lobby

кинозал
kinozal
cinema hall

экран
ekran
screen

словарь slovar' • vocabulary

комедия
komediya
comedy

триллер
triller
thriller

фильм ужасов
fil'm uzhasov
horror film

вестерн
vestern
western

мелодрама
melodrama
romance

научно-фантастический
фильм
nauchno-fantasticheskiy fil'm
science fiction film

приключенческий фильм
priklyuchencheskiy fil'm
adventure film

мультфильм
mul'tfil'm
animated film

оркестр orkestr · orchestra

струнные инструменты strunniye instrumenty · strings

арфа
arfa
harp

дирижёр
dirizhor
conductor

контрабас
kontrabas
double bass

скрипка
skripka
violin

дирижёрский подиум
dirizhorski podium
podium

альт
al't
viola

виолончель
violonchel'
cello

партитура
partitura
score

басовый ключ
basoviy klyuch
bass clef

скрипичный ключ
skripichniy klyuch
treble clef

нота
nota
note

нотный стан
notniy stan
staff

нотное письмо notnoye pis'mo | notation

пианино pianino | **piano**

словарь slovar' · vocabulary

увертюра uvertyura **overture**	**соната** sonata **sonata**	**пауза** pauza **rest**	**резкий** rezkiy **sharp**	**естественный** yestestvenniy **natural**	**гамма** gamma **scale**
симфония simfoniya **symphony**	**инструменты** instrumenty **instruments**	**высота звука** vysota zvuka **pitch**	**бемоль** bemol' **flat**	**тактовая черта** wtaktovaya cherta **bar**	**дирижёрская палочка** dirizhorskaya palochka **baton**

деревянные духовые инструменты derevyanniye dukhoviye instrumenty • **woodwind**

пикколо
pikkolo
piccolo

флейта
fleyta
flute

гобой
goboy
oboe

английский рожок
angliyskiy rozhok
cor anglais

кларнет
klarnet
clarinet

бас-кларнет
bas-klarnet
bass clarinet

фагот
fagot
bassoon

контрафагот
kontrafagot
double bassoon

саксофон
saksofon
saxophone

ударные инструменты udarniye instrumenty • **percussion**

вибрафон
vibrafon
vibraphone

бонго
bongo
bongos

малый барабан
maliy baraban
snare drum

литавра
litavra
kettledrum

гонг
gong
gong

тарелки
tarelki
cymbals

тамбурин
tamburin
tambourine

треугольник
treugol'nik
triangle

маракас
marakas
maracas

педаль
pedal'
foot pedal

медные духовые инструменты medniye dukhoviye instrumenty • **brass**

труба
truba
trumpet

тромбон
trombon
trombone

валторна
valtorna
French horn

туба
tuba
tuba

концерт kontsert • **concert**

динамик
dinamik
speaker

фанаты
fanaty
fans

солист
solist
lead singer

гитарист
gitarist
guitarist

микрофон
mikrofon
microphone

ударник
udarnik
drummer

рок-концерт rok-kontsert | **rock concert**

инструменты yuèqì • **instruments**

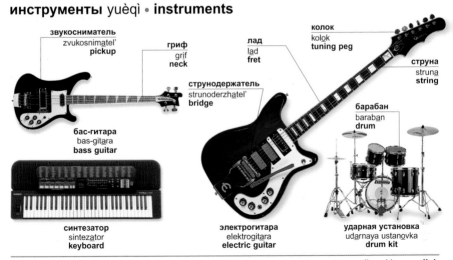

звукосниматель
zvukosnimatel'
pickup

гриф
grif
neck

лад
lad
fret

колок
kolok
tuning peg

струна
struna
string

струнодержатель
strunoderzhatel'
bridge

барабан
baraban
drum

бас-гитара
bas-gitara
bass guitar

синтезатор
sintezator
keyboard

электрогитара
elektrogitara
electric guitar

ударная установка
udarnaya ustanovka
drum kit

музыкальные стили muzykal'niye stili • musical styles

джаз dzhaz | **jazz**

блюз blyuz | **blues**

панк pank | **punk**

фолк folk | **folk music**

поп pop | **pop**

танцевальная музыка
tantseval'naya muzyka | **dance**

рэп rep | **rap**

хеви-метал
khevi-metal | **heavy metal**

классическая музыка
klasicheskaya muzyka
classical music

словарь slovar' • vocabulary

песня	текст песни	мелодия	ритм; темп	регги	кантри	прожектор
pesnya	tekst pesni	melodiya	ritm; temp	reggi	kantri	prozhektor
song	**lyrics**	**melody**	**beat**	**reggae**	**country**	**spotlight**

осмотр достопримечательностей osmotr dostoprimechatelnostey • **sightseeing**

турист
turist
tourist

маршрут
marshrut
itinerary

с открытым верхом
s otkrytym verkhom
open-top

This is an official London Sightseeing Bus.
LONDON PRIDE

туристический автобус
turisticheskiy avtobus | **tour bus**

достопримечательность
dostoprimechatel'nost' | **tourist attraction**

гид
gid
tour guide

организованная экскурсия
organizovannaya ekskursiya
guided tour

статуэтка
statuetka
statuette

сувениры
suveniry
souvenirs

словарь slovar' • **vocabulary**

открыто otkryto **open**	путеводитель putevoditel' **guidebook**	видеокамера videokamera **camcorder**	слева; налево; левый sleva; nalevo; leviy **left**	Где находится…? Gde nakhoditsya…? **Where is …?**
закрыто zakryto **closed**	фотоплёнка fotoplyonka **film**	фотоаппарат; камера fotoaparat; kamera **camera**	справа; направо; правый sprava; napravo; praviy **right**	Я заблудился. Ya zabludilsya **I'm lost.**
входная плата vkhodnaya plata **entrance fee**	батарейки batareyki **batteries**	указания; направления ukazaniya; napravleniya **directions**	прямо pryamo **straight on**	Как пройти/проехать к…? Kak proyti/proyekhat' k…? **Can you tell me the way to …?**

достопримечательности dostoprimech<u>a</u>tel'nosti • **attractions**

картина
kart<u>i</u>na
painting

экспонат
ekspon<u>a</u>t
exhibit

выставка
v<u>y</u>stavka
exhibition

исторические развалины
istor<u>i</u>cheskiye razv<u>a</u>liny
famous ruin

художественная галерея
khud<u>o</u>zhestvennaya galer<u>e</u>ya
art gallery

памятник
p<u>a</u>myatnik
monument

музей
muz<u>e</u>y
museum

историческое здание
istor<u>i</u>cheskoye zd<u>a</u>niye
historic building

казино
kazin<u>o</u>
casino

парк
p<u>a</u>rk
gardens

национальный парк
natsion<u>a</u>l'niy p<u>a</u>rk
national park

информация inform<u>a</u>tsiya • **information**

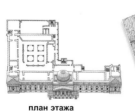

время
vr<u>e</u>mya
times

план этажа
plan etazh<u>a</u>
floor plan

карта
k<u>a</u>rta
map

расписание
raspis<u>a</u>niye
timetable

туристский информационный центр
tur<u>i</u>stskiy informatsi<u>o</u>nniy tsentr
tourist information

отдых на открытом воздухе <u>o</u>tdykh na otkr<u>y</u>tom v<u>o</u>zdukhe • **outdoor activities**

тропинка
trop<u>i</u>nka
footpath

солнечные часы
s<u>o</u>lnechnyye chas<u>y</u>
sundial

кафе
k<u>a</u>fe
café

парк p<u>a</u>rk | **park**

трава
trav<u>a</u>
grass

скамейка
skam<u>e</u>yka
bench

сад в классическом стиле
s<u>a</u>d v klas<u>i</u>cheskom st<u>i</u>le
formal gardens

американские горки
amerik<u>a</u>nskiye g<u>o</u>rki
roller coaster

территория ярмарки
terit<u>o</u>riya y<u>a</u>rmarki
fairground

тематический парк
temat<u>i</u>cheskiy p<u>a</u>rk
theme park

сафари-парк
saf<u>a</u>ri-p<u>a</u>rk
safari park

зоопарк
zoop<u>a</u>rk
zoo

занятия zanyatiya • **activities**

катание на велосипеде
kataniye na velosipede
cycling

бег трусцой
beg trustsoy
jogging

катание на скейтборде
kataniye na skeytborde
skateboarding

катание на роликах
kataniye na rolikakh
rollerblading

верховая тропа
verkhovaya tropa
bridle path

наблюдение за птицами
nablyudeniye za ptitsami
bird-watching

верховая езда
verkhovaya yezda
horse riding

пешеходный туризм
peshekhodniy turizmg
hiking

корзинка для пикника
korzinka dlya piknika
hamper

пикник
piknik
picnic

детская площадка detskaya ploshchadka • **playground**

песочница
pesochnitsa
sandpit

детский бассейн
detskiy baseyn
paddling pool

качели
kacheli
swing

доска-качели
doska-kacheli | **seesaw**

детская горка detskaya gorka | **slide**

лесенка lesenka | **climbing frame**

пляж plyazh · beach

отель otel' **hotel**	**пляжный зонт** plyazhniy zont **beach umbrella**	**пляжный домик** plyazhniy domik **beach hut**	**песок** pesok **sand**	**волна** volna **wave**	**море** more **sea**

пляжная сумка
plyazhnaya sumka
beach bag

бикини
bikini
bikini

загорать zagorat' | **sunbathe (v)**

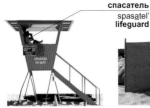

спасатель
spasatel'
lifeguard

спасательная вышка
spasatel'naya vyshka
lifeguard tower

ветролом
vetrolom
windbreak

набережная
naberezhnaya
promenade

шезлонг
shezlong
deck chair

солнцезащитные очки
solntsezashchitniye ochki
sunglasses

шляпа от солнца
shlyapa ot sontsa
sunhat

крем для загара
krem dlya zagara
suntan lotion

солнцезащитный крем
solntsezashchitniy krem
sunblock

пляжный мяч
plyazhniy myach
beach ball

плавательный круг
plavatel'niy krug
rubber ring

купальник
kupal'nik
swimsuit

лопатка
lopatka
spade

ведёрко
vedyorko
bucket

песочный замок
pesochniy zamok
sandcastle

ракушка
rakushka
shell

пляжное полотенце
plyazhnoye polotentse
beach towel

кемпинг k<u>e</u>mping • **camping**

туалеты
tual<u>e</u>ty
toilets

площадка для сбора мусора
ploshch<u>a</u>dka dlya sb<u>o</u>ra m<u>u</u>sora
waste disposal

душевые (кабины)
dush<u>e</u>vyie (kab<u>i</u>ny)
shower block

подключение к
электросети
podklyuch<u>e</u>niye k elektros<u>e</u>ti
electric hook-up

полог (палатки)
polog (pal<u>a</u>tki)
flysheet

трос
tros
guy rope

колышек для палатки
k<u>o</u>lyshek dlya pal<u>a</u>tki
tent peg

дом-фургон
d<u>o</u>m-furgon
caravan

площадка для кемпинга ploshch<u>a</u>dka dlya k<u>e</u>mpinga | **campsite**

словарь slov<u>a</u>r' • **vocabulary**

разбивать лагерь razbiv<u>a</u>t' l<u>a</u>ger' **camp (v)**	место для палатки m<u>e</u>sto dlya pal<u>a</u>tki **pitch**	стол для пикника stol dlya piknik<u>a</u> **picnic bench**	уголь ug<u>o</u>l' **charcoal**
офис директора кемпинга <u>o</u>fis dir<u>e</u>ktora k<u>e</u>mpinga **site manager's office**	разбивать палатку razbiv<u>a</u>t' pal<u>a</u>tku **pitch a tent (v)**	гамак gam<u>a</u>k **hammock**	растопка rast<u>o</u>pka **firelighter**
есть места (для палаток) yest' mest<u>a</u> (dlya pal<u>a</u>tok) **pitches available**	шест для палатки shest dlya pal<u>a</u>tki **tent pole**	автодом avtod<u>o</u>m **camper van**	разводить костёр razvod<u>i</u>t' kost<u>yo</u>r **light a fire (v)**
мест нет m<u>e</u>st net **full**	раскладушка rasklad<u>u</u>shka **camp bed**	трейлер tr<u>e</u>yler **trailer**	костёр kost<u>yo</u>r **campfire**

каркас
karkas
frame

подстилка
podstilka
ground sheet

рюкзак
ryukzak
backpack

термос
termos
vacuum flask

фляжка
flyazhka
water bottle

палатка
palatka
tent

репеллент
repelent
insect repellent

карманный фонарь
karmanniy fonar'
torch

москитная сетка
moskitnaya setka
mosquito net

термобельё
termobel'yo
thermals

туристические ботинки
turisticheskiye botinki
walking boots

непромокаемая одежда
nepromokayemaya
odezhda
waterproofs

спальный мешок
spal'niy meshok
sleeping bag

туристический коврик
turisticheskiy kovrik
sleeping mat

походная плита
pokhodnaya plita
camping stove

барбекю
barbekyu
barbecue

надувной матрац naduvnoy matrats | **air mattress**

домашние мультимедийные системы domashniye
mul'timediyniye sistemy • home entertainment

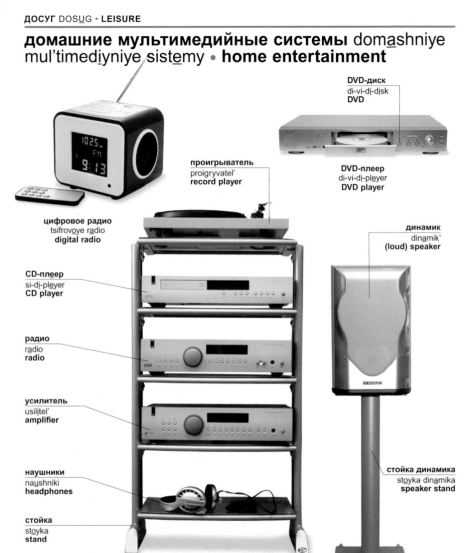

DVD-диск
di-vi-di-disk
DVD

проигрыватель
proigryvatel'
record player

DVD-плеер
di-vi-di-pleyer
DVD player

цифровое радио
tsifrovoye radio
digital radio

динамик
dinamik'
(loud) speaker

CD-плеер
si-di-pleyer
CD player

радио
radio
radio

усилитель
usilitel'
amplifier

наушники
naushniki
headphones

стойка
stoyka
stand

стойка динамика
stoyka dinamika
speaker stand

акустическая система hi-fi
akusticheskaya sistema khay-fay | **hi-fi system**

экран
ekr<u>a</u>n
screen

наглазник
nagl<u>a</u>znik
eyecup

декодер
dek<u>o</u>der
digital box

видеокамера
videokamera
camcorder

спутниковая тарелка
sputnikovaya tar<u>e</u>lka
satellite dish

телевизор с плоским экраном
televizor s pl<u>o</u>skim ekr<u>a</u>nom
flatscreen TV

игровая приставка
igrov<u>a</u>ya
prist<u>a</u>vka
console

быстрая перемотка вперёд
bystraya peremotka vper<u>yo</u>d
fast forward

запись
zapis'
record

громкость
gr<u>o</u>mkost'
volume

перемотка назад
peremotka naz<u>a</u>d
rewind

джойстик
dzh<u>o</u>ystik
controller

воспроизведение
vosproizved<u>e</u>niye
play

пауза
p<u>a</u>uza
pause

стоп
stop
stop

видеоигра videoigra | **video game**

пульт дистанционного управления
pul't distants<u>io</u>nnogo upravl<u>e</u>niya | **remote control**

словарь slov<u>ar</u>' • **vocabulary**

компакт-диск kompakt-disk **compact disc**	**платный канал** platniy kan<u>a</u>l **pay per view channel**	**программа** progr<u>a</u>mma **programme**	**художественный фильм** khud<u>o</u>zhestvenniy fil'm **feature film**	**смотреть телевизор** smotr<u>e</u>t' televizor **watch television (v)**
потоковый pot<u>o</u>koviy **streaming**	**реклама** rekl<u>a</u>ma **advertisement**	**стерео** st<u>e</u>reo **stereo**		**выключать телевизор** vyklyuch<u>a</u>t' televizor **turn the television off (v)**
высокое разрешение viysok<u>o</u>ye razresh<u>e</u>niye **high-definition**	**цифровой** tsifrov<u>o</u>y **digital**	**кабельное ТВ** k<u>a</u>bel'noye te-ve **cable television**	**переключать канал** pereklyuch<u>a</u>t' kan<u>a</u>l **change channel (v)**	
кассетный плеер kass<u>e</u>tniy pleyer **cassette player**	**кассета** kass<u>e</u>ta **cassette tape**	**вай-фай** vay-f<u>a</u>y **Wi-Fi**	**настраивать радио (на канал/волну)** nastr<u>a</u>ivat' radio (na kan<u>a</u>l/volnu) **tune the radio (v)**	**включать телевизор** vklyuch<u>a</u>t' televizor **turn the television on (v)**

фотография fotografiya • **photography**

спуск затвора
spusk zatvora
shutter release

кольцо управления диафрагмой
kol'tso upravleniya diafragmoy
aperture dial

объектив
ob-yektiv
lens

фильтр
fil'tr
filter

крышка объектива
kryshka ob-yektiva
lens cap

однообъективная зеркальная камера
odnoob-yektivnaya zerkal'naya kamera | **SLR camera**

лампа-вспышка
lampa-vspyshka
flash gun

экспонометр
eksponometr
light meter

зум-объектив
zum-ob-yektiv
zoom lens

штатив-тренога
shtativ-trenoga
tripod

типы фотоаппаратов tipy fotoaparatov • **types of camera**

вспышка
vspyshka
flash

поляроид
polyaroid
Polaroid camera

цифровой фотоаппарат
tsifrovoy fotoaparat
digital camera

камерофон
kamerofon
cameraphone

одноразовый фотоаппарат
odnorazoviy fotoaparat
disposable camera

фотографировать fotografirovat' • photograph (v)

катушка
плёнки
katushka
plyonki
film spool

плёнка
plyonka
film

фокусировать
fokusirovat'
focus (v)

проявлять
proyavlyat'
develop (v)

негатив
negativ
negative

пейзаж
peyzazh
landscape

портрет
portret
portrait

фотография fotografiya | **photograph**

фотоальбом
fotoal'bom
photo album

фоторамка
fotoramka
photo frame

проблемы problemy • problems

недоэкспонированный
nedoeksponirovanniy
underexposed

переэкспонированный
pereeksponirovanniy
overexposed

нерезкий
nerezkiy
out of focus

красные глаза
krasniye glaza
red eye

словарь slovar' • vocabulary

видоискатель
vidoiskatel'
viewfinder

чехол камеры
chekhol kamery
camera case

экспозиция
ekspozitsiya
exposure

проявочная; тёмная
комната
proyavochnaya; tyomnaya
komnata
darkroom

печать; отпечаток
pechat'; otpechatok
print

матовый
matoviy
matte

глянцевый
glyantseviy
gloss

увеличение
uvelicheniye
enlargement

Мне нужно проявить эту плёнку.
Mne nuzhno proyavit' etu plyonku
I'd like this film processed.

игры igry • games

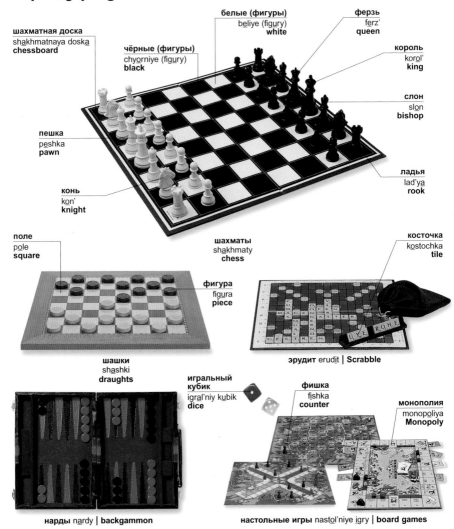

белые (фигуры)
beliye (figury)
white

ферзь
ferz'
queen

шахматная доска
shakhmatnaya doska
chessboard

чёрные (фигуры)
chyorniye (figury)
black

король
korol'
king

слон
slon
bishop

пешка
peshka
pawn

ладья
lad'ya
rook

конь
kon'
knight

поле
pole
square

шахматы
shakhmaty
chess

косточка
kostochka
tile

фигура
figura
piece

шашки
shashki
draughts

эрудит erudit | **Scrabble**

игральный кубик
igral'niy kubik
dice

фишка
fishka
counter

монополия
monopoliya
Monopoly

нарды nardy | **backgammon**

настольные игры nastol'niye igry | **board games**

филателия
filateliya
stamp collecting

пазл pazl | **jigsaw puzzle**

домино
domino | **dominoes**

мишень для
дротиков
mishen' dlya
drotikov
dartboard

яблочко
yablochko
bullseye

дартс darts | **darts**

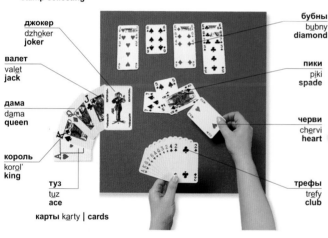

джокер
dzhoker
joker

валет
valet
jack

дама
dama
queen

король
korol'
king

туз
tuz
ace

карты karty | **cards**

бубны
bubny
diamond

пики
piki
spade

черви
chervi
heart

трефы
trefy
club

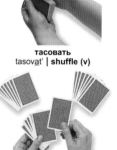

тасовать
tasovat' | **shuffle (v)**

сдавать sdavat' | **deal (v)**

словарь slovar' • vocabulary

ход khod **move**	**выигрывать** vyigryvat' **win (v)**	**проигравший** proigravshiy **loser**	**очко** ochko **point**	**бридж** bridzh **bridge**	**Бросай кубик.** Brosay kubik **Roll the dice.**
играть igrat' **play (v)**	**победитель** pobeditel' **winner**	**игра** igra **game**	**счёт** schyot **score**	**колода карт** koloda kart **pack of cards**	**Чья очередь?** Ch'ya ochered'? **Whose turn is it?**
игрок igrok **player**	**проигрывать** proigryvat' **lose (v)**	**пари** pari **bet**	**покер** poker **poker**	**масть** mast' **suit**	**Твой ход.** Tvoy khod **It's your move.**

искусства и ремёсла 1 iskustva i remyosla • arts and crafts 1

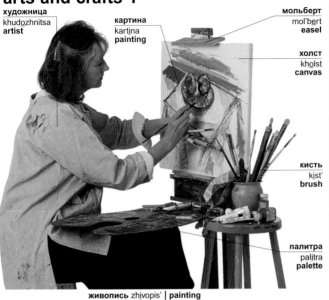

художница
khudozhnitsa
artist

картина
kartina
painting

мольберт
mol'bert
easel

холст
kholst
canvas

кисть
kist'
brush

палитра
palitra
palette

живопись zhivopis' | **painting**

краски kraski • paints

масляные краски
maslyaniye kraski
oil paints

акварель
akvarel'
watercolour paint

пастель
pastel'
pastels

акриловая краска
akrilovaya kraska
acrylic paint

гуашь
guash' | **poster paint**

цвета tsveta • colours

красный
krasniy | **red**

синий siniy | **blue**

жёлтый
zhyoltiy | **yellow**

зелёный
zelyoniy | **green**

оранжевый
oranzheviy | **orange**

фиолетовый
fioletoviy | **purple**

белый
beliy | **white**

чёрный
chyorniy | **black**

серый seriy | **grey**

розовый
rozoviy | **pink**

коричневый
korichneviy
brown

индиго
indigo | **indigo**

другие ремёсла drugiye remyosla • other crafts

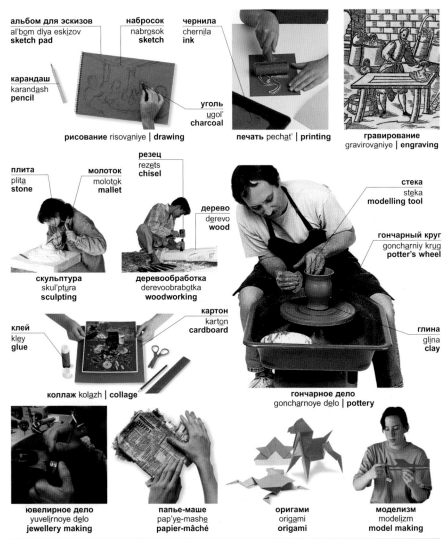

альбом для эскизов
al'bom dlya eskizov
sketch pad

набросок
nabrosok
sketch

чернила
chernila
ink

карандаш
karandash
pencil

уголь
ugol'
charcoal

рисование risovaniye | **drawing**

печать pechat' | **printing**

гравирование
gravirovaniye | **engraving**

плита
plita
stone

молоток
molotok
mallet

резец
rezets
chisel

дерево
derevo
wood

стека
steka
modelling tool

гончарный круг
goncharniy krug
potter's wheel

скульптура
skul'ptura
sculpting

деревообработка
derevoobrabotka
woodworking

клей
kley
glue

картон
karton
cardboard

глина
glina
clay

коллаж kolazh | **collage**

гончарное дело
goncharnoye delo | **pottery**

ювелирное дело
yuvelirnoye delo
jewellery making

папье-маше
pap'ye-mashe
papier-mâché

оригами
origami
origami

моделизм
modelizm
model making

искусство и ремёсла 2 iskustvo i remyosla • arts and crafts 2

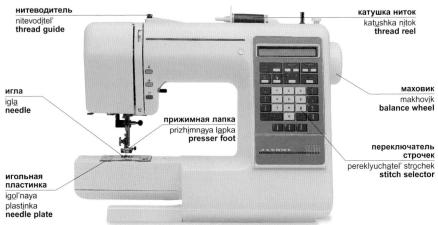

нитеводитель
nitevoditel'
thread guide

катушка ниток
katushka nitok
thread reel

игла
igla
needle

маховик
makhovik
balance wheel

прижимная лапка
prizhimnaya lapka
presser foot

переключатель строчек
pereklyuchatel' strochek
stitch selector

игольная пластинка
igol'naya plastinka
needle plate

швейная машина shveynaya mashina | **sewing machine**

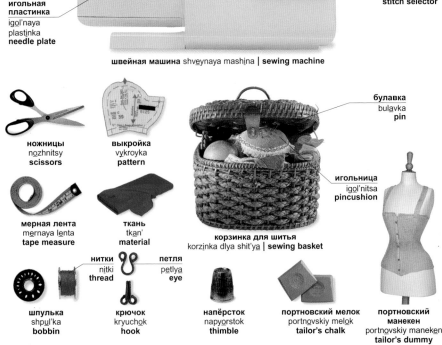

ножницы
nozhnitsy
scissors

выкройка
vykroyka
pattern

булавка
bulavka
pin

мерная лента
mernaya lenta
tape measure

ткань
tkan'
material

игольница
igol'nitsa
pincushion

корзинка для шитья
korzinka dlya shit'ya | **sewing basket**

нитки
nitki
thread

петля
petlya
eye

шпулька
shpul'ka
bobbin

крючок
kryuchok
hook

напёрсток
napyorstok
thimble

портновский мелок
portnovskiy melok
tailor's chalk

портновский манекен
portnovskiy maneken
tailor's dummy

продевать нить (в иглу)
prodevat' nit' (v iglu)
thread (v)

стежок
stezhok
stitch

шить
shit'
sew (v)

штопать
shtopat'
darn (v)

примётывать
primyotyvat'
tack (v)

резать
rezat'
cut (v)

вышивка по канве
vyshivka po kanve
needlepoint

вышивка
vyshivka
embroidery

крючок
kryuchok
crochet hook

вязание крючком
vyazaniye kryuchkom
crochet

макраме
makrame
macramé

пэчворк
pechvork
patchwork

квилтинг
kvilting
quilting

коклюшка
koklyushka
lace bobbin

ткацкий станок
tkatskiy stanok
loom

кружевоплетение
kruzhevopleteniye
lace-making

ткачество
tkachestvo
weaving

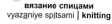

вязальная спица
vyazal'naya spitsa
knitting needle

вязание спицами
vyazaniye spitsami | **knitting**

шерсть
sherst'
wool

моток пряжи
motok pryazhi | **skein**

словарь slovar' • vocabulary

распарывать rasparyvat' **unpick (v)**	**нейлон** neylon **nylon**
ткань tkan' **fabric**	**шёлк** shyolk **silk**
хлопок khlopok **cotton**	**дизайнер** dizayner **designer**
лён lyon **linen**	**мода** moda **fashion**
полиэстер poliester **polyester**	**застёжка-молния** zastyozhka-molniya **zip**

окружающая среда okruzh<u>a</u>yushchaya sred<u>a</u>
environment

космос k_o_smos • **space**

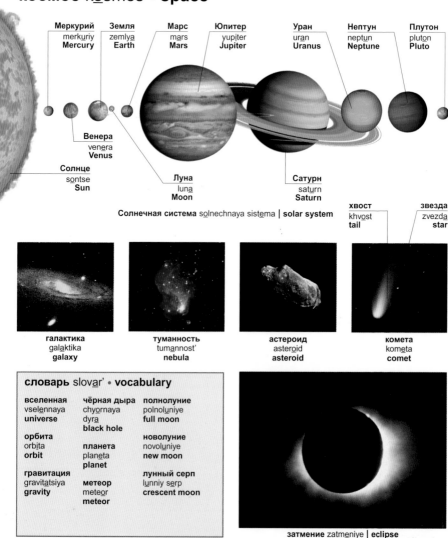

Меркурий
merkuriy
Mercury

Земля
zemlya
Earth

Марс
mars
Mars

Юпитер
yupiter
Jupiter

Уран
ur_a_n
Uranus

Нептун
neptun
Neptune

Плутон
pluton
Pluto

Венера
venera
Venus

Солнце
s_o_ntse
Sun

Луна
luna
Moon

Сатурн
saturn
Saturn

Солнечная система s_o_lnechnaya sist_e_ma | **solar system**

хвост
khv_o_st
tail

звезда
zvezd_a_
star

галактика
gal_a_ktika
galaxy

туманность
tum_a_nnost'
nebula

астероид
aster_o_id
asteroid

комета
kom_e_ta
comet

словарь slov_a_r' • **vocabulary**

вселенная
vsel_e_nnaya
universe

орбита
orb_i_ta
orbit

гравитация
gravit_a_tsiya
gravity

чёрная дыра
ch_yo_rnaya
dyr_a_
black hole

планета
plan_e_ta
planet

метеор
mete_o_r
meteor

полнолуние
polnol_u_niye
full moon

новолуние
novol_u_niye
new moon

лунный серп
l_u_nniy s_e_rp
crescent moon

затмение zatm_e_niye | **eclipse**

исследование космоса issledovaniye kosmosa • space exploration

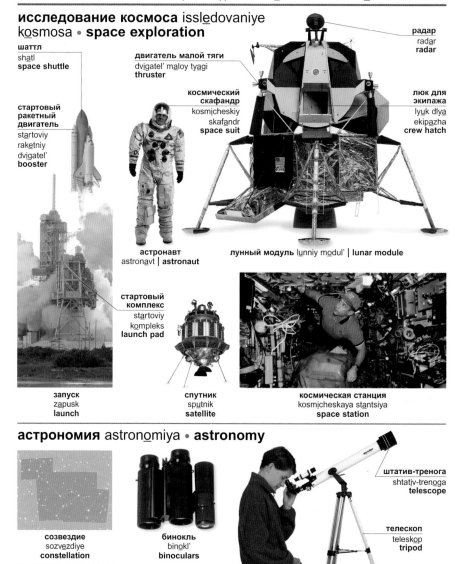

шаттл
shatl
space shuttle

двигатель малой тяги
dvigatel' maloy tyagi
thruster

радар
radar
radar

космический скафандр
kosmicheskiy skafandr
space suit

люк для экипажа
lyuk dlya ekipazha
crew hatch

стартовый ракетный двигатель
startoviy raketniy dvigatel'
booster

астронавт
astronavt | **astronaut**

лунный модуль lunniy modul' | **lunar module**

стартовый комплекс
startoviy kompleks
launch pad

запуск
zapusk
launch

спутник
sputnik
satellite

космическая станция
kosmicheskaya stantsiya
space station

астрономия astronomiya • astronomy

созвездие
sozvezdiye
constellation

бинокль
binokl'
binoculars

штатив-тренога
shtativ-trenoga
telescope

телескоп
teleskop
tripod

Земля zemlya • Earth

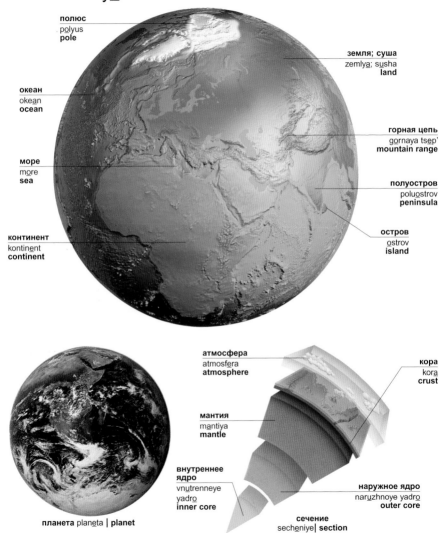

полюс
polyus
pole

земля; суша
zemlya; susha
land

океан
okean
ocean

горная цепь
gornaya tsep'
mountain range

море
more
sea

полуостров
poluostrov
peninsula

остров
ostrov
island

континент
kontinent
continent

атмосфера
atmosfera
atmosphere

кора
kora
crust

мантия
mantiya
mantle

внутреннее
ядро
vnutrenneye
yadro
inner core

наружное ядро
naruzhnoye yadro
outer core

планета planeta | **planet**

сечение
secheniye| **section**

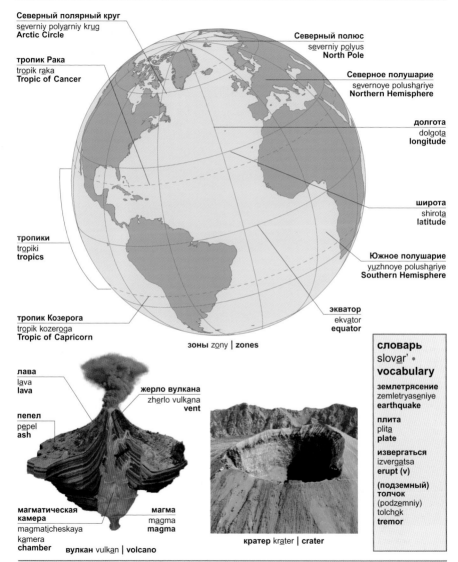

Северный полярный круг
severniy polyarniy krug
Arctic Circle

тропик Рака
tropik raka
Tropic of Cancer

Северный полюс
severniy polyus
North Pole

Северное полушарие
severnoye polushariye
Northern Hemisphere

долгота
dolgota
longitude

широта
shirota
latitude

тропики
tropiki
tropics

Южное полушарие
yuzhnoye polushariye
Southern Hemisphere

тропик Козерога
tropik kozeroga
Tropic of Capricorn

экватор
ekvator
equator

зоны zony | **zones**

лава
lava
lava

жерло вулкана
zherlo vulkana
vent

пепел
pepel
ash

магматическая камера
magmaticheskaya kamera
chamber

магма
magma
magma

вулкан vulkan | **volcano**

кратер krater | **crater**

словарь
slovar' •
vocabulary

землетрясение
zemletryaseniye
earthquake

плита
plita
plate

извергаться
izvergatsa
erupt (v)

(подземный) толчок
(podzemniy) tolchok
tremor

ландшафт landshaft • **landscape**

гора
gora
mountain

склон
sklon
slope

берег
bereg
bank

река
reka
river

речной порог
rechnoy porog
rapids

скалы
skaly
rocks

ледник lednik | **glacier**

долина dolina | **valley**

холм
kholm
hill

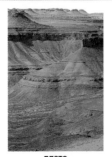

плато
plato
plateau

ущелье
ushchel'ye
gorge

пещера
peshchera
cave

равнина
ravnina | **plain**

пустыня
pustynya | **desert**

(густой) лес
(gustoy) les | **forest**

лес les | **wood**

тропический лес
tropicheskiy les
rainforest

болото
boloto
swamp

луг
lug
meadow

травянистая местность
travyanistaya mesnost'
grassland

водопад
vodopad
waterfall

ручей
ruchey
stream

озеро
ozero
lake

гейзер
geyzer
geyser

побережье
poberezh'ye
coast

утёс
utyos
cliff

коралловый риф
koraloviy rif
coral reef

устье
ust'ye
estuary

погода pogoda • **weather**

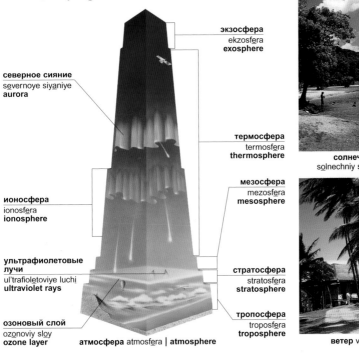

экзосфера
ekzosfera
exosphere

северное сияние
severnoye siyaniye
aurora

термосфера
termosfera
thermosphere

мезосфера
mezosfera
mesosphere

ионосфера
ionosfera
ionosphere

ультрафиолетовые лучи
ul'trafioletoviye luchi
ultraviolet rays

стратосфера
stratosfera
stratosphere

тропосфера
troposfera
troposphere

озоновый слой
ozonoviy sloy
ozone layer

атмосфера atmosfera | **atmosphere**

солнечный свет
solnechniy svet | **sunshine**

ветер veter | **wind**

словарь slovar' • **vocabulary**

дождь со снегом dozhd' so snegom **sleet**	**ливень** liven' **shower**	**жарко** zharko **hot**	**сухо** sukho **dry**	**ветрено** vetreno **windy**	**Мне жарко/холодно.** mne zharko/kholodno **I'm hot/cold.**
град grad **hail**	**солнечно** solnechno **sunny**	**холодно** kholodno **cold**	**дождливо** dozhdlivo **wet**	**буря** burya **gale**	**Идёт дождь.** idyot dozhd' **It's raining.**
гром grom **thunder**	**облачно** oblachno **cloudy**	**тепло** teplo **warm**	**влажно** vlazhno **humid**	**температура** temperatura **temperature**	**Сейчас… градусов.** seychas… gradusov **It's … degrees.**

облако <u>o</u>blako | **cloud**

дождь d<u>o</u>zhd' | **rain**

молния
m<u>o</u>lniya
lightning

гроза gr<u>o</u>za | **storm**

слабый туман
sl<u>a</u>biy tum<u>a</u>n | **mist**

сильный туман
s<u>i</u>l'niy tum<u>a</u>n | **fog**

радуга r<u>a</u>duga | **rainbow**

снег sn<u>e</u>g | **snow**

мороз mor<u>o</u>z | **frost**

лёд l<u>y</u>od | **ice**

сосулька
sos<u>u</u>l'ka
icicle

холод kh<u>o</u>lod | **freeze**

ураган
urag<u>a</u>n | **hurricane**

торнадо
torn<u>a</u>do | **tornado**

муссон
mus<u>o</u>n | **monsoon**

наводнение
navodn<u>e</u>niye | **flood**

горные породы gorniye porody • **rocks**

вулканические
vulkanicheskiye • **igneous**

гранит
granit
granite

обсидиан
obsidian
obsidian

базальт
bazal't
basalt

пемза
pemza
pumice

осадочные osadochniye • **sedimentary**

песчаник
peschanik
sandstone

известняк
izvesnyak
limestone

мел
mel
chalk

кремень
kremen'
flint

конгломерат
konglomerat
conglomerate

уголь
ugol'
coal

метаморфические
metamorficheskiye •
metamorphic

аспидный сланец
aspidniy slanets
slate

кристаллосланец
kristaloslanets
schist

гнейс
gneys
gneiss

мрамор
mramor
marble

драгоценные камни dragotsenniye kamni • **gems**

рубин
rubin
ruby

аметист
ametist
amethyst

алмаз
almaz
diamond

гагат
gagat
jet

опал
opal
opal

лунный камень
lunniy kamen'
moonstone

гранат
granat
garnet

топаз
topaz
topaz

аквамарин
akvamarin
aquamarine

нефрит
nefrit
jade

изумруд
izumrud
emerald

сапфир
sapfir
sapphire

турмалин
turmalin
tourmaline

минералы mineraly • **minerals**

кварц
kvarts
quartz

слюда
slyuda
mica

сера
sera
sulphur

гематит
gematit
hematite

кальцит
kal'tsit
calcite

малахит
malakhit
malachite

бирюза
biryuza
turquoise

оникс
oniks
onyx

агат
agat
agate

графит
grafit
graphite

металлы metally • **metals**

золото
zoloto
gold

серебро
serebro
silver

платина
platina
platinum

никель
nikel'
nickel

железо
zhelezo
iron

медь
med'
copper

олово
olovo
tin

алюминий
alyuminiy
aluminium

ртуть
rtut'
mercury

цинк
tsink
zinc

животные 1 zhiv_o_tniye • animals 1
млекопитающие mlekopit_a_yushchiye • mammals

усы
usy
whiskers

хвост
khv_o_st
tail

кролик
kr_o_lik
rabbit

хомяк
khom_ya_k
hamster

мышь
m_y_sh
mouse

крыса
kr_y_sa
rat

ёж
y_o_zh
hedgehog

белка
b_e_lka
squirrel

летучая мышь
let_u_chaya m_y_sh
bat

енот
yen_o_t
raccoon

лиса
lis_a_
fox

волк
v_o_lk
wolf

щенок
shch_e_nok
puppy

котёнок
koty_o_nok
kitten

детёныш
dety_o_nysh
pup

собака
sob_a_ka
dog

кошка
k_o_shka
cat

выдра
v_y_dra
otter

тюлень
tyul_e_n'
seal

ласт
l_a_st
flipper

дыхало
d_y_khalo
blowhole

морской лев
morsk_o_y l_e_v
sea lion

морж
m_o_rzh
walrus

кит
k_i_t
whale

дельфин
del'f_i_n
dolphin

олений рог
oleniy rog
antler

грива
griva
mane

копыто
kopyto
hoof

горб
gorb
hump

олень
olen'
deer

зебра
zebra
zebra

жираф
zhiraf
giraffe

верблюд
verblyud
camel

хобот
khobot
trunk

бивень
biven'
tusk

рог
rog
horn

бегемот
begemot
hippopotamus

слон
slon
elephant

носорог
nosorog
rhinoceros

тигр
tigr
tiger

грива
griva
mane

лев
lev
lion

обезьяна
obez'yana
monkey

горилла
gorila
gorilla

коала
koala
koala

сумка
sumka
pouch

коготь
kogot'
claw

панда
panda
panda

кенгуру
kenguru
kangaroo

медведь
medved'
bear

полярный медведь
polyarniy medved'
polar bear

животные 2 zhivotniye • animals 2
птицы ptitsy • birds

хвост
khvost
tail

канарейка; кенар
kanareyka; kenar
canary

воробей
vorobey
sparrow

колибри
kolibri
hummingbird

ласточка
lastochka
swallow

ворона
vorona
crow

голубь
golub'
pigeon

дятел
dyatel
woodpecker

сокол
sokol
falcon

сова
sova
owl

чайка
chayka
gull

орёл
oryol
eagle

пеликан
pelikan
pelican

фламинго
flamingo
flamingo

аист
aist
stork

журавль
zhuravl'
crane

пингвин
pingvin
penguin

страус
straus
ostrich

гусь gus' | **goose**

лебедь
lebed'
swan

павлин
pavlin
peacock

фазан
fazan
pheasant

индюк
indyuk
turkey

какаду
kakadu
cockatoo

клюв
klyuv
bill

перо
pero
feather

крыло
krylo
wing

коготь
kogot'
claw

попугай
popugay
parrot

рептилии reptiliy • **reptiles**

чешуя
cheshuya
scales

аллигатор
aligator
alligator

ящерица
yashcheritsa
lizard

игуана
iguana
iguana

панцирь
pantsir'
shell

морская черепаха
morskaya cherepakha
turtle

сухопутная черепаха
sukhoputnaya cherepakha
tortoise

змея
zmeya
snake

морда
morda
snout

крокодил
krokodil
crocodile

животные 3 zhiv<u>o</u>tniye • animals 3
земноводные zemnovodniye • amphibians

лягушка
lyagushka | **frog**

жаба
zh<u>a</u>ba | **toad**

головастик
golov<u>a</u>stik | **tadpole**

саламандра
salam<u>a</u>ndra | **salamander**

рыбы r<u>y</u>by • fish

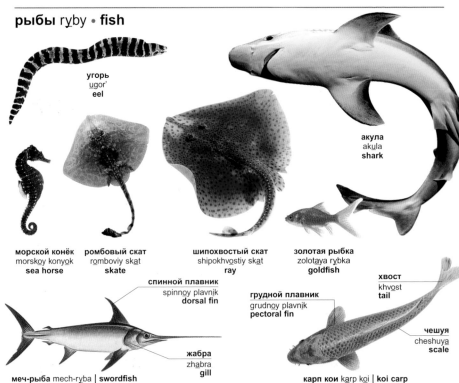

угорь
<u>u</u>gor'
eel

акула
ak<u>u</u>la
shark

морской конёк
morsk<u>o</u>y kony<u>o</u>k
sea horse

ромбовый скат
r<u>o</u>mboviy sk<u>a</u>t
skate

шипохвостый скат
shipokhv<u>o</u>stiy sk<u>a</u>t
ray

золотая рыбка
zolot<u>a</u>ya r<u>y</u>bka
goldfish

спинной плавник
spinn<u>o</u>y plavn<u>i</u>k
dorsal fin

хвост
khv<u>o</u>st
tail

грудной плавник
grudn<u>o</u>y plavn<u>i</u>k
pectoral fin

чешуя
cheshu<u>ya</u>
scale

жабра
zh<u>a</u>bra
gill

меч-рыба mech-r<u>y</u>ba | **swordfish**

карп кои k<u>a</u>rp k<u>o</u>i | **koi carp**

беспозвоночные bespozvon<u>o</u>chniye • invertebrates

муравей
mura<u>ve</u>y
ant

термит
term<u>i</u>t
termite

пчела
pchel<u>a</u>
bee

оса
os<u>a</u>
wasp

жук
zh<u>u</u>k
beetle

усик
<u>u</u>sik
antenna

таракан
tarak<u>a</u>n
cockroach

мотылёк
motyly<u>o</u>k
moth

бабочка
b<u>a</u>bochka
butterfly

кокон
k<u>o</u>kon
cocoon

гусеница
g<u>u</u>senitsa
caterpillar

жало
zh<u>a</u>lo
sting

сверчок
sverch<u>o</u>k | **cricket**

кузнечик
kuzn<u>e</u>chik
grasshopper

богомол
bogom<u>o</u>l
praying mantis

скорпион
skorpi<u>o</u>n
scorpion

сороконожка
sorokon<u>o</u>zhka
centipede

стрекоза
strekoz<u>a</u>
dragonfly

муха
m<u>u</u>kha
fly

комар
kom<u>a</u>r
mosquito

божья коровка
b<u>o</u>zh'ya kor<u>o</u>vka
ladybird

паук
p<u>a</u>uk
spider

слизняк
slizny<u>a</u>k
slug

улитка
ul<u>i</u>tka
snail

червяк chervy<u>a</u>k | **worm**

морская звезда
morsk<u>a</u>ya zvezd<u>a</u>
starfish

мидия
m<u>i</u>diya
mussel

краб
kr<u>a</u>b | **crab**

лобстер
l<u>o</u>bster | **lobster**

осьминог
os'min<u>o</u>g | **octopus**

кальмар
kal'm<u>a</u>r | **squid**

медуза
med<u>u</u>za | **jellyfish**

растения rasteniya • **plants**

дерево derevo • **tree**

ветка
vetka
branch

лист
list
leaf

веточка
vetochka
twig

кора
kora
bark

корень
koren'
root

ствол
stvol
trunk

дуб dub | **oak**

ива
iva
willow

тополь
topol'
poplar

эвкалипт
evkalipt
eucalyptus

лиственница
listvennitsa
larch

бук
buk
beech

берёза
beryoza
birch

сосна
sosna
pine

кедр
kedr
cedar

клён
klyon
maple

вяз
vyaz
elm

липа
lipa
lime

остролист
ostrolist
holly

ягода
yagoda
berry

пальма
pal'ma
palm

цветковое растение tsvetkovoye rasteniye • **flowering plant**

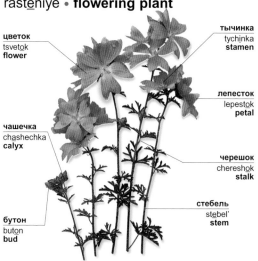

цветок
tsvetok
flower

тычинка
tychinka
stamen

лепесток
lepestok
petal

чашечка
chashechka
calyx

черешок
chereshok
stalk

стебель
stebel'
stem

бутон
buton
bud

лютик
lyutik
buttercup

ромашка
romashka
daisy

чертополох
chertopolokh
thistle

одуванчик
oduvanchik
dandelion

вереск
veresk
heather

мак
mak
poppy

наперстянка
naperstyanka
foxglove

жимолость
zhimolost'
honeysuckle

подсолнух
podsolnukh
sunflower

клевер
klever
clover

колокольчики
kolokol'chiki
bluebells

примула
primula
primrose

люпин
lyupin
lupins

крапива
krapiva
nettle

город gorod • city

улица
ulitsa
street

бордюр тротуара
bordyur trotuara
kerb

угол улицы
ugol ulitsy
street corner

магазин
magazin
shop

перекрёсток
perekryostok
intersection

односто-
роннее
движение
odnostoronneye
dvizheniye
**one-way
system**

тротуар
trotuar
pavement

офисное
здание
ofisnoye
zdaniye
office block

уличный
фонарь
ulichniy
fonar'
streetlight

переулок
pereulok
alley

стоянка
stoyanka
car park

дорожный знак
dorozhniy znak
street sign

оградительный
столбик
ograditel'niy stolbik
bollard

многоквартирный
жилой дом
mnogokvartirniy
zhiloy dom
apartment block

здания zd<u>a</u>niya • **buildings**

ратуша
r<u>a</u>tusha
town hall

библиотека
bibliot<u>e</u>ka
library

кинотеатр
kinote<u>a</u>tr
cinema

театр
te<u>a</u>tr
theatre

университет
universit<u>e</u>t
university

школа
shk<u>o</u>la
school

небоскрёб
neboskry<u>o</u>b
skyscraper

районы ray<u>o</u>ny • **areas**

промышленная зона
promyshlennaya z<u>o</u>na
industrial estate

город
g<u>o</u>rod
city

пригород
pr<u>i</u>gorod
suburb

деревня
der<u>e</u>vnya
village

словарь slov<u>a</u>r' • **vocabulary**

пешеходная зона
peshekh<u>o</u>dnaya z<u>o</u>na
pedestrian zone

проспект
prosp<u>e</u>kt
avenue

боковая улица
bokov<u>a</u>ya <u>u</u>litsa
side street

площадь
pl<u>o</u>shchad'
square

люк
lyuk
manhole

автобусная остановка
avt<u>o</u>busnaya ostan<u>o</u>vka
bus stop

водосточный жёлоб
vodost<u>o</u>chniy zh<u>o</u>lob
gutter

фабрика
f<u>a</u>brika
factory

церковь
ts<u>e</u>rkov'
church

водосток
vodost<u>o</u>k
drain

архитектура arkhitektura • architecture

здания и сооружения zdaniya i sooruzheniya • buildings and structures

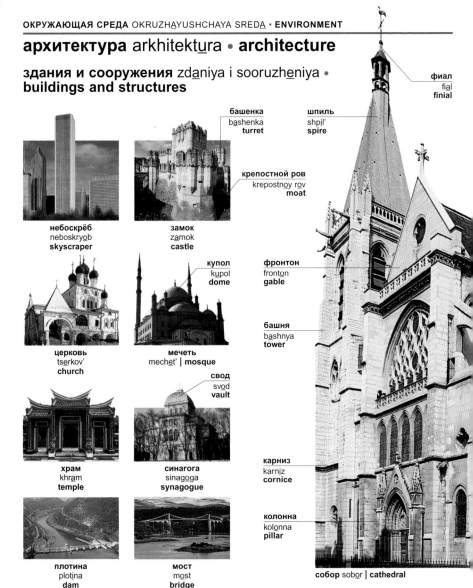

небоскрёб
neboskryob
skyscraper

башенка
bashenka
turret

замок
zamok
castle

крепостной ров
krepostnoy rov
moat

шпиль
shpil'
spire

фиал
fial
finial

купол
kupol
dome

церковь
tserkov'
church

мечеть
mechet' | **mosque**

фронтон
fronton
gable

башня
bashnya
tower

свод
svod
vault

храм
khram
temple

синагога
sinagoga
synagogue

карниз
karniz
cornice

колонна
kolonna
pillar

плотина
plotina
dam

мост
most
bridge

собор sobor | **cathedral**

стили stili • styles

архитрав
arkhitrav
architrave

барокко
barokko
Baroque

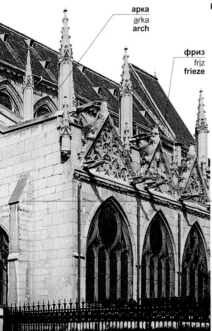

готика gotika | **Gothic**

Возрождение
vozrozhdeniye
Renaissance

арка
arka
arch

фриз
friz
frieze

хор
khor
choir

рококо
rokoko
Rococo

фронтон
fronton
pediment

контрфорс
kontrfors
buttress

неоклассический стиль
neoklasicheskiy stil'
Neoclassical

ар-нуво
ar-nuvo
Art Nouveau

ар-деко
ar-deko
Art Deco

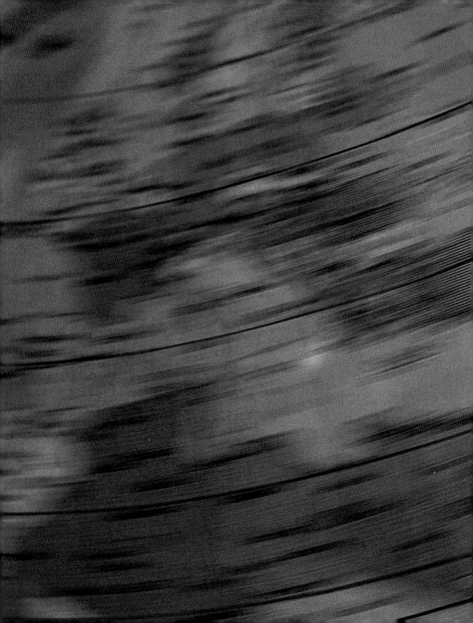

справка sprаvka
reference

время vremya · time

минутная стрелка
minutnaya strelka
minute hand

часовая стрелка
chasovaya strelka
hour hand

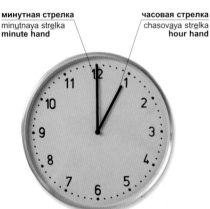

<table>
<tr><td colspan="3">словарь slovar' · vocabulary</td></tr>
</table>

секунда sekunda **second**	сейчас seychas **now**	четверть часа chetvert' chasa **a quarter of an hour**
минута minuta **minute**	позже pozhe **later**	двадцать минут dvatsat' minut **twenty minutes**
час chas **hour**	полчаса polchasa **half an hour**	сорок минут sorok minut **forty minutes**

Который час?
kotoriy chas?
What time is it?

Три часа.
Tri chasa
It's three o'clock.

часы
chasy
clock

пять минут второго
pyat' minut vtorogo
five past one

десять минут второго
desyat' minut vtorogo
ten past one

четверть второго
chetvert' vtorogo
quarter past one

двадцать минут второго
dvatsat' minut vtorogo
twenty past one

секундная
стрелка
sekundnaya
strelka
second hand

двадцать пять минут
второго
dvatsat' pyat' minut vtorogo
twenty five past one

половина второго
polovina vtorogo
one thirty

без двадцати пяти два
bez dvatsati pyati dva
twenty five to two

без двадцати два
bez dvatsati dva
twenty to two

без четверти два
bez chetverti dva
quarter to two

без десяти два
bez desyati dva
ten to two

без пяти два
bez pyati dva
five to two

два часа
dva chasa
two o'clock

день и ночь den' i noch' • **night and day**

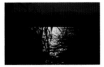
полночь
polnoch' | **midnight**

восход voskhod | **sunrise**

рассвет rassvet | **dawn**

утро utro | **morning**

закат
zakat
sunset

полдень
polden'
midday

сумерки sumerki | **dusk**

вечер vecher | **evening**

день den' | **afternoon**

словарь slovar' • **vocabulary**

рано
rano
early

вовремя
vovremya
on time

поздно
pozno
late

Вы пришли рано.
vy prishll rano
You're early.

Вы опоздали.
vy opozdali
You're late.

Я скоро там буду.
ya skoro tam budu
I'll be there soon.

Пожалуйста, приходите вовремя.
pozhaluysta, prikhodite vovremya
Please be on time.

Увидимся позже.
uvldimsya pozzhe
I'll see you later.

Когда это начинается?
kogda eto nachinayetsya?
What time does it start?

Когда это заканчивается?
kogda eto zakanchivayetsya?
What time does it finish?

Уже поздно.
uzhe pozno
It's getting late.

Сколько это продлится?
skol'ko eto prodlitsya?
How long will it last?

календарь kalend<u>a</u>r' • calendar

месяц
m<u>e</u>syats
month

год
g<u>o</u>d
year

день
d<u>e</u>n'
day

рабочий день
rab<u>o</u>chiy d<u>e</u>n'
workday

неделя
ned<u>e</u>lya
week

дата
d<u>a</u>ta
date

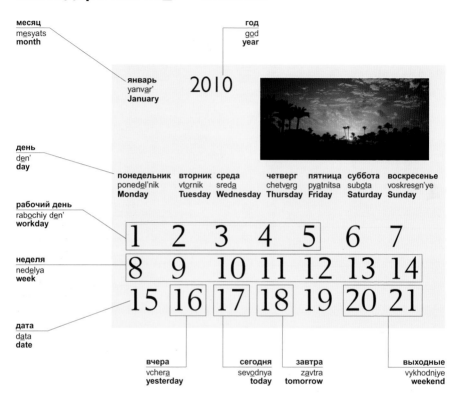

январь
yanv<u>a</u>r'
January

2010

понедельник	вторник	среда	четверг	пятница	суббота	воскресенье
poned<u>e</u>l'nik	vt<u>o</u>rnik	sr<u>e</u>da	chetv<u>e</u>rg	py<u>a</u>tnitsa	sub<u>o</u>ta	voskres<u>e</u>n'ye
Monday	**Tuesday**	**Wednesday**	**Thursday**	**Friday**	**Saturday**	**Sunday**

1	2	3	4	5	6	7
8	9	10	11	12	13	14
15	16	17	18	19	20	21

вчера
vcher<u>a</u>
yesterday

сегодня
sev<u>o</u>dnya
today

завтра
z<u>a</u>vtra
tomorrow

выходные
vykhodn<u>i</u>ye
weekend

словарь slov<u>a</u>r' • vocabulary

январь	**март**	**май**	**июль**	**сентябрь**	**ноябрь**
yanv<u>a</u>r'	m<u>a</u>rt	m<u>a</u>y	iyul'	senty<u>a</u>br'	noy<u>a</u>br'
January	**March**	**May**	**July**	**September**	**November**
февраль	**апрель**	**июнь**	**август**	**октябрь**	**декабрь**
fevr<u>a</u>l'	apr<u>e</u>l'	iyun'	<u>a</u>vgust	okty<u>a</u>br'	dek<u>a</u>br'
February	**April**	**June**	**August**	**October**	**December**

годы g<u>o</u>dy • **years**

1900   тысяча девятисотый t<u>y</u>syacha devyatis<u>o</u>tiy • **nineteen hundred**

1901   тысяча девятьсот первый t<u>y</u>syacha devyat's<u>o</u>t perviy • **nineteen hundred and one**

1910   тысяча девятьсот десятый t<u>y</u>syacha devyat's<u>o</u>t desyatiy • **nineteen ten**

2000   двухтысячный dvukht<u>y</u>syachniy • **two thousand**

2001   две тысячи первый dv<u>e</u> t<u>y</u>syachi p<u>e</u>rviy • **two thousand and one**

времена года vremen<u>a</u> g<u>o</u>da • **seasons**

весна	лето	осень	зима
vesn<u>a</u>	l<u>e</u>to	<u>o</u>sen'	zim<u>a</u>
spring	**summer**	**autumn**	**winter**

словарь slovar' • **vocabulary**

век; столетие
v<u>e</u>k; stol<u>e</u>tiye
century

десятилетие
desyatil<u>e</u>tiye
decade

тысячелетие
tysyachel<u>e</u>tiye
millennium

две недели
dv<u>e</u> ned<u>e</u>li
fortnight

на этой неделе
na <u>e</u>toy ned<u>e</u>le
this week

на прошлой неделе
na pr<u>o</u>shloy ned<u>e</u>le
last week

на следующей неделе
na sl<u>e</u>duyushchey ned<u>e</u>le
next week

позавчера
pozavcher<u>a</u>
the day before yesterday

послезавтра
poslez<u>a</u>vtra
the day after tomorrow

еженедельно
yezhened<u>e</u>l'no
weekly

ежемесячно
yezhem<u>e</u>syachno
monthly

ежегодно
yezheg<u>o</u>dno
annual

Какое сегодня число?
kak<u>o</u>ye sev<u>o</u>dnya chisl<u>o</u>?
What's the date today?

сегодня седьмое февраля, две тысячи семнадцатого года.
segodnya sed'm<u>o</u>ye fevraly<u>a</u>, dv<u>e</u> t<u>y</u>syachi semn<u>a</u>tsatogo g<u>o</u>da
It's February seventh, two thousand and seventeen.

цифры и числа tsifry i chisla • numbers

0	ноль nol' • **zero**	20	двадцать dvatsat' • **twenty**
1	один odin • **one**	21	двадцать один dvatsat' odin • **twenty-one**
2	два dva • **two**	22	двадцать два dvatsat' dva • **twenty-two**
3	три tri • **three**	30	тридцать tritsat' • **thirty**
4	четыре chetyre • **four**	40	сорок sorok • **forty**
5	пять pyat' • **five**	50	пятьдесят pyat'desyat • **fifty**
6	шесть shest' • **six**	60	шестьдесят shest'desyat • **sixty**
7	семь sem' • **seven**	70	семьдесят sem'desyat • **seventy**
8	восемь vosem' • **eight**	80	восемьдесят vosem'desyat • **eighty**
9	девять devyat' • **nine**	90	девяносто devyanosto • **ninety**
10	десять desyat' • **ten**	100	сто sto • **one hundred**
11	одиннадцать odinatsat' • **eleven**	110	сто десять sto desyat' • **one hundred and ten**
12	двенадцать dvenatsat' • **twelve**	200	двести dvesti • **two hundred**
13	тринадцать trinatsat' • **thirteen**	300	триста trista • **three hundred**
14	четырнадцать chetyrnatsat' • **fourteen**	400	четыреста chetyresta • **four hundred**
15	пятнадцать pyatnatsat' • **fifteen**	500	пятьсот pyat'sot • **five hundred**
16	шестнадцать shesnatsat' • **sixteen**	600	шестьсот shest'sot • **six hundred**
17	семнадцать semnatsat' • **seventeen**	700	семьсот sem'sot • **seven hundred**
18	восемнадцать vosemnatsat' • **eighteen**	800	восемьсот vosem'sot • **eight hundred**
19	девятнадцать devyatnatsat' • **nineteen**	900	девятьсот devyat'sot • **nine hundred**

1,000 **(одна) тысяча** (odna) tysyacha • **one thousand**

10,000 **десять тысяч** desyat' tysyach • **ten thousand**

20,000 **двадцать тысяч** dvatsat' tysyach • **twenty thousand**

50,000 **пятьдесят тысяч** pyat'desyat tysyach • **fifty thousand**

55,500 **пятьдесят пять тысяч пятьсот** pyat'desyat pyat' tysyach pyat'sot • **fifty-five thousand five hundred**

100,000 **сто тысяч** sto tysyach • **one hundred thousand**

1,000,000 **(один) миллион** (odin) milion • **one million**

1,000,000,000 **(один) миллиард** (odin) miliard • **one billion**

первый perviy • **first**

второй vtoroy • **second**

третий tretiy • **third**

четвёртый chetvyortiy • **fourth**

пятый pyatiy • **fifth**

шестой shestoy • **sixth**

седьмой sed'moy • **seventh**

восьмой vos'moy • **eighth**

девятый devyatiy • **ninth**

десятый desyatiy • **tenth**

одиннадцатый odinatsatiy • **eleventh**

двенадцатый dvenatsatiy • **twelfth**

тринадцатый trinatsatiy • **thirteenth**

четырнадцатый chetyrnatsatiy • **fourteenth**

пятнадцатый pyatnatsatiy • **fifteenth**

шестнадцатый shestnatsatiy • **sixteenth**

семнадцатый semnatsatiy • **seventeenth**

восемнадцатый vosemnatsatiy • **eighteenth**

девятнадцатый devyatnatsatiy • **nineteenth**

двадцатый dvatsatiy • **twentieth**

двадцать первый dvatsat' perviy • **twenty-first**

двадцать второй dvatsat' vtoroy • **twenty-second**

двадцать третий dvatsat' tretiy • **twenty-third**

тридцатый tritsatiy • **thirtieth**

сороковой sorokovoy • **fortieth**

пятидесятый pyatidesyatiy • **fiftieth**

шестидесятый shestidesyatiy • **sixtieth**

семидесятый semidesyatiy • **seventieth**

восьмидесятый vos'midesyatiy • **eightieth**

девяностый devyanostiy • **ninetieth**

сотый sotiy • **(one) hundredth**

меры и веса m<u>e</u>ry i ves<u>a</u> • **weights and measures**

площадь
plo<u>shch</u>ad' • **area**

квадратный фут	квадратный метр
kvadr<u>a</u>tniy fut	kvadr<u>a</u>tniy m<u>e</u>tr
square foot	**square metre**

расстояние
rasstoy<u>a</u>niye • **distance**

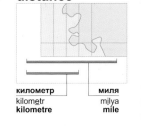

километр	миля
kilom<u>e</u>tr	m<u>i</u>lya
kilometre	**mile**

чаша весов
ch<u>a</u>sha ves<u>o</u>v
pan

фунт
f<u>u</u>nt
pound

унция
<u>u</u>ntsiya
ounce

килограмм
kilog<u>ra</u>m
kilogram

грамм
gram
gram

весы vesy | **scales**

словарь slov<u>a</u>r' • **vocabulary**

ярд	тонна	измерять
yard	t<u>o</u>nna	izmery<u>a</u>t'
yard	**tonne**	**measure (v)**
метр	миллиграмм	взвешивать
m<u>e</u>tr	milig<u>ra</u>m	vzv<u>e</u>shivat'
metre	**milligram**	**weigh (v)**

длина dlin<u>a</u> • **length**

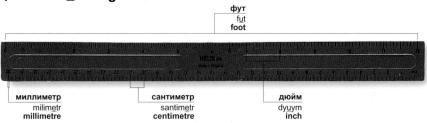

фут
f<u>u</u>t
foot

миллиметр	сантиметр	дюйм
milim<u>e</u>tr	santim<u>e</u>tr	dy<u>uy</u>m
millimetre	**centimetre**	**inch**

объём ob-y<u>o</u>m • capacity

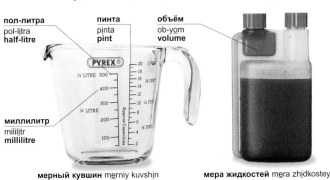

пол-литра
pol-litra
half-litre

пинта
p<u>i</u>nta
pint

объём
ob-y<u>o</u>m
volume

миллилитр
mil<u>i</u>litr
millilitre

мерный кувшин m<u>e</u>rniy kuvsh<u>i</u>n
measuring jug

мера жидкостей m<u>e</u>ra zhidkostey
liquid measure

словарь slov<u>a</u>r' • vocabulary

галлон
gal<u>o</u>n
gallon

кварта
kv<u>a</u>rta
quart

литр
l<u>i</u>tr
litre

контейнер kont<u>e</u>yner • container

картонная упаковка
kartonnaya upak<u>o</u>vka
carton

пакет
pak<u>e</u>t
packet

бутылка
but<u>y</u>lka
bottle

мешок
mesh<u>o</u>k
bag

контейнер
kont<u>e</u>yner | **tub**

банка b<u>a</u>nka | **jar**

консервная банка
kons<u>e</u>rvnaya b<u>a</u>nka
can

консервная банка
kons<u>e</u>rvnaya b<u>a</u>nka | **tin**

распылитель
raspyl<u>i</u>tel' | **liquid dispenser**

кусок
kus<u>o</u>k
bar

тюбик
ty<u>u</u>bik
tube

рулон
rul<u>o</u>n
roll

пачка
p<u>a</u>chka
pack

аэрозольный баллончик
aerozol'niy bal<u>o</u>nchik
spray can

карта мира karta mira · **world map**

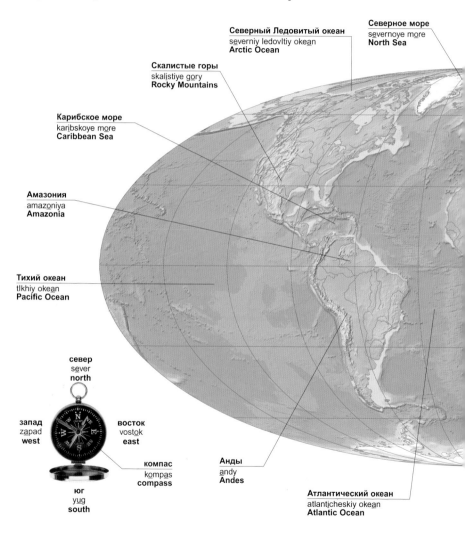

Северное море
severnoye more
North Sea

Северный Ледовитый океан
severniy ledovltiy okean
Arctic Ocean

Скалистые горы
skalistiye gory
Rocky Mountains

Карибское море
karibskoye more
Caribbean Sea

Амазония
amazoniya
Amazonia

Тихий океан
tlkhiy okean
Pacific Ocean

север
sever
north

запад
zapad
west

восток
vostok
east

компас
kompas
compass

Анды
andy
Andes

Атлантический океан
atlanticheskiy okean
Atlantic Ocean

юг
yug
south

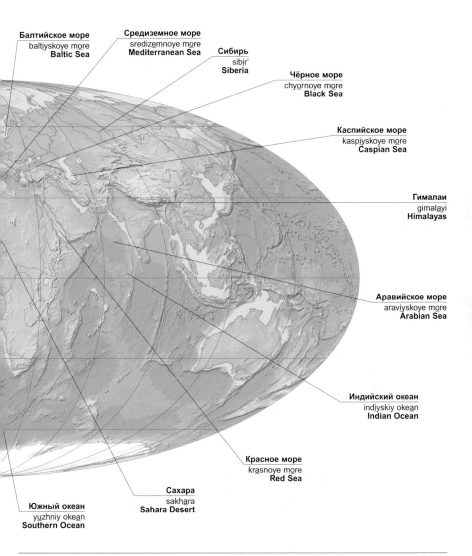

Балтийское море
baltiyskoye more
Baltic Sea

Средиземное море
sredizemnoye more
Mediterranean Sea

Сибирь
sibir'
Siberia

Чёрное море
chyornoye more
Black Sea

Каспийское море
kaspiyskoye more
Caspian Sea

Гималаи
gimalayi
Himalayas

Аравийское море
araviyskoye more
Arabian Sea

Индийский океан
indiyskiy okean
Indian Ocean

Красное море
krasnoye more
Red Sea

Сахара
sakhara
Sahara Desert

Южный океан
yuzhniy okean
Southern Ocean

Северная и Центральная Америка severnaya i tsentral'naya amerika · **North and Central America**

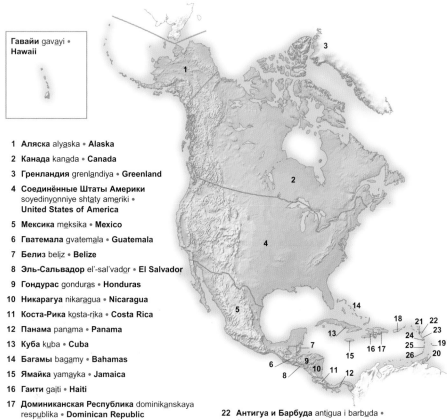

Гавайи gavayi ·
Hawaii

1 Аляска alyaska · **Alaska**

2 Канада kanada · **Canada**

3 Гренландия grenlandiya · **Greenland**

4 **Соединённые Штаты Америки**
soyedinyonniye shtaty ameriki ·
United States of America

5 Мексика meksika · **Mexico**

6 Гватемала gvatemala · **Guatemala**

7 Белиз beliz · **Belize**

8 Эль-Сальвадор el'-sal'vador · **El Salvador**

9 Гондурас gonduras · **Honduras**

10 Никарагуа nikaragua · **Nicaragua**

11 Коста-Рика kosta-rika · **Costa Rica**

12 Панама panama · **Panama**

13 Куба kuba · **Cuba**

14 Багамы bagamy · **Bahamas**

15 Ямайка yamayka · **Jamaica**

16 Гаити gaiti · **Haiti**

17 **Доминиканская Республика** dominikanskaya
respublika · **Dominican Republic**

18 Пуэрто-Рико puerto-riko · **Puerto Rico**

19 Барбадос barbados · **Barbados**

20 **Тринидад и Тобаго** trinidad i tobago ·
Trinidad and Tobago

21 **Сент-Китс и Невис** sent-kits i nevis ·
St Kitts and Nevis

22 **Антигуа и Барбуда** antigua i barbuda ·
Antigua and Barbuda

23 Доминикана dominikana · **Dominica**

24 Сент-Люсия sent-lyusiya · **St Lucia**

25 **Сент-Винсент и Гренадины** sent-vinsent i
grenadiny · **St Vincent and The Grenadines**

26 Гренада grenada · **Grenada**

Южная Америка yuzhnaya amerika • South America

1 Венесуэла venesuela • **Venezuela**

2 Колумбия kolumbiya • **Colombia**

3 Эквадор ekvador • **Ecuador**

4 Перу peru • **Peru**

5 Галапагосские острова
galapagosskiye ostrova •
Galápagos Islands

6 Гайана gayana • **Guyana**

7 Суринам surinam • **Suriname**

8 Французская Гвиана
frantsuzskaya gviana •
French Guiana

9 Бразилия braziliya • **Brazil**

10 Боливия boliviya • **Bolivia**

11 Чили chili • **Chile**

12 Аргентина argentina • **Argentina**

13 Парагвай paragvay • **Paraguay**

14 Уругвай urugvay • **Uruguay**

15 Фолклендские острова
folklendskiye ostrova • **Falkland Islands**

словарь slovar' • vocabulary

страна strana **country**	провинция provintsiya **province**	зона zona **zone**
нация natsiya **nation**	территория teritoriya **territory**	район rayon **district**
континент continent **continent**	колония koloniya **colony**	регион region **region**
государство gosudarstvo **state**	княжество knyazhestvo **principality**	столица stolitsa **capital**

Европа yevropa · Europe

1 **Ирландия** irlandiya · **Ireland**

2 **Великобритания** velikobritaniya · **United Kingdom**

3 **Португалия** portugaliya · **Portugal**

4 **Испания** ispaniya · **Spain**

5 **Балеарские острова** balearskiye ostrova · **Balearic Islands**

6 **Андорра** andorra · **Andorra**

7 **Франция** frantsiya · **France**

8 **Бельгия** bel'giya · **Belgium**

9 **Нидерланды** niderlandy · **Netherlands**

10 **Люксембург** lyuksemburg · **Luxembourg**

11 **Германия** germaniya · **Germany**

12 **Дания** daniya · **Denmark**

13 **Норвегия** norvegiya · **Norway**

14 **Швеция** shvetsiya · **Sweden**

15 **Финляндия** finlyandiya · **Finland**

16 **Эстония** estoniya · **Estonia**

17 **Латвия** latviya · **Latvia**

18 **Литва** litva · **Lithuania**

19 **Калининград** kaliningrad · **Kaliningrad**

20 **Польша** pol'sha · **Poland**

21 **Чехия** chekhiya · **Czech Republic**

22 **Австрия** avstriya · **Austria**

23 **Лихтенштейн** likhtenshteyn · **Liechtenstein**

24 **Швейцария** shveytsariya · **Switzerland**

25 **Италия** italiya · **Italy**

26 **Монако** monako · **Monaco**

27 **Корсика** korsika · **Corsica**

28 **Сардиния** sardiniya · **Sardinia**

29 **Сан-Марино** san-marino · **San Marino**

30 **Ватикан** vatikan · **Vatican City**

31 **Сицилия** sitsiliya · **Sicily**

32 **Мальта** mal'ta · **Malta**

33 **Словения** sloveniya · **Slovenia**

34 **Хорватия** khorvatiya · **Croatia**

35 **Венгрия** vengriya · **Hungary**

36 **Словакия** slovakiya · **Slovakia**

37 **Украина** ukraina · **Ukraine**

38 **Беларусь** belarus' · **Belarus**

39 **Молдова** moldova · **Moldova**

40 **Румыния** rumyniya · **Romania**

41 **Сербия** serbiya · **Serbia**

42 **Босния и Герцеговина** bosniya i gertsegovina · **Bosnia and Herzegovina**

43 **Албания** albaniya · **Albania**

44 **Македония** makedoniya · **Macedonia**

45 **Болгария** bolgariya · **Bulgaria**

46 **Греция** gretsiya · **Greece**

47 **Косово** kosovo · **Kosovo**

48 **Черногория** chernogoriya · **Montenegro**

49 **Исландия** islandiya · **Iceland**

Африка afrika · **Africa**

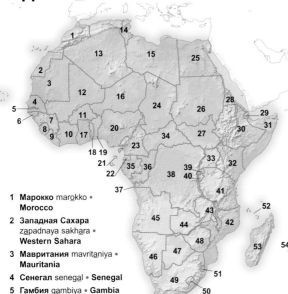

32 **Кения** keniya · **Kenya**

33 **Уганда** uganda · **Uganda**

34 **Центральноафриканская Республика** tsentral'noafrikanskaya respublika · **Central African Republic**

35 **Габон** gabon · **Gabon**

36 **Конго** kongo · **Congo**

37 **Кабинда** kabinda · **Cabinda**

38 **Демократическая Республика Конго** demokraticheskaya respublika kongo · **Democratic Republic of the Congo**

39 **Руанда** ruanda · **Rwanda**

40 **Бурунди** burundi · **Burundi**

41 **Танзания** tanzaniya · **Tanzania**

42 **Мозамбик** mozambik · **Mozambique**

43 **Малави** malavi · **Malawi**

44 **Замбия** zambiya · **Zambia**

45 **Ангола** angola · **Angola**

46 **Намибия** namibiya · **Namibia**

47 **Ботсвана** botsvana · **Botswana**

48 **Зимбабве** zimbabve · **Zimbabwe**

49 **Южная Африка** yuzhnaya afrika · **South Africa**

50 **Лесото** lesoto · **Lesotho**

51 **Свазиленд** svazilend · **Swaziland**

52 **Коморы** komory · **Comoros**

53 **Мадагаскар** madagaskar · **Madagascar**

54 **Маврикий** mavrikiy · **Mauritius**

1 **Марокко** marokko · **Morocco**

2 **Западная Сахара** zapadnaya sakhara · **Western Sahara**

3 **Мавритания** mavritaniya · **Mauritania**

4 **Сенегал** senegal · **Senegal**

5 **Гамбия** gambiya · **Gambia**

6 **Гвинея-Бисау** gvineya-bisau · **Guinea-Bissau**

7 **Гвинея** gvineya · **Guinea**

8 **Сьерра-Леоне** s'yerra-leone · **Sierra Leone**

9 **Либерия** liberiya · **Liberia**

10 **Берег Слоновой Кости** bereg slonovoy kosti · **Ivory Coast**

11 **Буркина-Фасо** burkina faso · **Burkina Faso**

12 **Мали** mali · **Mali**

13 **Алжир** alzhir · **Algeria**

14 **Тунис** tunis · **Tunisia**

15 **Ливия** liviya · **Libya**

16 **Нигер** niger · **Niger**

17 **Гана** gana · **Ghana**

18 **Того** togo · **Togo**

19 **Бенин** benin · **Benin**

20 **Нигерия** nigeriya · **Nigeria**

21 **Сан-Томе и Принсипи** san-tome i prinsipi · **São Tomé and Principe**

22 **Экваториальная Гвинея** ekvatorial'naya gvineya · **Equatorial Guinea**

23 **Камерун** kamerun · **Cameroon**

24 **Чад** chad · **Chad**

25 **Египет** yegipet · **Egypt**

26 **Судан** sudan · **Sudan**

27 **Южный Судан** yuzhniy sudan · **South Sudan**

28 **Эритрея** eritreya · **Eritrea**

29 **Джибути** dzhibuti · **Djibouti**

30 **Эфиопия** efiopiya · **Ethiopia**

31 **Сомали** somali · **Somalia**

Азия aziya · Asia

1 Турция turtsiya · **Turkey**

2 Кипр kipr · **Cyprus**

3 Российская Федерация rosiyskaya federatsiya · **Russian Federation**

4 Грузия gruziya · **Georgia**

5 Армения armeniya · **Armenia**

6 Азербайджан azerbaydzhan · **Azerbaijan**

7 Иран iran · **Iran**

8 Ирак irak · **Iraq**

9 Сирия siriya · **Syria**

10 Ливан livan · **Lebanon**

11 Израиль izrail' · **Israel**

12 Иордания iordaniya · **Jordan**

13 Саудовская Аравия saudovskaya araviya · **Saudi Arabia**

14 Кувейт kuveyt · **Kuwait**

15 Бахрейн bakhreyn · **Bahrain**

16 Катар katar · **Qatar**

17 Объединённые Арабские Эмираты ob-yedinyonniye arabskiye emiraty · **United Arab Emirates**

18 Оман oman · **Oman**

19 Йемен yemen · **Yemen**

20 Казахстан kazakhstan · **Kazakhstan**

21 Узбекистан uzbekistan · **Uzbekistan**

22 Туркменистан turkmenistan · **Turkmenistan**

23 Афганистан afganistan · **Afghanistan**

24 Таджикистан tadzhikistan · **Tajikistan**

25 Кыргызстан kyrgyzstan · **Kyrgyzstan**

26 Пакистан pakistan · **Pakistan**

27 Индия indiya · **India**

28 Мальдивы mal'divy · **Maldives**

29 Шри-Ланка shri-lanka · **Sri Lanka**

30 Китай kitay · **China**

31 Монголия mongoliya · **Mongolia**

32 Северная Корея severnaya koreya · **North Korea**

33 Южная Корея yuzhnaya koreya · **South Korea**

34 Япония yaponiya · **Japan**

35 Непал nepal · **Nepal**

36 Бутан butan · **Bhutan**

37 Бангладеш bangladesh · **Bangladesh**

38 Мьянма (Бирма) m'yanma (birma) · **Myanmar (Burma)**

39 Таиланд tailand · **Thailand**

40 Лаос laos · **Laos**

41 Вьетнам v'yetnam · **Vietnam**

42 Камбоджа kambodzha · **Cambodia**

43 Малайзия malayziya · **Malaysia**

44 Сингапур singapur · **Singapore**

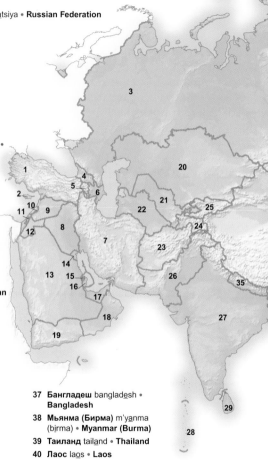

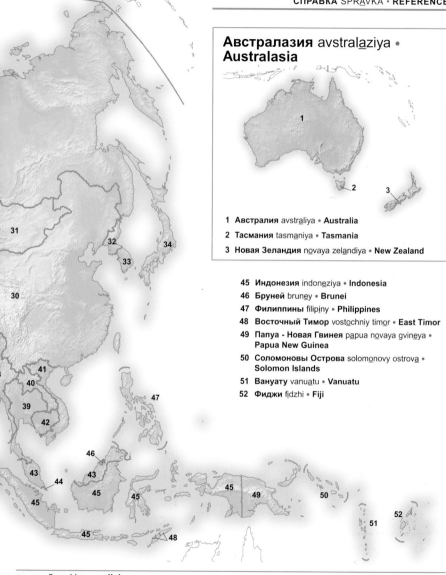

Австралазия avstralaziya • Australasia

1 **Австралия** avstral<u>a</u>liya • **Australia**

2 **Тасмания** tasm<u>a</u>niya • **Tasmania**

3 **Новая Зеландия** n<u>o</u>vaya zel<u>a</u>ndiya • **New Zealand**

45 **Индонезия** indon<u>e</u>ziya • **Indonesia**

46 **Бруней** brun<u>e</u>y • **Brunei**

47 **Филиппины** filip<u>i</u>ny • **Philippines**

48 **Восточный Тимор** vost<u>o</u>chniy tim<u>o</u>r • **East Timor**

49 **Папуа - Новая Гвинея** p<u>a</u>pua n<u>o</u>vaya gvin<u>e</u>ya • **Papua New Guinea**

50 **Соломоновы Острова** solom<u>o</u>novy ostrov<u>a</u> • **Solomon Islands**

51 **Вануату** vanu<u>a</u>tu • **Vanuatu**

52 **Фиджи** f<u>i</u>dzhi • **Fiji**

предлоги и антонимы predlogi i antonimy · particles and antonyms

к k to	**от** ot from	**для** dlya for	**на** na towards
над nad over	**под** pod under	**вдоль** vdol' along	**поперёк, через** poperyok, cherez across
впереди, перед vperedi, pered in front of	**позади, сзади** pozadi, zzadi behind	**с** s with	**без** bez without
на (поверхность) na (poverkhnost') onto	**в** v; vnutr' into	**перед** pered before	**после** posle after
в v in	**из** iz out	**к** k by	**до** do until
над, (с)выше nad, (s)vyshe above	**под** pod below	**рано** rano early	**поздно** pozdno late
внутри vnutri inside	**снаружи** snaruzhi outside	**сейчас** seychas now	**позже** pozhe later
вверх vverkh up	**вниз** vniz down	**всегда** vsegda always	**никогда** nikogda never
у, около u, okolo at	**за** za beyond	**часто** chasto often	**редко** redko rarely
сквозь, через skvoz', cherez through	**вокруг** vokrug around	**вчера** vchera yesterday	**завтра** zavtra tomorrow
наверху naverkhu on top of	**рядом с** ryadom s beside	**сначала** snachala first	**в последнюю очередь** v poslednyuyu ochered' last
между mezhdu between	**напротив** naprotiv opposite	**каждый** kazhdiy every	**некоторый, несколько** nekotoriy, neskolki some
близко blizko near	**далеко** daleko far	**около** okolo about	**точно** tochno exactly
здесь zdes' here	**там** tam there	**немного** nemnogo a little	**много** mnogo a lot

большой
bol'shoy
large

маленький
malen'kiy
small

широкий
shirokiy
wide

узкий
uzkiy
narrow

высокийа
vysokiy
tall

короткий
korotkiy
short

высокий
vysokiy
high

низкий
nizkiy
low

густой
gustoy
thick

тонкий
tonkiy
thin

лёгкий
lyohkiy
light

тяжёлый
tyazholiy
heavy

твёрдый
tvyordiy
hard

мягкий
myahkiy
soft

мокрый
mokriy
wet

сухой
sukhoy
dry

хороший
khoroshiy
good

плохой
plokhoy
bad

быстрый
bystriy
fast

медленный
medlenniy
slow

правильный
pravil'niy
correct

неправильный
nepravil'niy
wrong

чистый
chistiy
clean

грязный
gryazniy
dirty

красивый
krasiviy
beautiful

уродливый
urodliviy
ugly

дорогой
dorogoy
expensive

дешёвый
deshyoviy
cheap

тихий
tikhiy
quiet

шумный
shumniy
noisy

горячий
goryachiy
hot

холодный
kholodniy
cold

открытый
otkrytiy
open

закрытый
zakrytiy
closed

полный
polniy
full

пустой
pustoy
empty

новый
noviy
new

старый
stariy
old

светлый
svetliy
light

тёмный
tyomniy
dark

простой
prostoy
easy

сложный
slozhniy
difficult

свободный
svobodniy
free

занятый
zanyatiy
occupied

сильный
sil'niy
strong

слабый
slabiy
weak

толстый
tolstiy
fat

худой
khudoy
thin

молодой
molodoy
young

старый
stariy
old

лучше
luchshe
better

хуже
khuzhe
worse

чёрный
chyorniy
black

белый
beliy
white

интересный
interesniy
interesting

скучный
skuchniy
boring

больной
bol'noy
sick

здоровый
zdoroviy
well

начало
nachalo
beginning

конец
konets
end

полезные фразы polezniye frazy • useful phrases

необходимые фразы
neobkhodimiye frazy •
essential phrases

Да
da
Yes

Нет
net
No

Возможно
vozmozhno
Maybe

Пожалуйста
pozhaluysta
Please

Спасибо
spasibo
Thank you

Пожалуйста
pozhaluysta
You're welcome

Простите
prostite
Excuse me

Извините
izvinite
I'm sorry

Не надо
ne nado
Don't

ОК, хорошо
okey, khorosho
OK

Хорошо
khorosho
That's fine

(Это) верно/правильно
(eto) verno/pravil'no
That's correct

Вы ошибаетесь/Это не так
vy oshibayetes'/eto ne tak
That's wrong

приветствия
privetstviya • **greetings**

Здравствуйте
zdrastvuyte
Hello

До свидания
do svidaniya
Goodbye

Доброе утро
dobroye utro
Good morning

Добрый день
dobriy den'
Good afternoon

Добрый вечер
dobriy vecher
Good evening

Спокойной ночи
spokoynoy nochi
Good night

Как дела?
zdrastvuyte/kak dela?
How are you?

Меня зовут...
menya zovut...
My name is ...

Как Вас/тебя зовут?
kak vas/tebya zovut?
What is your name?

Как его/её зовут?
kak yego/yeyo zovut?
What is his/her name?

Можно представить...
mozhno predstavit'...
May I introduce ...

Это...
eto...
This is ...

Приятно познакомиться
priyatno poznakomit'sya
Pleased to meet you

Увидимся
uvidimsya
See you later

объявления
ob-yavleniya • **signs**

Туристическое бюро
turisticheskoye byuro
Tourist information

Вход
vkhod
Entrance

Выход
vykhod
Exit

Запасной/аварийный выход
zapasnoy/avariyniy vykhod
Emergency exit

От себя
ot sebya
Push

Опасность
opasnost'
Danger

Курение запрещено
kureniye zapretscheno
No smoking

Не работает
ne rabotayet
Out of order

Часы работы
chasy raboty
Opening times

Вход бесплатный
vkhod besplatniy
Free admission

Сниженная цена
snizhennaya tsena
Reduced

Распродажа
rasprodazha
Sale

Стучите (перед тем, как войти)
stuchite (pered tem, kak voyti)
Knock before entering

По газонам не ходить
po gazonam ne khodit'
Keep off the grass

помощь pomoshch'
help

Не могли бы Вы мне помочь?
ne mogli by vy mne pomoch'?
Can you help me?

(Я) не понимаю
(ya) ne ponimayu
I don't understand

(Я) не знаю
(ya) ne znayu
I don't know

Вы говорите по-английски?
vy govorite po-angliyski?
Do you speak English?

Я говорю по-английски
ya govoryu po-angliyski
I speak English

Пожалуйста, говорите помедленней
pozhaluysta, govorite pomedlenney
Please speak more slowly

Пожалуйста, запишите мне это
pozhaluysta, zapishite mne eto
Please write it down for me

Я потерял...
ya poteryal...
I have lost ...

направление
napravleniya ·
directions

Я заблудился
ya zabludilsya
I am lost

Где (находится)…?
gde (nakhoditsya)…?
Where is the …?

Где ближайший…?
gde blizhayshiy…?
Where is the nearest …?

Где (находятся) туалеты?
gde (nakhodyatsya) tualety?
Where are the toilets?

Как добраться до…?
kak dobrat'sya do…?
How do I get to …?

Направо
napravo
To the right

Налево
nalevo
To the left

Прямо
pryamo
Straight ahead

Как далеко (находится)…?
kak daleko (nakhoditsya)…?
How far is …?

дорожные знаки и указатели
dorozhniye znaki i ukazateli · **road signs**

Все направления
vse napravleniya
All directions

Внимание
vnimaniye
Caution

Въезд запрещён
v-yezd zapreshchyon
No entry

Снизь(те) скорость
sniz'(te) skorost'
Slow down

Объезд
ob-yezd
Diversion

Держитесь правой стороны
derzhites' pravoy storony
Keep to the right

Скоростная дорога
skorostnaya doroga
Motorway

Парковка запрещена
parkovka zapreshchena
No parking

Дорога идёт в тупик
doroga idyot v tupik
No through road

Дорога с односторонним движением
doroga s odnostoronnim dvizheniyem
One-way street

Только для жителей
tol'ko dlya zhiteley
Residents only

Уступи дорогу
ustupi dorogu
Give way

Дорожные работы
dorozhniye raboty
Roadworks

Опасный поворот
opasniy povorot
Dangerous bend

проживание
prozhivaniye ·
accommodation

У меня заказан номер
u menya zakazan nomer
I have a reservation

Где столовая?
gde stolovaya?
Where is the dining room?

В какое время/когда завтрак?
v kakoye vremya/kogda zavtrak?
What time is breakfast?

Я вернусь в … часов
ya vernus' v … chasov
I'll be back at … o'clock

Я уезжаю завтра
ya uyezhayu zavtra
I'm leaving tomorrow

приём пищи
priyom pishchi ·
eating and drinking

Ваше/ твоё здоровье!
vashe/ tvoyo zdorov'ye!
Cheers!

Это очень вкусно/не очень вкусно
eto ochen vkusno/ne ochen vkusno
It's delicious/awful

Я не курю/пью
ya ne kuryu/p'yu.
I don't drink/smoke

Я не ем мясо
ya ne yem myaso
I don't eat meat

Спасибо, для меня этого достаточно
spasibo, dlya menya etogo dostatochno
No more for me, thank you

Можно мне ещё немного?
mozhno mne yeshchyo nemnogo?
May I have some more?

Можно счёт?
mozhno schyot?
May we have the bill?

Можно чек?
mozhno chek?
Can I have a receipt?

Место для курения
mesto dlya kureniya
Smoking area

здоровье
zdorov'ye · **health**

Мне нехорошо
mne nekhorosho
I don't feel well

Меня тошнит
menya toshnit
I feel sick

Здесь больно/болит
zdes' bol'no/bolit
It hurts here

У меня температура
u menya temperatura
I have a temperature

Я на … месяце беременности
ya na … mesyatse beremennosti
I'm … months pregnant

Мне нужен рецепт на…
mne nuzhen retsept na…
I need a prescription for …

Обычно я принимаю…
obychno ya prinimayu…
I normally take …

У меня аллергия на…
u menya alergiya na…
I'm allergic to …

Он/она будет в порядке?
on/ona budet v poryadke?
Will he/she be alright?

русский указатель ruskiy ukazatel' • **Russian index**

ruskiy

ruskiy

ruskiy

ruskiy

ruskiy

ruskiy

ruskiy

ruskiy

ruskiy

английский указатель angliyskiy ukazatel' • English index

english

english

english

english

english

english

english

english

english

english

english

благода́рности blagodárnosti • acknowledgments

DORLING KINDERSLEY would like to thank Christine Lacey for design assistance, Georgina Garner for editorial and administrative help, Kopal Agarwal, Polly Boyd, Sonia Gavira, Cathy Meeus, Antara Raghavan, and Priyanka Sharma for editorial help, Claire Bowers for compiling the DK picture credits, Nishwan Rasool for picture research, and Suruchi Bhatia, Miguel Cunha, Mohit Sharma, and Alex Valizadeh for app development and creation.

The publisher would like to thank the following for their kind permission to reproduce their photographs:

Abbreviations key: (a-above; b-below/bottom; c-centre; f-far; l-left; r-right; t-top)

123RF.com: Andrey Popov / andreypopov 23bc; Andriy Popov 34tl; Brad Wynnyk 172bc; Daniel Ernst 179rc; Hongqi Zhang 24cla, 175cr; Ingvar Bjork 60c; Kobby Dagan 259c; leonardo255 269c; Liubov Vadimovna (Luba) Nel 39cla; Ljupco Smokovski 75crb; Oleksandr Marynchenko 60bl; Olga Popova 33c; oneblink 49bc; Robert Churchill 94c; Roman Gorielov 33bc; Ruslan Kudrin 35bc, 35br; Subbotina 39cra; Sutichak Yachaingkham 39tc; Tarzhanova 37tc; Vitaly Valua 39tl; Wavebreak Media Ltd 188bl; Wilawan Khasawong 75cb; **Action Plus:** 224bc; **Alamy Images:** 154t; A.T. Willett 287bcl; Alex Segre 105ca, 195cl; Ambrophoto 24rca; Blend Images 168cr; Cultura RM 33r; Doug Houghton 107fbr; Hugh Threlfall 35tl, 176tr; Ian Allenden 48br; Ian Dagnall 270t; Levgen Chepil 250bc; Imagebroker 199tl, 249c; Keith Morris 178c; Martyn Evans 210b; MBI 175tl; Michael Burrell 213cra; Michael Foyle 184bl; Oleksiy Maksymenko 105tc; Paul Weston 168br; Prisma Bildagentur AG 246b; Radharc Images 197tr; RBtravel 112tl; Ruslan Kudrin 176tl; Sasa Huzjak 258t; Sergey Kravchenko 37ca; Sergio Azenha 270bc; Stanca Sanda (iPad is a trademark of Apple Inc., registered in the U.S. and other countries) 176bc; Stock Connection 287bcr; tarczas 35cr; Vitaly Suprun 176cl; Wavebreak Media ltd 39cl, 174b, 175tr; **Allsport/Getty Images:** 238cl; **Alvey and Towers:** 209 acr, 215bcl, 215bcr, 241cr; **Peter Anderson:** 188cbr, 271br. **Anthony Blake Photo Library:** Charlie Stebbings 114cl; John Sims 114tcl; **Andyalte:** 98tl; **Arcaid:** John Edward Linden 301bl; Martine Hamilton Knight, Architects: Chapman Taylor Partners, 213cl; Richard Bryant 301br; **Argos:** 41tcl, 66cl, 66cl, 66br, 66bl, 69cl, 70bcl, 71t, 77tl, 269tc, 270tl; **Axiom:** Eitan Simanor 105bcr; Ian Cumming 104; Vicki Couchman 148cr; **Beken Of Cowes Ltd:** 215cbc; **Bosch:** 76tcr, 76tc, 76tcl; **Camera Press:** 38tr, 256t, 257cr; Barry J. Holmes 148tr; Jane Hanger 159cr; Mary Germanou 259bc; **Corbis:** 78b; Anna Clopet 247br; Ariel Skelley / Blend Images 52l; Bettmann 181tl, 181br; Blue Jean Images 48bl; Bo Zauders 156t; Bob Rowan 152bl; Bob Winsett 247cbl; Brian Bailey 247br; Chris Rainer 247ctl; Craig Aurness 215bl; David H.Wells 249cbr; Dennis Marsico 274bl; Dimitri Lundt 236bc; Duomo 211tl; Gail Mooney 277ctcr; George Lepp 248c; Gerald Nowak 239b; Gunter Marx 248cr; Jack Hollingsworth 231bl; Jacqui Hurst 277cbr; James L. Amos 247bl, 191ctr, 220bcr; Jan Butchofsky 277cdc; Johnathan Blair 243cr; Jose F. Poblete 191br; Jose Luis Pelaez.Inc 153tc; Karl Weatherly 220bl, 247tcr; Kelly Mooney Photography 191tr; Kevin Fleming 249bc; Kevin R. Morris 105tr, 243tl, 243tc; Kim Sayer 249tcl; Lynn Goldsmith 258t; Macduff Everton 231bcl; Mark Gibson 249bl; Mark L. Stephenson 249tcl; Michael Pole 115tr; Michael S. Yamashita 247ctcl; Mike King 247cbl; Neil Rabinowitz 214br; Pablo Corral 115bc; Paul A. Sounders 169br, 249ctcl; Paul J. Sutton 224c, 224br; Phil Schermeister 227b, 248tr; R. W Jones 309; Richard Morrell 189bc; Rick Doyle 241ctr; Robert Holmes 197br, 277ctc; Roger Ressmeyer 169tr; Russ Schleipman 229; The Purcell Team 211ctr; Vince Streano 194t; Wally McNamee 220br, 220bcl, 224bl; Wavebreak Media LTD 191bc; Yann Arhus-Bertrand 249bl; **Demetrio Carrasco / Dorling Kindersley (c) Herge / Les Editions Casterman:** 112ccl; **Dorling Kindersley:** Banbury Museum 35c; Five Napkin Burger 152t; **Dixons:** 270cl, 270cr, 270bl, 270bcl, 270bcr, 270ccr; **Dreamstime.com:** Alexander Podshivalov 179tr, 191cr; Alexxl66 268tl; Andersastphoto 179tc; Andrey Popov 191bl; Arne9001 190tl; Chaoss 26c; Designsstock 269cl; Monkey Business Images 26clb; Paul Michael Hughes 162tr; Serghei Starus 190bc; **Education Photos:** John Walmsley 26tl; **Empics Ltd:** Adam Day 236br; Andy Heading 243c; Steve White 249cbc; **Getty Images:** 48bcl, 94tr, 100t, 114bcr, 154bl, 287tr; George Doyle & Ciaran Griffin 22cr; David Leahy 162tl; Don Farrall / Digital Vision 176c; Ethan Miller 270bl; Inti St Clair 179tl; Liam Norris 188br; Sean Justice / Digital Vision 24br; **Dennis Gilbert:** 106tc; **Hulsta:** 70t; **Ideal Standard Ltd:** 72r; **The Image Bank/Getty Images:** 58; **Impact Photos:** Eliza Armstrong 115cr; Philip Achache 246t; **The Interior Archive:** Henry Wilson, Alfie's Market 114bl; Luke White, Architect: David Mikhail, 59tl; Simon Upton, Architect: Phillippe Starck, St Martins Lane Hotel 100bl, 100br; **iStockphoto.com:** asterix0597 163tl; EdStock 190br; RichLegg 26bc; SorinVidis 27cr; **Jason Hawkes Aerial Photography:** 216t; **Dan Johnson:** 35r; **Kos Pictures Source:** 215cbl, 240cc, 240tr; David Williams 216b; **Lebrecht Collection:** Kate Mount 169bc; **MP Visual.com:** Mark Swallow 202t; **NASA:** 280cr, 280ccl, 281tl; **P&O Princess Cruises:** 214bl; **P A Photos:** 181br; **The Photographers' Library:** 186bl, 186bc, 186t; **Plain and Simple Kitchens:** 66t; **Powerstock Photolibrary:** 169tl, 256t, 287tc; **PunchStock:** Image Source 195tr; **Rail Images:** 208c, 208 cbl, 209br;

Red Consultancy: Odeon cinemas 257br; **Redferns:** 259br; Nigel Crane 259c; **Rex Features:** 106br, 259tc, 259tr, 259bl, 280b; Charles Ommaney 114tcr; J.F.F Whitehead 243cl; Patrick Barth 101tl; Patrick Frilet 189cbl; Scott Wiseman 287bl; **Royalty Free Images:** Getty Images/Eyewire 154bl; **Science & Society Picture Library:** Science Museum 202b; **Science Photo Library:** IBM Research 190cla; NASA 281cr; **SuperStock:** Ingram Publishing 62; Juanma Aparicio / age fotostock 172t; Nordic Photos 269tl; **Skyscan:** 168t, 182c, 298; Quick UK Ltd 212; **Sony:** 268bc; **Robert Streeter:** 154br; **Neil Sutherland:** 82tr, 83tl, 90t, 118c, 188ctr, 196tl, 196tr, 299cl, 299bl; **The Travel Library:** Stuart Black 264t; **Travelex:** 97cl; **Vauxhall:** Technik 198t, 199tl, 199tr, 199cl, 199ctcl, 199cr, 199ctl, 199ctr, 199tcr, 200; **View Pictures:** Dennis Gilbert, Architects: ACDP Consulting, 106t; Dennis Gilbert, Chris Wilkinson Architects, 209trr; Peter Cook, Architects: Nicholas Crimshaw and partners, 208t; **Betty Walton:** 185br; **Colin Walton:** 2, 4, 7, 9, 10, 28, 40l, 42, 56, 92, 95c, 99tl, 99tcl, 102, 116, 120t, 138t, 146, 150t, 160, 170, 191ctcl, 192, 218, 252, 260br, 260l, 261tr, 261c, 261cr, 271cbl, 271cbr, 271ctl, 278, 287br, 302.

DK PICTURE LIBRARY:

Akhil Bahkshi; Patrick Baldwin; Geoff Brightling; British Museum; John Bulmer; Andrew Butler; Joe Cornish; Brian Cosgrove; Andy Crawford and Kit Hougton; Philip Dowell; Alistair Duncan; Gables; Bob Gathany; Norman Hollands; Kew Gardens; Peter James Kindersley; Vladimir Kozlik; Sam Lloyd; London Northern Bus Company Ltd; Tracy Morgan; David Murray and Jules Selmes; Musée Vivant du Cheval, France; Museum of Broadcast Communications; Museum of Natural History; NASA; National History Museum; Norfolk Rural Life Museum; Stephen Oliver; RNLI; Royal Ballet School; Guy Ryecart; Science Museum; Neil Setchfield; Ross Simms and the Winchcombe Folk Police Museum; Singapore Symphony Orchestra; Smart Museum of Art; Tony Souter; Erik Svensson and Jeppe Wikstrom; Sam Tree of Keygrove Marketing Ltd; Barrie Watts; Alan Williams; Jerry Young.

Additional photography by Colin Walton.

Colin Walton would like to thank:
A&A News, Uckfield; Abbey Music, Tunbridge Wells; Arena Mens Clothing, Tunbridge Wells; Burrells of Tunbridge Wells; Gary at Di Marco's; Jeremy's Home Store, Tunbridge Wells; Noakes of Tunbridge Wells; Ottakar's, Tunbridge Wells; Selby's of Uckfield; Sevenoaks Sound and Vision; Westfield, Royal Victoria Place, Tunbridge Wells.

All other images © Dorling Kindersley
For further information see: www.dkimages.com

ру́сский ruskiy • english